Praise for SYNC YOUR RELATIONSHIP

"Time has been called the 'new currency' in today's world with too much to do and not enough time to do it. Yet each of us manages these pressures in different ways. In a fascinating new book, Peter Fraenkel shows us how our approaches to time and the rhythms of our lives spill over into our couple relationships. Even more importantly, he offers practical suggestions for improving."
—Ellen Galinsky, President, Families
and Work Institute, author of *Mind in the Making*

"Peter Fraenkel offers an original and profoundly accessible way for people to think about their relationships. His book is alive with insights and examples that enable the readers to observe their relationships freshly, with easily applicable tools."
—Janet Reibstein, author of *The Best-
Kept Secret: Men's and Women's Stories of Enduring Love*

"Couples today are time starved and out of sync. Peter Fraenkel has devised a powerful set of tools to help couples take on the challenges of time pressure, overstuffed work schedules, and contemporary life's frenetic pace, so that partners can reconnect, revitalize, and preserve their relationship."
—Evan Imber-Black, author of *The Secret Life of Families*

"A very timely book on a topic that all couples deal with... Peter Fraenkel helps us understand that our internal pace and couple rhythm are hidden under virtually all issues, and he uncovers the mystery of time in ways that will amaze and engage all readers."
—Howard Markman, Co-director of the Center for
Marital and Family Studies and author of *Fighting for Your Marriage*

"Peter Fraenkel puts forth some of the most pertinent and useful ideas about the time famine that afflicts couples today. You must take the time to read this timely book and find out how you can redeem your relationship from the time crunch. Peter Fraenkel is an inspiring writer and an inspired therapist. You are sure to enjoy your time with him."
—Esther Perel, author of *Mating in
Captivity: Reconciling the Domestic and the Erotic*

"Peter Fraenkel has written an outstanding guide for couples and families who want to take charge of the time crunch and transform their lives for the better. In a highly readable and often humorous style, *Sync Your Relationship* gathers the evidence for why we need to take back our time, and then he shows us how to do it. If you want to build a happy, healthy relationship, read this book!"
—John de Graaf, co-author of *Affluenza*
and Executive Director of Take Back Your Time

"Peter Fraenkel analyzes, with immaculate timing and much humour, common dysfunctional couple 'arrhythmias,' and he provides many solutions to stuck 'dance routines' as well as terrific tips on how partners can jazz up their relationship. Unique and most refreshing!"

—Eia Asen, M.D., author of *Multi-Family Therapy* and Visiting Professor, University College London

"Most things in life come and go, but time only goes. Often the love goes with it. In this remarkably creative new look at relationships, Peter Fraenkel helps us see how our invisible relationship to time shapes our lives and our intimate connections with others. Then he gently and compassionately guides couples away from the despair of core differences and into an appreciative dance of complementary personalities. I heartily recommend this book for any couple that wants to get 'that swing' back into their marriage."

—Christopher K. Germer, Ph.D.,
author of *The Mindful Path to Self-Compassion*
and Clinical Instructor, Harvard Medical School

"Some say 'sex,' some say 'money,' but Peter Fraenkel says 'time.' In this brilliant book, Peter Fraenkel, master clinician, teacher, and researcher, illuminates how couples construct and manage time—the 'hidden dimension' in couples' lives. This book will help couples and therapists understand the critical but seldom acknowledged role that time plays in couple conflicts, alienation, and loss of intimacy. Even more importantly, Fraenkel presents the guidelines he has evolved over years of practice and reflection to help couples learn to manage time more effectively—to get in sync with each other. The goal of 'flow' and the road to get there are the great contributions of this wonderful book."

—William Pinsof, President,
The Family Institute at Northwestern University

"Whether you play in a band, do corporate work, are an air traffic controller, or are part of a comedy troupe, timing and teamwork are essential. Peter Fraenkel's new book deftly shows how couples will thrive once they start playing the same tune."

—John Riley, jazz drummer

"All couples struggle with the rhythms of family, business, and personal priorities. So your relationship had better be in sync. Peter Frankel sheds light on the key challenges couples face and addresses them in a way that is extremely consumable, and most importantly, actionable."

—Gregory T. Rogers, founder and President, RayLign Advisory

Sync Your Relationship,
Save Your Marriage

FOUR STEPS TO
GETTING BACK ON TRACK

PETER FRAENKEL, PH.D.

palgrave
macmillan

Names and identifying characteristics of individuals mentioned have been changed.

First published in 2011 by
PALGRAVE MACMILLAN®
in the United States—a division of St. Martin's Press LLC,
175 Fifth Avenue, New York, NY 10010.

Where this book is distributed in the UK, Europe and the rest of the world,
this is by Palgrave Macmillan, a division of Macmillan Publishers Limited,
registered in England, company number 785998, of Houndmills,
Basingstoke, Hampshire RG21 6XS.

Palgrave Macmillan is the global academic imprint of the above companies
and has companies and representatives throughout the world.

Palgrave® and Macmillan® are registered trademarks in the United States,
the United Kingdom, Europe and other countries.

ISBN: 978–0–230–61814–5

Library of Congress Cataloging-in-Publication Data

Fraenkel, Peter.
    Sync your relationship, save your marriage : four steps to getting back
on track / Peter Fraenkel.
        p. cm.
    Includes index.
    ISBN 978–0–230–61814–5
    1. Marriage counseling. I. Title.

HQ10.F65 2011
646.7′8—dc22   2010035421

A catalogue record of the book is available from the British Library.

Design by Newgen Imaging Systems (P) Ltd., Chennai, India.

First edition: March 2011

10 9 8 7 6 5 4 3 2 1

Printed in the United States of America.

Contents

To my family, Heike, Lena, and Noah, for our precious time together every day

Time and Rhythm: The Hidden Dimension of Intimacy

IT WAS JUST ABOUT 20 years ago when I started noticing the power of time and rhythm to improve intimate relationships—and to mess them up. I was a newly minted Ph.D. in clinical psychology, in my first year of postdoctoral training in couple and family therapy at the renowned New York University Medical School. I was also a professional jazz drummer, the guy who sets the beat and helps the combo keep time together. Walking into the consulting room for their first session with me were John and Tina.[1] Trim, blond, and lanky, his face just starting to show the signs of middle age, John exuded a laid-back temperament. With a nervous grin he plopped down on the couch, a battered pair of sneakers peeking out from under his slightly frayed chinos. At his side, perched on the edge of the sofa sat Tina, a slender, fine-featured brunette in her early 30s, dressed immaculately in a sharp business suit, no-nonsense pumps, and pearls.

I welcomed them, and asked them to tell me about the problems bringing them to couple therapy. Before I could complete the sentence, Tina jumped in, speaking in rapid-fire staccato: "Well, you see, John and I met a couple of years ago, and actually we really get along most of the time, so it's not really us that's the problem per se but how to deal with Tim, John's son from a previous marriage."

Having run out of breath, Tina stopped long enough for me to interject, "So, John, what's your point of view about this?" John took a few seconds to consider the question before he opened his mouth to speak. But before he could complete a sentence, Tina jumped in, a hint of exasperation curling the corners of her mouth, and declared, "Oh, yeah, and that's another thing—this always happens: John's never willing to talk about our problems!" John's eyes met mine with eyebrows raised in a plaintive glance, as he slowly intoned, "I am *trying* to, but I just take a while to get my words out is all!"

By the session's end, it was clear that whatever problems they had with John's son, Tina and John differed drastically in their life rhythms, especially in one aspect that I call life pace: the speed of everyday activities such as walking, talking, eating, and getting ready to leave the house. Not surprisingly, their professional choices matched their personal rhythms—Tina was an investment banker and John a private boat captain who took small, elite groups on private cruises around Manhattan. Like so many couples, those very pace differences formed a powerful force of attraction when they first met: Tina loved John's mellow style—"he calmed me down," she sighed, remembering the early days of their infatuation—and John was drawn to Tina's up-tempo energy—"she was so exciting!" And yet, like so many couples, over time those same differences became major sources of irritation and misunderstanding between them.

What force draws us inexorably to the person who will become our soul mate, our life partner? And why is it that—though inconceivable in those heady beginning days and weeks and months of lust and love as we are flooded with the hormones that make our hearts pound and our heads swim[2]—this same soul mate also inevitably becomes the person with whom we wrestle emotionally, struggling with our frightening feelings of dependency and need?[3] The person toward whom we stoke simmering, overwhelming, self-righteous resentment; the one by whom we feel controlled, pushed away, misunderstood? The person alongside of whom we experience the most intense, confusing, painful loneliness imaginable?

Over the past 30 years, truckloads of self-help books have stocked shelves describing the most common relationship problems and how to solve them. Books for couples on money management. Books on improving couple communication. Books on reaching the pinnacle of sexual satisfaction. Although useful in many ways, none of these books help couples reveal the *hidden dimension of time and rhythm* that keeps their dysfunctional dance going. Time is everywhere—we swim in it and we breathe it, yet because we can't see it, we don't recognize its fundamental power in structuring our lives and our relationships.

After more than 20 years of working with couples and researching the causes of couple conflict and satisfaction, it's clear to me that unless couples can "hear the beat" of their conflict, they can't change it. You can't understand your anger with your partner until you realize the huge, underlying differences in your *pace,* your *tempo*—that what's angering you is how slowly he gets things done around the house, while he feels frustrated that you're always trying to complete tasks at the speed of light. Nor can you solve your persistent arguments about spending or saving money unless you realize that she focuses on the future (not just about money but in general) while you live more for the moment—a difference in what's called time perspective.

You can't overcome the fact that you never communicate, never make love, rarely have a date, or haven't had a quiet evening together in months until you realize that your work schedules are out of sync. And you can't explain to yourself (or to him) why you melt down when your partner is five minutes late to a date until you realize that being punctual is a key to keeping you calm and, moreover, that it was a point of pride in your family. And he can't explain why he feels you're incredibly rigid and unforgiving until you both realize that his family's strict rules about being on time made him feel oppressed in his youth.

In all these examples, your rhythms mismatch, you do not dance to the same beat, and, therefore, you struggle. And yet, when you go back to those early days and weeks and months of your love, you will find that, "surprise!" lo and behold, the very time differences that now drive you nuts about your partner were, unbeknownst to you, one of the things that most attracted you to each other. You *liked* his fast pace and high energy; he *loved* your laid-back side. You respected her incredible organizational skills, her focus on the future, and she dug your beach-bum, catch-the-wave approach to life. You both wanted someone talented and competitive and dedicated to his or her career—and you got it, but not much time for each other. And you sometimes couldn't stand your own uptightness about being on time, and he was often embarrassed by his own lateness, so you each unconsciously looked to the other to provide a punctuality corrective, but when it was offered, it was too different.

When we can hear the beat beneath our conflicts, perceive the time patterns that govern daily existence, rediscover the positives about them, and revise the patterns that lock us in distress, we can bring our relationship to new heights of connection and joy. In *Sync Your Relationship, Save Your Marriage,* I will teach you how to hear the clashing rhythms inside your flashpoints. You will learn the powerful four-step Relationship Rhythms Analysis:

1. Reveal your couple rhythms
2. Revalue the rhythms that work
3. Revise the rhythms that don't
4. Rehearse—practice the new rhythms

Before you can do something about a problem, you've got to diagnose it accurately. That's where the Relationship Rhythms Analysis comes in. It's the couple's equivalent of what any good physician does for us—our doctor takes our pulse, listens to the regularity of our heartbeat, determines the rate and balance between our systolic and diastolic blood pressure, and listens to the rhythm of our breathing. When the body's rhythms are off, it's a sure sign of disease. Same goes for relationship rhythms—when rhythms are off between partners, it's a sign that something's wrong.

To get a quick sense of where your time troubles lie, complete this brief version of the Couples in Time Questionnaire (the full version is available on my Web site, www.syncyourrelationship.com):

COUPLES IN TIME QUESTIONNAIRE: BRIEF VERSION

By answering these questions, you will get a snapshot of how greatly time issues affect the quality of your relationship. For each aspect of time, circle one number from 0 to 3 that describes the degree to which you experience this as a problem in your relationship.

**0 = not at all a problem, 1 = a little problem,
2 = somewhat a problem, 3 = definitely a problem**

1.	Finding adequate amount of time together	0	1	2	3
2.	Sense of time pressure	0	1	2	3
3.	Mismatch in daily schedules	0	1	2	3
4.	Mismatch in life paces (speed of walking, talking, eating)	0	1	2	3
5.	Differences in caring about or being punctual	0	1	2	3
6.	Differences in desire for time alone as a couple	0	1	2	3
7.	Differences in when we wake up or go to bed	0	1	2	3
8.	Differences in our focus on past, present, or future	0	1	2	3
9.	Differences in concern about using time effectively	0	1	2	3
10.	Different preferences about how to spend leisure time	0	1	2	3
11.	Match in satisfaction with progress toward life goals	0	1	2	3
12.	Differences in when we have the most energy during the day	0	1	2	3
13.	Balance of work and personal time	0	1	2	3

Total Score: _____

If you scored:

0–7: You're in the Groove! (little or no problems with couple time)
8–15: A Little out of Sync (mild difficulties: need a couple time tune-up)

16–23: Missing Some Beats (moderate difficulties: need to examine and change some rhythms)

24–31: Out of Step (notable difficulties: attention needed to several aspects of your couple time)

32–39: Couple Arrhythmia (significant problems with couple time: need major overhaul)

If you scored between 32 and 39, you may be suffering from a case of couple arrhythmia: Like a heart that's beating irregularly, you're significantly out of sync with your partner, and your relationship might be at risk. A score of 24–31 means you've got some notable difficulties connecting with one another in time, and your couple rhythms need immediate attention. A score of 16–23 says you've probably got some moderate difficulties getting together in time. A score of 8–15 indicates mild difficulties; if you scored between 0 and 7, congratulations, you have no time problems—except you're probably clueless or lying to yourself! From what I've seen in working with hundreds of couples over 20 years, time differences are endemic to couple life. And they can be solved. You are not alone.

Being out of sync in one or more aspect of time almost always plays a part in creating or sustaining conflict in couples, but it's often not the overt problem for which couples seek therapy. Many of the common problematic interaction patterns that distressed couples find themselves in play out in conflicts about time. As I describe these common couple problems, I'll also introduce you to some of the things therapists can help couples do right from the start to understand the nature of distress. And I'll give you examples of how these patterns play out in the arena of couple time.

The Sources of Couple Suffering and the Steps Toward Change

Couples suffer—and some come to therapy to relieve that suffering—because one or both partners are unhappy and view their unhappiness to be at least in part caused by the other person and the qualities of the relationship. This statement might seem obvious, but it's worth delving into a few details. By the time *most* couples seek help, both partners agree something's not working well. And that's no surprise, because one study found that the average length of time couples are distressed before seeking therapy is six years![4] Even if initially one partner is more unhappy than the other, after six years (but usually long before) we'd expect that the other partner is unhappy too—if only because of sensing his or her partner's discontent. Partners often disagree about the cause of problems and usually blame each other, but usually agree that there *is* a problem and that they are both unhappy.

However, both partners don't *always* admit that there's a problem. Sometimes, even by the time they first show up for therapy, one partner is significantly more unhappy or, at least, more vocal about it.

As a couple therapist, my first step in figuring out the pair's problems is to establish that both partners acknowledge a dynamic worth changing. I do this by getting a sense of whose idea it was to seek therapy and why, and if it wasn't a mutual decision, how the other partner feels about coming (and if they don't want to, why). By the end of the first or second session, both partners need to become stakeholders in the change process, to find something they could get out of it, or else the therapy will resemble their relationship—with one partner naming the problems and the other defensively denying their existence.

Identifying Polarizing Patterns

One of the most frequent polarizing patterns is known as the "pursuer/distancer" pattern. This occurs when one partner attempts to raise an issue, often in a perfectly reasonable manner, but the other feels unfairly criticized, blamed, or attacked, unable to acknowledge or verbalize his (or sometimes her) vulnerable feelings, and withdraws, refusing to talk about "it," whatever "it" is. Meanwhile, the partner raising the issues now feels unfairly burdened with all the responsibility of starting the conversation. She feels wrongly characterized as an attacker when, at least initially, she simply tried to raise legitimate concerns. As one person makes a demand, the other shrinks back and grows defensive.[5] The louder one knocks, the less willing the other is to open the door.

In heterosexual relationships, it's more often men who withdraw from conflict and women who then are stuck trying to get men back to the table to talk. Underlying this pattern is often a power struggle in which the man refuses to be influenced by his female partner. This refusal to be influenced is sometimes based on the man's conscious or unconscious belief that it would be "unmanly" for him to accept critical input about his behavior, or to agree to change something if that request for change comes from a woman—especially his intimate partner. Men often learn this belief about gender and power through what they observed in their parents' or other adult family members' relationships. These beliefs are then reinforced by movies, television shows, photos, news stories, popular songs, and other sources of messages about relationships that pervade most of the world's cultures—despite, and sometimes it seems in reaction to, feminist gains toward the equality of women and men. As a result, not only may the male partner be unwilling to respond to the specific requests or concerns of his female partner, but also his refusal to be influenced by her may show up in not being willing to talk at all.

Even more often, men refuse to converse about their partners' concerns in order to protect themselves emotionally. This is due to another rule of the constricting male code: Thou shalt not experience or express vulnerable emotions.[6] (Actually, those gender-power beliefs have stayed in place to be relied on by generations of men in part *because* they serve to safeguard them, at least partially and temporarily, from dealing with negative emotions.) Starting when they are infants, men and women are still raised with different expectations about their needs, abilities, rights, and responsibilities to experience and express uncomfortable emotions such as anxiety, fear, sadness, weakness, loneliness, shame, and guilt, or to listen to and empathize with expressions of those feelings by others.[7] Despite the cultural revolution of the 1960s that encouraged both men and women to "let it all hang out," "get in touch with your feelings," "be real," and "be intimate and empathic," boys and men generally continue to get the message that it's OK to express and act on emotions associated with strength (like anger), to assert themselves, and to say "no," but that it's not OK to have emotions associated with vulnerability (like embarrassment), or to "give in" to others' needs and requests. In contrast, girls and women continue to be trained to feel and express the emotions associated with vulnerability, and to take care of the vulnerable feelings of others. And women as a group are still generally discouraged from asserting themselves in business or in their personal lives,[8] or from openly expressing dissatisfaction or outright anger.

Unfortunately, when the man withdraws, it may only stimulate the woman to increase the intensity with which she raises the original issue, as she may feel even more pressed to initiate a conversation about it. Although he may show little emotion, the withdrawing partner is likely experiencing the uncomfortable physiological signals associated with the body's fight-or-flight response—increased anxiety, increased heart rate, shallow breathing, and other signs of stress.[9] The other partner also experiences these symptoms of stress, along with feeling frustrated, abandoned, or disrespected.

Here's a good juncture for me to note that when I describe general patterns about men and women in relationships—how they handle difficult emotions or common patterns of couple interactions—it is almost always based either on research, carefully studied clinical cases discussed in professional articles (mine and those of other experienced therapists), or both. As much as possible, I'll let you know in the back of the book the sources that support what I describe about couples. But even when my statements are based on some of the best research or clinical observations in the field, these general statements about couples are always based on averages. Every person and couple may be different. For instance, in any particular couple argument, or for a particular couple in general, it may be the woman who withdraws and the man who is trying to raise issues, and the woman who's less comfortable with vulnerable emotions and the man more so. And this pattern by no means occurs only in heterosexual couples. Although many same-sex/gay or lesbian couples attempt to avoid some of the problematic aspects of stereotypic heterosexual relationship patterns and roles, and although in many same-sex couples both partners may be relatively comfortable experiencing and discussing feelings, in others, one partner pursues, the other withdraws. So, many gay or lesbian couples resemble heterosexual couples in their gender roles and problematic patterns. In other words, men and women, gay or straight, may act in ways traditionally associated with the societally defined gender roles of masculine or feminine, or may act differently than those roles. Likewise, men and women, gay or straight, vary widely in their degree of comfort with vulnerable emotions. The good news is that relationship patterns and comfort experiencing and expressing emotions are behaviors that can change and can be learned.

In any case, once the pursuer/distancer pattern captures a couple, each partner may feel manipulated by the other's seemingly self-serving behavior. Over time and repetition, each comes to view the other's behavior in this pattern as reflective of the worst aspects of their partner's personality and as unlikely to change. Yet, as I've noted, there are usually some good intentions underlying each one's behavior: The pursuer is trying to get the withdrawer to talk, solve the problem, and end the conflict, while the withdrawer is trying to minimize conflict in the moment. Each is earnestly trying to reestablish harmony, but they are working in an uncoordinated way, at cross-purposes. Each one's efforts interlocks with the other's like two perfectly fitted components of an ill-fated device that then spins out of control, creating greater polarization.

The pursuer/distancer is only one of a number of polarizing patterns couples fall into, and a skilled couple therapist can begin to identify these patterns within the first session or two (and now, with the information I've provided, hopefully, so can you!). Another frequent one is called the "overfunctioning/

underfunctioning" pattern: One partner takes much more of the lead in effectively organizing the household, finances, social events, parenting, or other aspects of daily life, while the other rarely shows initiative or skill in managing these things. The more one exerts his or her competence, the less the other demonstrates his or hers. Although some couples seem patterned this way from the get-go, more often the differences develop over time, with each one's contribution becoming increasingly unequal. The partner who, when he lived alone or with another partner, was quite skilled in all manner of life management tasks, now finds himself feeling that his partner always has a better way to do the laundry, cook a sauce, or keep track of finances. Rather than acknowledging her greater skills and accepting her invitation to learn her way of doing things, or suggesting his own twist and possible improvement to what she does, he pulls back and stops contributing—sometimes sullenly (e.g., "well, if she doesn't like my way of doing things, then I guess I'll just let her do it"), and sometimes because she tells him not to bother trying since he always does a substandard (that is, according to her standards) job anyway. Likewise, the partner who's taking over more and more responsibilities might wish that her partner would take charge of more of these tasks, yet as long as she insists on her way as the only way, or goes ahead and does it before he gets a chance, that's not likely to happen. The result? She feels burdened, he feels useless, and each blames the other. And, by the way, I've worked with just as many couples in which it's the man rather than the woman who believes he's got all the best ways to do things around the home, and who doesn't value and adopt any of her ways, leading her to feel disrespected and disempowered. I've also worked with plenty of gay and lesbian couples for whom the same dynamic occurs.

One of the core ideas in couple therapy is that polarized patterns like the pursuer/distancer or overfunctioning/underfunctioning are much more powerful than partners' personalities in determining the quality and longevity of couple relationships. Research shows that, for the most part, no one personality style has a better or worse chance of a happy relationship.[10] Each partner brings his or her personality style and associated skills, tendencies, sensitivities, and vulnerabilities into the relationship. You are more verbal, he is less so. She is more anxious, you are calmer. You consider yourself a realist, he always sees the positive, the possible, the humorous. She is more organized and obsessive, you are more spontaneous but a bit chaotic. You are more social and enjoy big parties, while she prefers dinner for two. More important than the initial personality styles each partner brings to the relationship, it's how these styles play off one another that determines the impact of personality on their joint happiness. For instance, as one partner becomes the flag bearer for organizing time efficiently, the other champions a looser, take-it-as-it-comes approach, and then the more one insists on the correctness of her approach to time, the more the other argues for the correctness of his approach. In other words, through the centrifuge of a couple's circular conflicts, a wide range of personality differences can spin out into polarizing patterns.

Both the pursuer/distancer and the overfunctioning/underfunctioning patterns had just started to take over John and Tina's relatively new relationship when they came to see me. Tina interpreted John's slower pace of responding in their conversations about problems as evidence that he didn't want to talk about her feelings and their issues. True, John was not as comfortable experiencing anxiety as Tina was, nor was he as adept as she at speaking about those feelings. That meant she was the one to pursue the issue of the weekend time crunch on their relationship when John's son, Tim, came to visit twice a month, and John sometimes didn't want to talk about it because he didn't know how to solve the problem. He said he felt "stuck between a rock and a hard place," trying to please Tina while fulfilling his responsibilities to his son and his ex-wife, who relied on those every-other-weekends apart from Tim to catch up on her work and spend time with her new romantic partner. Meanwhile, Tina felt frustrated that she had to take charge of raising the issue and offering possible solutions.

To free them from the grip of these polarizing patterns, I taught the couple some powerful communication skills that you will learn in chapter 9, skills developed and tested by Howard Markman, Scott Stanley, and their colleagues at the University of Denver's Center for Marital Studies,[11] and which I've taught to hundreds of couples in my private practice and at the New York University Family Studies Program.[12] These skills create a safe space for experiencing and talking about unpleasant feelings.

For Tina and John, these skills helped equalize the pace of their conversation, so that the couple's differences in speaking speed did not interfere with their communication. They moved onto problem solving, and with the pace of conversation now more equalized between them, it turned out John had some great ideas about creating a regular weekend rhythm when Tim visited that Tina liked and helped refine. In this rhythm, John would spend the morning with Tina until Tim woke up, then make brunch for everyone, then go play ball with Tim for a few hours (giving Tina some much-needed time for herself), followed by an activity together as a threesome—taking in a movie, going for a walk, playing a board game. Tina and

John would then make dinner, order in, or they'd all go out for pizza, and then they'd decide together what to do with the evening until Tim's bedtime. After Tim was in bed, the couple would have a little cuddle time. The couple tried it the next weekend, and it worked, and through this approach to talking and solving the problem, we had disrupted all of the polarizing patterns—pursuer/distancer, overfunctioning/underfunctioning, fast pace/slow pace—that had begun to take hold of their love.

Personality differences like those between John and Tina are not only normal. Appreciated and used positively, they can be among the couple's greatest assets. Just as partners' different levels of skill in managing finances, interior decorating, home repair, and cooking can complement one another's abilities, differences in emotional styles can allow a natural division of labor for the psychological management of a loving relationship. If one partner is more social and the other shyer, that can translate into a better balance between time with others and time alone as a couple than either might have achieved with someone exactly like them. If one tends to envision the future with more hope and confidence and the other is more clear-eyed about potential setbacks, those different perspectives can combine to provide an approach that both reaches for the stars and touches the ground. If one partner has an exploratory streak while the other hews to the tried-and-true pleasures, this can result in a life filled with both adventurous novelty and comforting reliability. If one partner wants to discuss feelings associated with problems and the other jumps right to solutions, they can learn to combine these inclinations sequentially. Either approach alone is limiting.

In other words, it's not differences per se that cause problems in couples. It's how those differences are utilized. When partners understand their own and each other's personality styles and tendencies, when they recognize the value of each other's styles and discuss them respectfully, and when partners can put these differences to use, they reap the full benefits of being part of a "we" instead of just a "me."

While we're on the topic of utilizing rather than trying to eliminate the differences, let's examine a contemporary myth that many couples labor under: trying to establish a relationship in which each partner contributes exactly 50 percent in all life tasks. In fact, having a fair, equitable "peer marriage"[13] does not require each partner to do exactly 50 percent of everything and to develop equal skill in all areas. Indeed, the myth of the 50–50 marriage is an unreasonable standard that often makes couples feel deficient. The key to fairness is that neither partner feels forced by the other to take on a particular role and responsibility. For instance, as often happens, when working women feel forced by their male partners to do a disproportionate amount of the housework or childcare—either because of his financial advantage, his dead-set belief that men earn the money and women tend to the home and children, or because he just doesn't fulfill commitments to do his share—this can result in women feeling the relationship is extremely unfair. And among other effects, the sense that the relationship is unfair acts like an anti-aphrodisiac—when women feel the relationship is unfair, they become much less interested in sexual intimacy.[14] (Which is why one of my first recommendations to men who want more sex with their partners is that the men should do more housework.) But as long as partners don't feel unduly burdened with one or another task or emotional role, and as long as one partner doesn't feel that the other refuses to allow joint control or decision making, it can work well that one partner is the leader and the other the assistant in certain domains. Or at least, that one is initially the teacher, the other the learner, and then both can function equally "on the job." For instance, one may be the better cook, but the other can serve as sous-chef. Or one may be Ms. Fix-It, and the other can be the journeyman. Or one may be highly skilled in organizing finances, but the other can learn the system and share the work.

As some of my examples so far have illustrated, the general tendency for partners to polarize is one of the key ways that differences about time become a couple's problem. Like John and Tina, one is slower, one faster, and this initially appealing pace difference transforms from asset to annoyance as it gets more extreme. Other couples differ on punctuality, with one always on time or early, the other more relaxed about promptness. Although both tendencies have value in different circumstances, conflict ensues when each insists on the exclusive correctness of their approach. Or when one insists on detailed planning for the future and the other insists on detailed enjoyment of the here and now, partners miss the opportunity for a complementary combining of their equally important time perspectives. Instead, they're stuck in a polarized pattern, with the result that they neither enjoy the present nor prepare well for the future. Or one partner is a morning person, the other a night owl. I worked with one couple with a two-year-old child for whom this became the make-or-break issue. He, regularly in bed by 11:30 P.M. and up at 6 A.M. to go to work, was terrified that his wife, who regularly stayed up until 1 A.M. and rose at 10 A.M., would not be able to get up earlier in the morning when it came time to bring their daughter to preschool in two years, and that they would need to rely on their expensive live-in nanny forever. And she refused to change her diurnal rhythms until the daughter came of age for preschool, saying she'd always been late to bed and late to rise.

That's where I come in. By naming the polarizing pattern, letting the couple know they are not the first (and won't be the last) to fall into it, by explaining how they each contribute to it, by identifying the honorable intentions behind each one's behavior, and by noting that the pattern can change, I provide the couple some initial hope and relief. By showing that I understand each one's perspective, by showing them that it's not one of them that's to blame for the conflict but rather it's a dance they do together, I validate each one's feelings and model one of the key things partners must learn to do with one another when in conflict: to put aside their own needs, pain, and frustration for a moment and see the relationship and themselves from the other's point of view. This is simple to say, and again, perhaps obvious, but it's not so simple to do. Much of couple therapy centers on helping partners feel safe enough to acknowledge, first to themselves, and then to their partners, their most vulnerable feelings—feelings of hurt, fear, loneliness, disappointment, despair. And as hard as it may be, they need to hear the other's feelings, really take them in, and imagine what the relationship feels like from the point of view of the partner. I then help partners re-value the differences between them that likely served as a powerful source of attraction in the first place. And help them find ways to synthesize those differences into a more usefully complex "we," so that they escape the battle between "me" and "me."

Building Mutual Awareness: From Me versus You to We

The capacity to listen and to understand the other, to imagine the feelings and honorable intentions beneath the other's annoying behavior, and to tolerate knowing that there are differences between oneself and one's partner goes by various names—positive attributions, empathy, intersubjectivity, reflective functioning—depending on the specific psychological theory. But despite some important distinctions among them, all of these concepts highlight a core capacity that both partners need in order to thrive in an intimate relationship over time. For some of the couples with whom I've worked to facilitate this act of deep listening, it's the first time one or both partners has realized that his or her partner is not a mirror image of him or herself, but rather, has his or her own feelings, perceptions, needs, sensitivities, and capacities, which may vary quite radically from his or her own.

As individuals' projections of who their partners are (and who they wish they would be) dissolve, and as they come to see and hear each other more clearly, couples often move from initial anger and frustration to sadness and an unexpected sense of aloneness. The expectation of blissful, seamless merging promised by the early, heady, biochemically infused days of romance transitions to a renewed sense of separateness, a stepping back from assumed unity to a fuller appreciation of differences and of the need to negotiate compromises. Suddenly, being in a relationship seems like it's going be "hard work," and that can feel discouraging. My role at this moment is to normalize this as an inevitable stage in the development of intimate relationships and to help couples see it as a major step toward becoming much more fully appreciative of one another, and in most cases, more fully and enjoyably connected in a deeper, more realistic, and ultimately more satisfying "we."

Building mutual awareness helps avoid the four major destructive patterns of communication identified by research with thousands of couples: Escalation (one partner says something with critical or contemptuous affect, and the other responds in kind, in a kind of Ping-Pong match of negativity); Withdrawal (which we've discussed in detail already, when one partner gives verbal or nonverbal signals that he or she is avoiding or pulling out of the conversation); Invalidation (putting down the partner's point of view or efforts, often with critical or contemptuous facial expressions and voice tone, or minimizing the concerns by underresponding to the distress); and Negative Interpretations (developing a kind of theory of "mal-intent," an explanation of how the partner's unpleasant behavior is motivated by his or her secret, pervasive, deep-seated, malevolent intentions and feelings—usually expressed in phrases such as my partner doesn't really love me, is trying to control me, doesn't respect me, is not truly committed to me—revealing deeper "hidden issues" that go well beyond the specific distressing behavior).[15]

Let's look at some examples of Escalation, Invalidation, and Negative Interpretations as they occur when couples argue about time.

Escalation

Jim to Linda (with an impatient tone): "Why are you so late—again?"

Linda to Jim (equally terse): "Because I had things to get done—for *our* family."

Jim to Linda (with a rising tone of outrage in his voice): "Are you implying that I don't do enough for this family?"

Linda to Jim (sarcastically): "Got that one right, big guy. Why is it that we both work full-time jobs but I get to do all the shopping and other chores?"

Jim (loudly): "Right, right, you are so burdened, it's just horrible, what a terrible life you have—I only work about 10 hours more a week than you, do you ever think of that? If you could manage your time better, you'd get everything done twice as fast."

Linda (shouting now): "And if I had a husband that even once would offer to pick up the dry cleaning on his way home, I'd get things done twice as fast."

And on and on they go, until either Jim or Linda leaves the house, angrily slamming the door behind. The way to avoid these kinds of escalations is to stop as soon as they begin and shift to using the communication skills described in chapter 9, with each partner getting a chance to speak while the other listens and paraphrases, with both avoiding critical and contemptuous statements.

Invalidation

A couple I worked with hadn't had a night out and away from their toddler in almost a year. So they bought tickets to the opera, which in their "pre-child years" was one of their joint passions. Joanne, who'd left her job to raise their daughter full time, shed her "mommy clothes" and dressed up for the first time in months, arrived early to pick up tickets, and then took her place at their old meeting spot, just to the left of the fountain in front of the theater. She smiled. It felt good to be doing this again, and standing in that old meeting place brought back a flood of warm memories of the early, indulgent years of their love. But as curtain time approached with no sign of her husband, Tom, she started to worry. As other well-dressed patrons started to leave the plaza and file into the theater, she started to panic and to feel a bit annoyed as well—what could have happened? Was there yet another last-minute work crisis that Tom had to attend to? She understood his work was demanding right now as he sought to become a partner in a law firm, and she was eager to see him advance his career, but this was their first special night out in a long time. Surely nothing at work could be that urgent. And why hadn't he called? As it reached 8:05 P.M., she felt flooded with disappointment, tinged with frustration—no chance of seeing the first act now, the curtain was up, and doors would be closed.

At 8:20, Tom finally showed up in a cab. It seemed to Joanne that he took forever to pay the taxi driver and that his slow saunter toward her didn't match the moment's urgency or her own agitation. Nevertheless, not wanting to spoil the evening further with anger and realizing she should give him the benefit of the doubt—who knows, maybe he had a good excuse?—she stifled her frustration, greeted him, then said in a tone of obvious disappointment, "Tom, what happened? We've missed the first act!"

Rather than offering a ready apology and showing that he recognized, understood, and shared her disappointment, Tom shrugged his shoulders and said almost nonchalantly, "Hey, what can I say? I left in plenty of time, but the crosstown traffic was terrible, and my phone battery died so I couldn't call. Let's just go get a drink or something before the second half."

Joanne was stunned: "Tom, we've been planning this for months, this was our big night out, I'm not blaming you for being late, but I'm really disappointed and frustrated, can't you see that? Aren't you?" Tom looked at her coolly and said with controlled emotion, "Hey, come on, Joanne, get over it. It's just the opera. We'll catch the second half." Joanne exploded in angry tears, Tom turned away; then they fought right there at the fountain and passersby were treated to a very personal operatic tragedy.

As we discussed the event in their first couple therapy session a week later, Joanne felt that Tom's words and behavior completely dismissed her legitimate feelings of disappointment, worry, and frustration. Although she was upset that he was late, she wasn't even blaming him and yet he seemed so defensive. Or, she thought, maybe he really wasn't looking forward to this big night out as much as she was.

For his part, Tom felt he'd done what he could to get there on time. He had a habit of running late, of trying to do too much in too little time, and he was determined not to be late to their date. He'd really been looking forward to this evening and made special efforts to block any last-minute phone calls that might keep him late at the office. He just about burst a vein sitting in that cab stuck in traffic and felt mad at himself for forgetting to charge his phone that day. He'd tried to calm down before he got to the theater, but when he saw Joanne so upset, he felt bad, and the frustration welled up in him. He was trying to help her calm down by keeping his cool and by trying to put this disappointment in perspective so they could enjoy the rest of the evening, but when Joanne seemed to get even more upset after he explained what happened, he felt she must be blaming him even though she said she didn't. He felt that wasn't fair and started to feel angry, but again, to keep from spoiling the evening, he squelched his feelings and tried again to stay cool and put the disappointment in perspective. But when Joanne then started crying and seemed so angry, he "lost it."

This kind of unfortunate event is all too common in the lives of couples. One partner inadvertently slips up, inconveniences, hurts, or annoys the other. Although there are to my knowledge no research findings on this, clinical researchers estimate that in all but the most distressed couples, about 90 percent of the things partners do that hurt one another are unintentional, not deliberate attempts to cause pain. But we seem to have a hard time apologizing to our partners for the unintended impact of our behavior. Instead, we focus on the fact that we didn't "mean it." That leaves our partner feeling hurt, angry, and invalidated.

To avoid having an experience similar to Joanne and Tom's, my suggestion to couples is that they make a clear distinction between the impact and the intent of their behavior, and learn to apologize for the impact of their unwittingly hurtful behavior, allow their partner to vent, sit with their partner's emotion and empathize with it. In turn, the responsibility of the hurt partner is to avoid taking advantage of the partner's apologetic stance by going on and on about the incident, or by using it as an opportunity to vent about all manner of other, past insults and injuries (as in, "this is just like the time when you…"). Instead, the hurt partner needs to allow him or herself to be comforted by the inadvertently hurtful partner's apologies and to move on together.

Negative Interpretations

Joanne had already started to develop a theory about Tom's frequent lateness: that he really preferred spending time at work to spending time with her and their child. In the course of addressing the incident of his lateness to the opera, Joanne expressed her emerging negative interpretation in what we call a "negative mind-reading statement"— "Face it, Tom, you just like being at work more than you like being with me!" Tom was stunned and hurt by this accusation. From his point of view, he had difficulty saying no to authority and setting boundaries on work, especially now that they had a child and other colleagues had lost their jobs. It was important for Joanne to hear this from Tom, but it was also clear he needed to assert himself with his boss and set some boundaries on work, even if it meant jeopardizing his job, if she was going to be able to dismiss her emerging negative theory. He talked to his boss, and to his amazement, his boss smiled slightly, nodded, and said, "Tom, I completely understand. I wish I'd had the guts to stand up to my boss years ago… it could've saved my marriage."

Although more often than not our theories of mal-intent about our partners are wrong—at least in our sense of their degree or breadth—unfortunately, sometimes our theories are not entirely off-base. For instance, it may actually be that our constantly late partner really *doesn't* respect us much (or our time), or *doesn't* want to spend time with us, or balks at our attempts to share control of the schedule, or *is* more invested in work, parents, friends, or video games. But given that our partners haven't spontaneously shared with us their control issues or their diminished love, respect, or concern for us, telling them definitively that we *know* what's behind their bad behavior (because, after all, we can read their minds) is a surefire way to get off on the wrong foot. Instead, a better way to bring it up is to say, "Sometimes I wonder if you really don't want to be with me, when you are frequently late for our dates," or "When you won't negotiate the weekend schedule with me, it seems to me that you won't give me any control, and that's upsetting." Rather than saying that you definitively *know* what your partner's intentions are, these statements tell the partner what you are thinking about his or her behavior and give your partner space to affirm or disconfirm your impressions.

The Place of Time in Couple Problems and Solutions

One of the major issues that couples argue about and that also affects *how* couples argue, is time. That is one of the reasons I have found time to be such a useful focus in helping couples change. Consider again John and Tina, whose radically different paces created a polarizing pattern that precluded clear communication and left each feeling controlled by the other. This unrecognized temporal pattern was so powerful that they couldn't make headway on the explicit time problem they'd come to therapy to discuss—how to balance time together as a couple with time for John's son. And eventually, the solution to their problem was to create a new rhythm, a new time structure for when Tim visited them on weekends. Time issues underlie all the other common problems couples argue about, and changing couple time patterns is often the key to dissolving those problems.

When I tell people that I work with couples to help them solve their problems with time, they frequently say, "Oh, you mean how nobody has any time for relationships anymore?" For sure, if there's one common cry from couples today, it's "We have no time!" Partners are stretched to the max with demanding work schedules that are cranked up by technologies that link them to the workplace twenty-four hours a day, seven days a week. The ever-increasing work hours and the speeding up of our lives through technology over the past two decades have definitely challenged couples' abilities to synchronize their lives. When stressed couples sense that the work-life balance equation is impossible to solve, burnout sets in.

Burnout is a state of emotional, mental, and physical exhaustion caused by excessive and prolonged stress. It shows up as disengagement or loss of interest and motivation for a work role that one originally sought, reduced energy, feelings of helplessness, hopelessness, cynicism, resentment, and lowered self-worth and self-efficacy.[16] Burnout damages not only partners' psychological and physical well-being, but by lowering productivity on the job, it affects the corporate bottom-line, and ultimately, the nation's economy.

But besides the time famine most often emphasized in the media, I've discovered that there are many other ways that couples come into conflict about time. Ever since I became a clinical psychologist and therapist, I've been struck by how many of the conflicts couples experience result from falling out of sync and out of rhythm. Because partners inevitably differ in at least one or more of the ways that they view time, prefer to use time, and organize their lives in time, I can safely say that all couples face time challenges.

Maybe it's my background as a conservatory-trained percussionist and my continued parallel life as a jazz drummer that especially tuned me in to the rhythms of relationships. After all, I'm the guy who sets the beat and helps the combo keep time together. I know that a jazz group can't swing together if they're not keeping time, if they don't have the same understanding of beat, tempo, and rhythm. And I see the same thing in couples—if they can't "get in the groove" together, nothing else seems to work well.

Or maybe it's partly my personal time challenges, juggling two busy careers as a psychologist and jazz drummer with being a husband and a father of two kids; my own imperfect attempts to balance fast-paced periods in my work and personal life with time for slowness, relaxation, and reflection; my own struggles to immerse fully in the present moment while still effectively planning my future, and while remembering to pause long enough to cherish and learn from my past.

Whatever led me to discover it, I've found that one of my most efficient, powerful therapeutic methods is to observe, reveal, and help couples change the ways they think about and utilize time.

Consider the following vignettes. All are real-life couples I worked with, couples for whom identifying and changing the time problems underlying their other conflicts (about money, intimacy, in-laws, and the like) was the key to improving their relationships.

Money Problems That Hide Time Problems

In my first session with Cindy and Jerry, I witnessed their constant conflicts about how much money to spend or save. At base, Cindy and Jerry's conflicts were just one outgrowth of a fundamental difference between their respective *time perspectives*—how much a person values and focuses on the past versus the present versus the future.

Cindy was a responsible and competent personnel manager in an advertising agency who grew up in a future-focused family in which every activity was carefully scheduled and planned weeks or months in advance. Finding this oppressively constraining, Cindy vowed to live her adult life making the most of the present moment. She invited friends over for impromptu dinner parties with just a day's notice (or less). She once decided on a whim to fly off for a short vacation to a distant city over a long weekend. She would pop into a new restaurant she'd just walked by rather than calling ahead for reservations. And although fiscally responsible by most standards, she believed it foolish to save everything for a future that might never come and preferred to spend a high percentage of her discretionary income on present pleasures and passions.

Her husband, Jerry, came from a family similar in some ways to Cindy's, with lots of regular routines, hard-working parents who scrimped and saved and planned in order to secure their future. But unlike Cindy, who had largely abandoned living for the future, Jerry was convinced that this was the only responsible and satisfying way to live. He preferred to plan social events and make restaurant reservations well in advance, plan vacations a year ahead, and carefully managed the couple's investments for long-term growth. He regarded Cindy's desire to "live for the present moment" as "flighty" and "irresponsible." She increasingly found him "uptight" and "anal," and complained that he was boring and unimaginative.

Pace Differences That Create Conflicts about Chores

On the surface, Mary-Lou and Bill were troubled by the frequency and intensity of their arguments over every aspect of maintaining the house. Bill took much longer to complete chores and fix-it tasks, while Mary-Lou started immediately and worked extremely rapidly. He saw her speediness as reflecting an attempt to get things done as quickly as possible, irrespective of the quality of her work; she regarded him as a tinkerer who dragged things out because he resented doing them. Although initially attracted to his laid-back style, over years of living together she became irritated not only by his slower pace of completing chores, but by his slower pace of walking, eating, and talking. In turn, although at first he found her fast pace exciting and enlivening, now he complained of feeling constantly rushed by her.

Eroded Trust and Asynchronous Daily Rhythms

Roger, a corporate lawyer, and Tim, an interior designer, sought therapy with me for what they described as "trust issues." Tim had engaged in a number of casual affairs, all after Roger started working later. Their newly asynchronous schedules had led Tim to feel lonely. Although Roger was not against either of them occasionally having casual sexual encounters with others, Roger was devastated that Tim did so without telling him and while he was putting in longer hours at the office. Tim stated that he loved Roger and was quite committed, but complained that he got frustrated "waiting around" for Roger. Roger bitterly countered that he was the main breadwinner, and that if Tim worked a more demanding job, Tim would understand the pressure.

Mismatched Personal Timelines

Marcia and Fred, both academics, were out of sync in how they thought about the link between their present and their future. They had differences in what I call *life plan timelines,* one's personal chronology of an imagined or planned future.

Both in their late 30s, Marcia was now desperate to start a family, and she wanted Fred to "grow up," which meant to stop being a student and assume adult responsibilities. Fred, who had recently begun postdoctoral studies in his discipline, argued that if having children were so important to Marcia, she should have met someone earlier with whom to start a family. He angrily rejected her implication that he was depriving her of this experience. The more Marcia insisted on her vision of their joint timeline, the more Fred held to his current plans. Each partner infuriated the other. Deadlocked, Marcia and Fred turned to me, gazing imploringly for a solution.

Arguments about Time Allocation

Many couples argue about how to spend or divide their time. One couple I worked with struggled over how much time to spend on the weekend with in-laws versus just the two of them and their young son. She wanted to visit her traditional Italian-American family every Sunday, while he, desperate to leave behind that same traditional culture in which he also was raised, thought Christmas and Easter were quite enough contact. He felt the visits with her parents got in the way of connecting with his son, whom he rarely saw during the work week. In contrast, she relished the opportunity to hand over child care and cooking to her mother once a week.

Struggles over Sequence: When to Do What

In yet another twist on time problems, a couple I consulted with argued about how to *sequence* activities over time. He preferred to make love before tackling the housework on a weekend morning, while she described feeling restless and distracted until all the chores were complete. They also argued about *when*—within a day, across the weeks, months, and year—to do a variety of things. When to wake up and go to bed (she was an early riser, he a night owl). When to take vacations (he preferred the winter, she, the summer). When to tackle the taxes (for her, as soon as the W-2's arrive, for him, in the last possible week). The only activity they seemed not to argue about was when to argue. With all these differences around when to do everything else, they argued all the time.

The Power of Punctuality

Another couple came to me in great distress, on the brink of divorce, because he felt so insulted whenever she was late (which was, by both their accounts, constantly). He was raised in New York City and tightly wound. She was raised in Rio de Janeiro, Brazil, and more laid back. He became anxious when not on time; she became anxious when she *was* on time (punctuality reminded her of her "snobby parents," who tried to distinguish themselves from stereotypes about "lazy" Brazilians by being "superpunctual").

Rhythm Problems That Lead to Intimacy Problems

Sunita and Bhanu sat at opposite ends of the long couch in my therapy office. They'd come to see me to set their marriage back on course. Bhanu fidgeted anxiously forward, his torso tightly folded over his knees and polished shoes. Sunita slouched with legs crossed at the ankles, head resting askew on a cushion, as she absently twirled a long strand of her jet-black hair. The couple looked discouraged and exhausted. Both had recently completed highly competitive residencies at prestigious New York City medical centers. Bhanu was on the fast track to a career in cardiology while Sunita was taking time off, turning down offer after offer for positions in pediatrics, wanting to "get off the treadmill for a little while." The couple had married four years earlier, and although Sunita and Bhanu were once madly in love, they now warily eyed one another. "I have no faith that he wants anything to do with me, really," Sunita sighed, a distinct hint of bitterness in her exhaling breath.

He jumped, clearly injured by this assessment. "What are you talking about?" Bhanu said. "Haven't I been making an effort lately?"

"You mean, in the last week, since we've decided to come here?" she countered.

Bhanu simmered quietly, before responding, "You know, I am also lonely. I feel like you never want to touch me anymore."

Sunita's eyes darted as she said, "When should I? When you come home and just sit like a vegetable on the couch until you pass out?"

He shrugged. She grimaced and turned away.

You don't have to be a professional therapist to see that Bhanu and Sunita were out of touch both physically and emotionally. Seated at opposite ends of the couch, never touching, they couldn't even make eye contact. Each felt unloved. They struggled with many of the most common couple problems: decreased intimacy, blocked communication, conflict about the in-laws, her resentment about the amount of time she spent on chores, his concerns about disparities in how much money each earned and spent. They also engaged in some common polarizing patterns: He expressed more positive emotions and hopefulness; she expressed more negative emotions and hopelessness. She overfunctioned and he underfunctioned in the area of planning enjoyable events for their leisure time. He tended to pursue while she withdrew in problem discussions.

But beneath these apparent problems in communication and intimacy—what therapists call "the presenting problems"—was the hidden time dimension of their relationship, their unique couple arrhythmia. As we talked further, I was quickly able to help them understand that while their operating rhythm worked for them professionally, it put a constant strain on their relationship. Few couples grasp the connection between time and love, and even fewer realize that this problem can be approached and solved.

To illustrate how I work with couples to solve their underlying problems with time, I'll describe how I helped Sunita and Bhanu. My first step was to draw their attention to the power of time in their personal lives. I aimed to highlight their sources of time pressure, their chronic state of couple arrhythmia, and the lack of reliable, protected time for togetherness on a daily and weekly basis. They had grossly underrated the obvious strain sustained from years of long hours of study and patient care. Both were from hard-working, high-achieving families, in which it was assumed that their lives would focus on higher education and career. But with my encouragement, they reflected on how much relationship time they had done without in doggedly pursuing professional goals, and their mood softened.

It had also never occurred to Sunita and Bhanu how much their emotional distance was maintained and even worsened by their different times of going to bed and getting up (he early, she late on both ends of the day), the absence of an established time to reconnect at the end of the day, the absence of any rhythm of pleasurable activities on the weekend, his 24/7 accessibility by mobile phone to hospital staff and patients, as well as his constant accessibility to his ailing mother and two worried sisters.

Our unhappiness in a relationship may begin for reasons other than time. It may derive from negative reactions to the tone in our partner's voice when they criticize us. Or how our partner touches us (or doesn't) in the act of making love. Or how our partner talks to our parents or disciplines the kids, or scatters clothes all over the apartment and never picks them up. But the negative feelings launched by these issues may be sent into orbit by partners being temporally out of sync, because there's no time to talk about, repair, and resolve these issues, and because there is little reliable pleasurable time together to balance out the difficult moments. Like many couples, Bhanu and Sunita overrated the power of their initial attraction to keep them connected, neglected to repair the fabric of their love when it started to fray, and ignored the need to preserve pleasure time to buffer themselves against difficult periods.

Before Bhanu and Sunita left our first session, I gave them two homework assignments designed to jump start their couple rhythms. First, I asked them to create a nightly sequence designed to help each of them unwind from the day's pressures, to set aside as best they could the work responsibilities and the unpleasant emotions that accompany these, so that they could reconnect with less distraction and with renewed energy. I call this exercise the "decompression chamber," a metaphor meant to conjure up an image of a remedial tank used for deep-sea divers when they've changed pressure levels too quickly by speeding to the surface, risking illness or even death. The decompression chamber allows the diver to more gradually reduce the water and air pressure and adjust to being back out of the ocean's depths. Similarly, we often rush directly from the pressures of work outside or inside the home (including child care) into attempts at couple time. Bhanu and Sunita expected that they could readily chill and reconnect. But instead of chilling, they spilled stress left over from the day, turning what could have been enjoyable, healing time together into just another night of irritation, disappointment, and lonely disconnection.

To prepare Sunita and Bhanu to try the decompression chamber over the next week, I asked them to tell each other what they most needed in order to slow down, relax, and transition into the rest of the evening. For a moment, they looked at each other blankly and then exploded in simultaneous laughter. "We have no idea!," she exclaimed, as he nodded vigorously in agreement. It was the first bit of levity and consensus to enter our meeting.

Like many couples, Sunita and Bhanu had not yet found a way to deal with periods of what I call sustained stressful situations—work difficulties or other life problems that are extremely unpleasant, often complicated, somewhat or largely out of our control, and not easy to change. Clearly, we had to find a way to balance Bhanu's need to talk about the stressful aspects of his work and his mother's health with a response to Sunita's understandable feelings of being saturated with his unremitting stress. So I suggested a time-based strategy I've found extremely useful for setting a boundary between couple time and these sustained stressful situations. While they would still "decompress" together each night, I recommended that they create a less frequent subrhythm for talking about Bhanu's ongoing stressors.

They agreed to talk about these once a week, barring some urgent new development. During other nightly decompression times, he could say something like, "Ah, you know, same old same old—no big headlines today." Bhanu also liked my suggestion that he try reporting every day on one positive thing that happened at work. He added that it might help him move into a better mood before talking with Sunita if he'd first spend 20 minutes riding the stationary bike that had been gathering dust in a corner of their bedroom for the last six months.

Having spelled out the elements and sequence of their nightly decompression chamber routine, I introduced their second homework assignment. On one weekend day or evening, they were to go somewhere in the city that neither had been before, and spend the time walking around and appreciating the sights, sounds, and smells together, but with one constraint: no talking. To reduce the risk that they might spoil the time by sliding into discussions about their problems, I stipulated that they could only communicate through hand gestures and facial expressions.

A week later Sunita and Bhanu returned, and things were much improved. They'd gone for a nature walk on a Sunday afternoon and had fun wordlessly pointing out special trees and guiding each other to sniff intoxicating flowers. And they'd managed to enact their decompression chamber most nights, talking and relaxing together more than they had in years. Interestingly, talking less about his work and his mom's health problems seemed to galvanize Bhanu into action to make some changes. He started a more earnest search for another position and found a better specialist to treat his mom.

Having identified time as a major underlying source of their disconnection, and having demonstrated that some simple shifts in how they used time could have dramatic effects, over the next few weeks we examined their other temporal differences. His faster and her slower pace of walking, talking, and eating often led him to feel she was purposefully "dragging her heels," signaling that she was reluctant to connect with him. In turn, she felt his pace was just another way that he pushed her around. Exploring their initial attraction to one another when they met in their third year of medical school, pace differences figured prominently. Bhanu said he'd found her bright, beautiful, that she "really cared about making a difference for patients...and I liked that she was more laid back than me, she helped me relax."

In turn, Sunita found Bhanu brilliant yet "not stuck up or sexist like so many other male doctors, and incredibly energetic. It seemed like he could do things so quickly. I found that inspiring at times when I felt like giving up."

In subsequent weeks, they agreed to get their bedtimes and wake times in sync, especially on the weekends. They came to a compromise about how much time to spend on weekends with each other versus with in-laws (he had wanted to spend more time with his mother and sisters than she did). We examined their respective life plan timelines, and they discovered to their relief that their visions of the future were more similar than they'd feared, especially regarding when to start trying to have a child. In addition, by getting in sync in the now, they'd created a platform of positive feeling and trust that enabled them to step away from the painful events of the last few years and put these truly in the past. They'd also created satisfying rhythms that would carry them forward, like a river's steady current, into their shared and hope-filled future.

Time and Your Relationship

This book will help you rethink the way in which time creates problems in your intimate relationships and show you how to use time as a resource to make those relationships better. I'll reveal the many ways time functions as the hidden dimension in your relationships and offer you straightforward, creative solutions for deploying time to transform those relationships.

Time in Mind: Revealing and Balancing Your Basic Time Types

CHRIS AND SUSAN FOUGHT almost every day about the same thing: he needed to use his time effectively, to have something to show for practically every waking minute. He was up early, worked hard all day, and once home, after a short dinner, would often dive into books to improve his skills in computer programming and marketing as he hoped to create a software company. When he and Susan spent time together, he felt it important that they "make every minute count," and he always wanted to plan out their couple time so that they would get the most pleasure out of every moment. His attention to the clock and to making his and their time productive drove Susan nuts. In her time off from work as an assistant director of a successful art gallery where the pace often became stressful, she preferred yoga, meditation, and wandering around and exploring neighborhoods new to her—anything that would help her "stop time" and allow her to "float." Chris's approach to time made her feel tense, while Chris viewed Susan's approach to time as "wasteful and irresponsible." This difference about how to spend their time had created such stress that they were now considering a separation.

As I helped them to see, their dissimilar ideas about how to use their time were linked to extremely different, but potentially complementary and balancing, worldviews on the nature of time itself. For each of them, their strong endorsements of these different views were not abstract and intellectual but visceral and emotional. I understood this because from years of studying time in people's intimate relationships, I have learned that how we think about time affects what we do with our time and how we feel in our day-to-day lives. Chris was a devotee of the clock and calendar. It made him feel safe and calm to order his days with work tasks and pleasurable activities. This allowed him to account for his time and to view his life as having value and meaning. These values came directly from his family. He'd grown up in a family that had been wealthy for several generations, and Chris had a trust fund and other money he'd eventually inherit that could have allowed him never to work a day in his life. But his parents inculcated in him the importance of living a life of value, and in his family, one's value depended on how one used time.

Susan had grown up in an equally well-to-do family, but it was her father who had made the climb from a working-class background to the higher reaches of business success. In contrast to Chris's family, her parents encouraged her to use the benefits of their financial support to enjoy life, which in their family meant to balance hard work with unstructured time for pleasure and exploration—a kind of time mostly unavailable to Susan's parents and their parents before them, who had to keep their noses to the grindstone to eke out a living in factory jobs and small businesses. From their perspective (and now Susan's), to spend all your time working and worrying about being accountable to the clock sounded like being in a factory—what was money for if not to provide some freedom from the daily grind? Susan's interests in Eastern religions, yoga, and meditation, and the year she spent after college backpacking around Europe with no real plan, all emerged from her family's support to live life free of a constant concern about accounting for her time. In contrast to Chris who felt best when he could say exactly what he'd done in clock and calendar time, Susan felt best when she could step away from linear time and just immerse in the timeless moment. She also looked for moments in time that rose above the mundane and seemed particularly poignant and powerfully meaningful. It was the search for both timelessness and precious time that led her to become a painter and to obtain a degree in art history.

It helped Chris and Susan to learn that their different ways of inhabiting time were linked to larger, ancient conceptions about its nature. These time conceptions, time orientations, or time "types"[1] can all be useful resources in our lives, and couples can learn to move fluidly among markedly different ways of being in time to make their relationships richer and more fulfilling. This chapter is all about how our beliefs about time affect how we inhabit and use time, and how we can shift among different ways of thinking and doing in time to change how we feel emotionally in our bodies and in our relationships. So before you start being a "time traveler," you need an orientation to these different realms of time.

How Real Is Time?

If there's one thing to learn from the history of scholarly reflection on the topic of time, it's that we tend to view time as an objective, given aspect of reality when it is much more a human creation. Time seems to just be there, like all the other fundamental aspects of our world—up and down, close or far, large and small, the ground, the sky, the water, the air. Time, like space, seems to be a dimension or element that we just enter into when we're born and leave when we die (although some religions believe that after we die we enter a different kind of time). But as generations of scholars have discovered, to their surprise, we can create time and live in it differently if we choose to.

In fact, that other core dimension of our reality, space, isn't all that real, either! We view space and the "things" that fill space as just being there. We go about our days viewing our world's seemingly stable objects as solid matter. The roofs over our heads, the floors we walk on, the chairs we sit in, the windows we look out, the trains, planes, and automobiles we ride to get from one place to the next, the food and drink we consume—all seem "there" just the way we see, touch, smell, hear, and taste them. So does the "empty space" between these objects—it's "there" too, in an empty sort of way. Things seem pretty solid and "there" unless we are particle physicists. They know that all these objects and the spaces between them are different configurations of atoms and energy in constant motion, which appear to us as they do because of the nature of the interactions of light, the atomic makeup of these objects, and the capacities of our particular sensory-perceptual system.

We inhabit time in the same unquestioning way, as if it was a substance that we can have more or less of, lose, gain, save, and spend. Unless we've recently imbibed a mind-altering substance that changes our perception of the flow of time, or are in a hypnotic trance, or experienced a traumatic brain injury, or are in the late stages of a progressive brain illness like Alzheimer's that can erase our sense of past or future, we fully expect time to flow along at pretty much the same pace every day.[2] And we expect to wake up to a sense that we have a past, a present, and a future—just as we wake up everyday expecting to find the dimensions of length, width, and height in our physical environment.

We mindlessly go about our business in time, using it as a given aspect of reality within which we organize and conduct our lives. But once we start asking questions like "What is time?" and "Does time move or stand still?" and "Where does our sense of time come from?" our confidence about the reality of time slips away rather quickly.

Another important question with real implications for our experience of time individually and as a couple is, "Who in the relationship controls the time?" The story of Chris and Susan is one example of how a couple's happiness largely depended on whether they could bring together and flexibly balance their different time orientations.

Musicians, especially drummers like me, know that the "time feel" greatly affects the emotional experience of music, for both the other musicians and the audience. Musical time has a kind of texture. A groove might be described as tight or loose, straight ahead, swinging, funky, or choppy, simple or thick, hard-driving or easygoing, light or heavy, lively or down and dirty. For drummers, it's deeply meaningful to distinguish playing in front of, on top of, or behind the beat, and one of the biggest compliments awarded a drummer is when the bandleader describes one's playing as "totally in the pocket"—meaning supremely solid and, well, "in the groove."

Of course, different types of music are largely defined by their different rhythms and time feels. Just think of how differently *you* feel listening to a hard-swinging jazz classic by Frank Sinatra with a big band, like "New York, New York," versus a slow blues by B. B. King, versus a funky soul tune by Stevie Wonder or James Brown, versus a heavy metal tune by AC/DC or Van Halen, versus a slowly grooving hip-hop or contemporary rhythm and blues tune by Erykah Badu or Jay-Z, versus a smooth-as-silk country song by George Jones or Loretta Lynn, or a lively honky-tonk by Dolly Parton or Trace Adkins. (If you don't know the musicians I'm referring to, just compare the feelings you have in some tunes by artists you know.) Trust me: The time feel, the basic rhythm of the music, has a huge effect on your experience of it—as much or more than the melody, harmony, and words. If you want further proof, check out a wonderful album called *Rock Swings* by the great singer Paul Anka. Anka took classic rock tunes—like grunge band Nirvana's classic "Smells Like Teen Spirit"—and sang them set to a jazz big-band feel. Same tune, totally different experience!

Drummers learn the fine distinctions between and within these different time feels. And drummers and other musicians can argue for hours about the fine points of one versus another drummer's jazz swing beat, or one versus another's funk groove.[3]

You don't have to be a drummer to sense differences in how you feel under different time conditions. Here's a sample of adjectives commonly used to capture the feel of time: pressuring, tight, invigorating, boring, peaceful, hectic, stagnant, flowing, standing still, buoyant, wide open, restricted, focused, chaotic, smooth, overwhelming, special. And there are many others. What words would you use to describe the time feel of the following situations?

- You have a long, busy week at work, with back-to-back meetings each day and several tasks to complete, all with urgent deadlines
- You have two weeks off in a place you find extremely relaxing, and the weather is perfect day after day
- You've got a weekend to yourself but no clear sense of what you want to do with it
- You've finally finished catching up with a lot of paperwork and demanding projects, and there's nothing really on your plate at the moment.

Now imagine that you and your partner are experiencing the same kinds of situations simultaneously (e.g., both busy at work, or both relaxing on a vacation). How does it feel to be matched in your time situations? It could feel good or not so good—for instance, when both partners are frantic at work, they may bounce off each other like balls ricocheting around a pool table! Likewise, when both partners feel lethargic and uninspired about the weekend, they can feed off each other and descend into a state of total, dull inertia.

But now imagine that you are experiencing quite different time circumstances—one of you is quite busy with work and will need to tote some tasks along on vacation (along with the skis or surfboard), while the other is ready to completely unwind and play. How might being in the same place time-wise, or in two different places, affect your respective time feels and sense of being in sync? And what if your degree of match in time feel and circumstances was not specific to one day or week but typical of your lives together?

All this is just to say that how we live in time brings certain powerful feelings, and when couple partners, like Chris and Susan, differ in their basic feel and approach to time, conflict often ensues.

The Three Times of Ancient Greece

Stepping back in historical time, the ancient Greeks recognized and named three different types of time, distinctions that remain useful today: *aion* (in English, aeon, and related to the word "eon"), meaning the unchanging eternity, the forever; *chronos*, or measurable time that is viewed as moving in an inexorable sequence of uniform units—seconds, minutes, and hours, days, months, and years, and extending along a linear, yet ever-growing path from past to present to future; and *kairos*, time viewed as meaningful episodes, events. Interestingly, *kairos* also carries the connotation of a special, significant, right, expedient, and "opportune" moment, one in which deep immersion in the present can have a powerful and positive impact both in the now and on the future.

Family systems theorists and time scholars L. Boscolo and P. Betrando note that of these three ancient definitions and senses of time, aeon is most related to religious belief and spiritual experience; chronos underlies the world of planning and schedules, time as an objective quantity; and kairos captures the sense of the subjective quality of experienced time.[4] Although chronos is often described as "objective," quantifiable time, and kairos as "subjective," experienced, qualitative time (aeon is left out of this distinction altogether), both chronos and kairos have "objective," observable aspects, and all three types of time affect our subjective experience and relationships in profoundly different ways.

To help you recognize how differently you feel when inhabiting each of these times, and to help you become a time traveler who can move among these three times at will, let's take a more careful look at them. As you read the following sections—a kind of "brief history of time"[5]—think about the following questions:

- Which time type or orientation do you experience most on a daily basis?
- What are moments or activities when you experience a different orientation to time? And what do you do to make the shift between one time feel and another?
- Which orientation to time do you find most appealing and why?
- Which do you find least appealing and why?
- Do you and your partner share the same general time orientation? If not, how does that become apparent in your relationship?

Chronos: The Time of the Clock and Calendar

First, let's enter chronos. Chances are you're already deeply immersed in it. You probably can quickly answer the questions, "What day is it? What month? What year?" Indeed, along with knowing *where* you are and *who* you are (not in the deep, existential, or spiritual sense, just facts about your identity such as your name and where you live), knowing the time—at least the day, month, and year—is one of the three pillars of being psychologically oriented. Being oriented to time, place, and person is a key component of one's mental status, routinely checked by mental health professionals when patients are brought to a psychiatric emergency room. When one's orientation to time is faulty, it's often a first sign of something serious, either a brain injury, progression in longer-term brain function degeneration, effects of drugs or other ingested substances, or psychosis.

Aside from these basics, you likely know the calendar date and the clock time—or you have ready access to several calendars or clocks to provide that information. These time-keeping devices are omnipresent. Most of us spend most of our days in this world of chronos. We frequently check our watches (or the clocks on our computers or mobile phones) to see if we are early, on time, or late, ahead of the game, right on schedule, or falling behind. We're planning our futures, checking off the days on our calendars as they pass. We fret about never having enough of this kind of time or, occasionally, more than we know what to do with. There's a conveyer belt sense in this kind of time—time is moving along, we can't stop it, and the best we can do is use it effectively and stay on the time track.

The linear, quantitative conception of time and ways to measure its progress likely date back to earliest humankind: Artifacts from the Paleolithic era indicate that early humans used the moon to calculate the passage of time. And our contemporary clocks and calendars evolved from systems devised in ancient Egypt. But it was the rise of capitalism and industrialism in the nineteenth and early twentieth centuries under the stewardship of a small group of powerful men at the helm of those economic movements that led to the increasing dominance of chronos in contemporary life—and with it came the increased emphasis on structuring our everyday lives in smaller units of time and the need to account for how we use our time. The factory whistle signaling the start and end of work (as well as break times) became the modern symbol of the power of chronos, lampooned so brilliantly by Charlie Chaplin in the film *Modern Times*. The advent of scientific management, as formulated in a classic 1911 work by Frederick W. Taylor, along with the creation of machines that could get more done in less time, resulted in the sense of a greatly speeded-up world and an emphasis on efficiency.[6]

If we could easily leave this highly structured sense of time at the workplace and readily shift into a more relaxed, off-the-clock experience of time in our personal lives, partners might conflict less about how to use their leisure time together. But many couples, like Chris and Susan, have at least one partner who has firmly internalized clock time as the best or only way to think about all aspects of their lives, including how much time they allot for sex, communication, fun, and other forms of intimacy.

Interestingly, this tendency to apply a highly structured approach to using time in our off-from-work hours is no accident. The scientific management approach of Taylorism was extended not only to scheduling workers' time on the job but to their leisure activities as well. Scheduling pleasurable leisure time was touted as a means of ensuring adequate rest and morally sound recreation for workers and their families. Still, scheduled leisure was clearly in the service of the companies' central goal, to maximize production. The current emphasis on creating smaller and smaller bits of "quality time" with partners and families—the limits of which we will discuss later in this chapter—grew in part from this practice of scheduling leisure. As chronos has increasingly become the world's dominant conception of time, we've come to live our lives almost exclusively by the clock and calendar, focused on whether we are effectively utilizing smaller and smaller chunks of what we view as an ever-diminishing, precious resource.

To be sure, clocks and calendars enable people to plan, make it possible to come together to share an event, to coordinate their efforts to create new things, and to specify when to attain steps toward a goal. The problem comes when chronos dominates our lives to the exclusion of all other ways of being in time. And the dominance of chronos has led to the prevalence of five myths about relationship time that interfere greatly with achieving pleasurable intimacy. These myths set an unrealistic bar or standard for how relationship time is supposed to come about at all, and limit our ideas about what types of activities represent true intimacy and fulfilling, quality time together. In addition to being an outgrowth of the dominance of chronos, these myths stem from other broad guiding beliefs in our culture—beliefs in personal freedom, in the attainability of perfection, in individual control over our destinies.

Five Myths about Relationship Time

The Myth of Spontaneity

The Myth of Spontaneity represents a kind of desperate but ultimately misguided backlash against the dominance of chronos. It shows our longing to protect our relationships from the same schedule mania that runs the rest of our lives. This myth suggests that great sex, as well as other forms of genuine fun and connection with our partners, must happen without planning, only when the spirit moves us. We think that a little deliberation or preparation for intimacy will douse the flames of desire. The power of this myth is revealed whenever I suggest to a couple that if fun and romance are to happen, they need to set aside time for it—actively and consistently. In other words, they need to put chronos to use to create time for connection and pleasure. The typical couple's reaction is a deep, discouraged sigh, sometimes accompanied by a knowing, shared glance that says, "We've heard *this* idea before." They turn back to me and groan that the last thing they want to do is "schedule sex" as if it were just another chore.

And with that reaction, I quite agree. *Scheduling*—a word associated with modern work practices—does not belong in conversations about intimacy. The word *routines* is no better. Both are antithetical to the mood of desire and play required for enjoyable sex and other forms of pleasure, fun, and intimacy. But given couples' overall busy-ness, some way of setting aside regular time for sex, fun, and connection is essential. For couples to feel inspired to do so, they need alternatives to the temporal metaphors of the work world.

To these couples, I suggest the idea of *creating rhythms of couple time*. The metaphor of creating regular rhythms of sex and intimacy carries a totally different set of connotations much more attractive and encouraging to couples. Unlike *schedules*, *rhythms* are as old as the universe and planet Earth itself. Rhythms are an essential aspect of the movement of planets, the eternal sequence of the seasons, the growth, death, and reemergence of plants and crops. As I'll discuss in chapter 4, rhythms are at the heart of the intricate, multilayered linkages among bodily systems in all living beings, and in the cycles of holidays and other human cultural events. Couples are much more likely to agree to try setting "rhythms of intimacy" in motion than they are to "schedule sex."

The Myth of Perfection

The Myth of Perfection is a direct extension of our valiant attempts to live in and control clock and calendar time. It holds that if we can organize our time and energy effectively, we *can* have it all—plenty of satisfying time with our partners, with our children, with extended family and friends; energetic, effective time at work; time for exercise and other health-promoting activities; for hobbies, community participation, and worship; and time for the weekly chores. By this account, the full, successful life results from skillful time management and successful multitasking.

Yet emerging research indicates that we are less productive and less satisfied with our work when multitasking than when unitasking.[7] And the electronic calendars on our computers, BlackBerries, iPhones, and other PDAs—with their capacity to fragment time into one-minute segments—create an unrealistic promise. We find that we can't fit it all in, no matter how organized we are.

Instead of trying to have it all at once, we need to make choices, to learn to say "no" or "not now" to some things so that we can say a more complete "yes" to others.[8] By doing this, we embrace the reality of different periods in our lives in which we will have to do some things and not others, and hope that our life lines will extend long enough to attain things not yet realized or to return to things temporarily left to the side. As it is said in Ecclesiastes, "For everything there is a season, and a time for every purpose under heaven." We have to make choices, sometimes tough ones, about what to invest our time in, when, and for how long, and what to let go, at least for the time being.

The Myth of Total Control

The Myth of Total Control is closely related to the Myth of Perfection. It holds that we are the masters of our destinies, no matter what sorts of time pressures are exerted on us—whether by our workplaces, by the needs of our families, by acute or chronic health issues (our own or those of our partners or family members) that may require time for care and downshifting life's pace, and even by large-scale events that affect society, such as the attacks on September 11 or Hurricane Katrina.

This is the time version of the foundational American myth of the "rugged individual" standing above and apart from his or her context, manipulating (indeed, at times exploiting) resources at will. It is also related to that other foundational myth, America, the land of limitless opportunity. When it comes to these myths about economic attainment, as sociologists Richard Sennett and Jonathan Cobb demonstrated in their classic book *The Hidden Injuries of Class*,[9] far fewer opportunities exist than the myths suggest. Those who strive and don't make it believe they have no one to blame but themselves.

These beliefs about our capacity to make money are paralleled by our beliefs about our ability to make time. So when we find ourselves buffeted

TABLE 2.1   THE FIVE MYTHS OF RELATIONSHIP TIME

Myths	The Wrong Idea	The Antidote
Myth of Spontaneity	All couple fun, pleasure, and sexuality must occur unplanned and spontaneously to be worthwhile.	Time for fun, pleasure, and sex must be set aside and preserved—but within that time, be spontaneous!
Myth of Perfection	Through careful scheduling and time management, we can do everything we want to for as long as we want.	Set priorities and make choices—What is most important and necessary to do at this phase of your life? What can you let go of, or do less of, for now?
Myth of Total Control	We are masters of our time. If we fail to achieve everything we want or need to do, it's completely our fault. We simply haven't mastered time management, or we are weaklings who cannot stand up for ourselves.	Recognize the powerful forces that determine our time—work schedules determined by employers and clients, children's and elders' needs, health issues, transportation schedules and resources, etc. Be gentle in your assessment of yourself and one another when it comes to making and preserving couple time!
Myth of Quality Time	As long as you are focused and attentive, it doesn't matter how small the segments of time you have for one another.	Focus and attentiveness are great, but quantity of time is important! Be sure to set aside sufficient time to hang out and let spontaneous things happen. See Myth of Spontaneity above!
The Housework-Fun Incompatibility Myth	Mundane chores of life must be cordoned off from the sublime pleasures of intimacy.	Utilize the natural, necessary rhythms and mindlessness of chores as time to connect!

by various real-life pressures rather than fully in command, we turn a critical eye on ourselves. And when it's our partners who are struggling to take charge of their time and failing to a greater or lesser degree, we blame them, resulting in conflict and poisoning the little time left for each other. Yet, by compassionately acknowledging the realistic temporal constraints on ourselves and our partners, we paradoxically create more opportunities to support each other in making small but significant changes toward a better balance of time for our relationships.

The Myth of Quality Time

This is the myth that as long as we are fully focused during the time we spend with our partners, our kids, or others we care about, small amounts of time together are just as good as more extended time. One unintentional result of this emphasis on quality time is that we allocate less and less time for our intimate relationships, believing we can do just fine with bits of contact. After all, if the time-management techniques pioneered during the advent of industrialism demonstrated that factories could produce more widgets (or their contemporary equivalents) while maintaining high quality, and if creating a sense of urgency[10] and a culture of high speed are viewed as the keys to corporate success,[11] why can't we produce high-quality relationship pleasure and connection even with smaller, faster bits of time?

The idea of inhabiting our time with loved ones more fully and intentionally has merit: Buddhism has long demonstrated, and the emerging Western science of flow corroborates,[12] that we enjoy our lives more and reduce our stress levels when we bring ourselves more fully into the present moment. But coupled with the increasing sense of time pressure and fragmentation exerted in the postindustrial version of chronos, the belief in quality over quantity time places unrealistically high demands on ourselves and our partners (and others) for making the most of our time.

Prominent work-life researcher Ellen Galinsky and her colleagues conducted a national survey about children's perspectives on their parents' work-family balance. She reported that children desire not just quality time but unstructured periods of time to "hang out" with parents.[13] My own research found that children, rather than parents, typically initiate family time—but this requires parents and children to be present and available to each other long enough for kids to start something up.

The same goes for couples. By attempting to make every minute count, and expecting high quality in all our togetherness time, we leave no room for the unplanned, for serendipity, for silence that becomes sound, for floating and dreaming and grooving together—not to mention awkward silences, transition time from thoughts about work, gradually getting in sync rhythmically and emotionally, or what could be called relationship sync-up time. Questioning the myth of quality time adds further impetus to couples' attempts to carve out and protect more substantial time.

The Housework–Fun Incompatibility Myth

This myth holds that the mundane chores of life must be cordoned off from the sublime pleasures of intimacy. This myth is a logical conclusion from all the previously described myths. In this view, chores are viewed generally as an unromantic drag, as far from passionate relationship *spontaneity* as one can get. Chores are usually experienced as an unpleasant but necessary part of the daily and weekly schedule, the unsavory side of life over which we attempt to exert *control* in creating the *perfectly* time-managed life. Pick up any women's home life management magazine, from the old stalwart *Good Housekeeping* to the cooler, contemporary *Real Simple*, and you're sure to find an article with 52 (or more, or less) tips to new and improved organization strategies designed to get the chores done efficiently and with as little effort and emotional investment as possible. Indeed, these articles appear in women's rather than in men's magazines because, at least in heterosexual couples, even when both partners work an equal number of hours, women do two-to-three times the number of routine chores that men do.[14] Same-sex couples divide chores more evenly.[15] As I'll discuss in greater detail in chapter 7, in many heterosexual couples, the doing of chores may evoke quite the opposite of loving or sexy impulses—instead, the doing of chores is often associated with feelings of resentment, unfairness, and bitterness.[16] And finally, because we (or at least she, and sometimes he) have to do all these chores on top of work, child care and homework supervision, elder care, and other responsibilities, the time needed to spend on chores contributes to the myth of *quality time*, leading us to feel we've got to jam time for relationships into the tiny cracks and crevices between all these other activities.

For all these reasons, it is assumed that love time and chore time cannot comingle.

And that is a big mistake. Because chores tend to have daily, weekly, or monthly rhythms of their own, couples that keep chores and intimacy separated miss many regular opportunities to hang out, chat, catch up, and experience a sense of joint purpose and achievement. Washing and drying dishes, sweeping up the kitchen and tidying up the countertops, folding laundry, changing the litter box or brushing the dogs, raking the leaves, grocery shopping, even paying the bills and assembling the tax records... the list of ready-made rhythms for couple time provided by necessary household tasks and chores are as numerous as a pile of leaves in autumn. And if partners are using chore time as time for intimacy, it goes a long way toward equalizing who shoulders the burden and responsibility for them, reducing the sense of unfairness. This is especially true for women, whose assessments of the overall fairness of the relationship are strongly associated with their perceptions of how equally housework and child care are distributed.[17] And when both partners feel the relationship is fair, they are more inclined to have sex.

Although we're focusing on your couple relationship, it's also worth noting that the daily quotient of pleasurable time between parents and kids can dramatically increase when kids and parents do chores together. And if you, like many couples, put time together last—after meeting work, parenting, and household responsibilities—by using chores as a time to connect with kids, you can free up more time for you and your partner.

In short, by recognizing and acting in opposition to the Housework-Fun Incompatibility myth, you can dramatically increase pleasurable couple time because you'll jump in on the existing rhythms devoted for chores, you'll become more efficient in getting those chores done, you'll increase the sense of partnership and fairness, and have more fun with the mundane aspects of life.

These five myths about couples, intimacy, and time pervade American culture and most other postindustrial societies ruled by the clock and the calendar. By becoming aware of how these myths pile on unnecessary pressure and keep you from seeing all the possibilities for enjoyable time together, you will be freer to proactively create and protect couple time.

In order to be able to step out of chronos, it's useful to be aware of other ways of experiencing time and how to shift into them. The very existence of other conceptions of time may surprise you since we don't often venture into these other temporal rivers. Yet they flow well within our reach and accessing them is essential to escaping the prison of the tick-tock. Let's look at what the ancient Greeks had to say about a completely different sense of time: Aeon.

Aeon: The Sense of Timelessness

Imagine that you are floating in a timeless, eternal void—or, in other views of the eternal, in an endless, unchanging expanse of "time-fulness." In either version (no time, or full time), nothing changes, nothing moves. There is no past, no future, only an endless present. Seeking contact with some version of this eternal time, believed to lie beyond the transitory world of chronos, has been the ultimate but elusive aim of most of the world's major religions.

Over the past two decades, there's been an exploding popularity of books, TV shows, courses, retreats, CDs, and DVDs providing guidance toward inhabiting the present moment,[18] attaining mindfulness,[19] and accessing the "power of now."[20] This search for some version of timelessness clearly attests to a hunger to step off the treadmill and experience true stillness.

A new wave of psychotherapies holds that psychological disorders and emotional suffering have a strong temporal component. For instance, a hallmark of depression is that time seems to move too slowly, making the future seem indistinguishable from the painful present. In anxiety disorders, time seems to move at a breakneck pace, the approaching future is filled with risk and worry, and persons feel pressured to the point of breaking. Research has found that helping patients gently immerse in, rather than try to run from, the emotionally fraught present moment can bring a tremendous amount of relief from suffering.[21]

Like Chris and Susan, Bhanu and Sunita differed in how much they prioritized adherence to chronos versus the pursuit of aeon. And for Bhanu, his sense of the relentless pressure to abide by clock and calendar time contributed to developing a constant state of anxiety, at times verging on panic. From the age of 5, his life had been dominated by academic achievement. After medical residency he worried about future positions and a seemingly endless stream of steps, tests, and evaluations to pass. When he was presented with a choice of jobs, he felt hopeless—not only about how to decide but about his career, as he already couldn't imagine a professional future that would not be dominated by worry.

As you'll recall from chapter 1, Sunita was raised with similar high academic pressures and expectations, and a few months before the couple came to see me, shortly after completing a prestigious medical residency in her specialty, she'd decided to pause for a year and see what life was like without all this future focus and pressure. In contrast to Bhanu's anxiety, the constant focus on the future and achievement had left her depleted and depressed. During her time off she had grown to appreciate activities that had nothing to do with furthering her education and career—spending time with friends, shopping and decorating their apartment, reading for pleasure, taking a course in painting, and "just hanging out" in her pajamas. She had finally come to appreciate the present moment, which made it all the more difficult to connect with the ever-worrying, future-focused Bhanu.

When it was clear that Bhanu felt paralyzed trying to decide his occupational future, I decided to take a different tack. Rather than continue to consider the specifics of which job might suit him best, I focused on helping him immerse more in the here and now. I observed to him that he was too caught up in chronos, which led him to feel tremendous anxiety about the future. He needed to cultivate the ability to be in the present moment, even as he continued to need to make choices about his future. After reimmersing in the here and now of his work, he'd be better able to answer some key questions: What are the moments in his work now that he enjoyed? How similar or different would those moments likely be in the new position? What moments did he not enjoy or even loathe? How much would the new job require him to immerse in similar moments? What different, appealing sorts of moments would the new position likely provide? And what different, less appealing ones would he have to immerse in?

Our work lives (indeed, our lives in general) are like a river ever flowing, sometimes more quickly, sometimes more slowly. When we are immersed fully in the work flow, even when things are moving quickly, we can often do quite well and even enjoy the energy of fast movement (as long as there are periods when things slow down). But when we climb out of the river and sit on the riverbank and watch the river of our lives moving past, we often can't imagine how we could ever cope with it. Bhanu had been spending way too much time on the riverbank of his life, especially his work life, and as result of all this river watching, he was becoming increasingly anxious about how he could ever manage.

Interestingly, for all their work-related links to the clock and calendar of linear time, both Bhanu and Sunita were practicing Hindus, a religion famous for its belief in circular time and in the unreality of the future. When I asked about how Bhanu's obsession with the future squared with his religious beliefs, he noted, with a self-deprecating, ironic smile, "Well, I guess that's one part of the religion I don't practice too well!" He and Sunita agreed that the Western model of education had the power to override their other, religion-based beliefs about time. "It's hard to believe the future doesn't exist when you've got to schedule patients weeks in advance and when getting trained as a doc is all about meeting rigidly set deadlines," she acknowledged.

Our discussions about the importance of presentness in the Hindu conception of time helped Bhanu realize he could draw on his religious-cultural time beliefs to provide a counterbalance to, and a break from, the overriding, anxiety-provoking influence of the clock and calendar in his life. And as they further explored this important cultural link between them, it brought him and Sunita closer through their joint desire to balance these two ways of experiencing time.

To provide them with further support for their joint efforts to immerse in the present, I e-mailed them a photo of a brush drawing by Thich Nhat Hanh, the great Vietnamese Buddhist leader and author of many books on mindfulness practice in contemporary society.[22] The drawing is of a simple circle, although the manner in which it was drawn suggests dynamic, circular motion filled with and surrounded by emptiness and stillness. I suggested that they, especially Bhanu, think about the significance of all the space created by this simple circle, and that during the week he try to create more space within and around the dynamic motion of his busy workday. I also suggested a few books on mindfulness (listed in this chapter's notes).

The following week, Bhanu exclaimed, with great excitement, that our metaphoric conversation about work, rivers, and riverbanks, space in time, dynamic movement, and emptiness led him to a powerful emotional breakthrough. He suddenly realized that this was precisely what he most lacked and longed for in his life—the ability to pause and to step back from the constant flow of work, from the overwhelming list of responsibilities, from the sense of being a "prisoner of time" construed as an endless sequential progression of scheduled tasks stretching from now into the future. On my suggestion he tried some classes in mindfulness meditation, which he embraced enthusiastically. As his ability to step out of chronos and into aeon improved, and as he immersed more fully in the various aspects of his work, he became clearer about those aspects he enjoyed most and least.

Realizing this led him to make the difficult choice of stepping away from the brilliant but time-consuming academic career his mentors had predicted for him and into a position that focused more on training and clinical work.

As a result, the couple's relationship improved markedly. They had more pleasurable, relaxed time together on a daily and weekly basis, deliberately leaving certain evenings during the week or days of the weekend completely unscheduled to spend however the spirit moved them in the moment. And when Bhanu left his job, he took three months off before starting the next one, during which he and Sunita did some long-postponed traveling.

Shifting between Chronos and Aeon

Like Bhanu and Sunita, you may feel your relationship is too dominated by the clock and calendar of chronos, with every hour and minute scheduled and accounted for. If so, follow their example—try leaving some times unstructured, just for hanging out or for activities you decide to do on a spontaneous whim. Try meditation, deep breathing exercises, or other mindfulness activities designed to create a sense of stillness and immersion in the present moment. Try doing these sorts of activities together. It's often hard for one partner to fully immerse in meditation or otherwise chill out in the moment while the other is busily handling affairs of the day. By doing these activities together, you can create your own couple culture of calmness, amplifying and reinforcing the level of peacefulness you would achieve alone.

Although I've been emphasizing some of the psychological and relationship hazards of an overfocus on chronos and touting the benefits of exploring aeon, sometimes we feel stuck doing the same thing day in and day out. Like Bill Murray's character in the classic comedy *Groundhog Day*, we can feel that we wake up every day to exactly the same routine. It's as if the chronos aspects of our lives—our daily and weekly schedule—become so repetitive that they become aeonic in quality. When this occurs, it's useful to try altering your daily or weekly rhythms even slightly. This can provide you with unexpected novelties that have always been available, but you've missed them because of your unchanging, repetitive schedule.

For instance, getting up a little earlier or staying up a little later, you might notice a different quality to the light or darkness, or a different smell or feel in the morning or evening air. You might find that you like seeing the sunrise although up until now you've missed it, or you might enjoy sighting the moon high in the sky. Cutting back on work time by just a half hour, getting in a little earlier or even—though I don't usually recommend this!—staying at work a little bit longer, you might find you get more done, or find your can enjoy some quiet time at the office that's usually overwhelmingly frantic and noisy. You might try a small change in the rhythm of your week. Doing the grocery shopping on a different day, you might find the vegetables and fruits are fresher, or the store less crowded, or that you run into more of the neighbors and have newfound opportunities for a chat. You might try taking off part of a weekday (if not every week, then at least once a month) and doing something different with the time, such as going to a museum or out for a coffee with a friend. And you might try changing when in the year you take your vacation, or on which holidays you visit relatives.

The same time techniques apply to creating novelty in a stuck relationship. Research shows that engaging in exciting new activities together can increase a couple's relationship satisfaction. The research focuses only on doing a new and exciting *type* of activity—going to a music concert, play, or interesting lecture, skiing or hiking, dancing, and in two experiments, being strapped together and having to walk on hands and knees on gym mats and crossing a barrier while balancing a pillow between them (the things psychologists come up with for experiments!).[23] Although I don't yet have the research data to back up this claim, I've found that couples can get a similar charge of novelty and excitement simply by changing the time of day, the time of week, of month, or year when they do any of their typical but now somewhat boring activities. Making love in the morning instead of the evening. Vacations in the fall instead of the summer. Staying up really late talking once in a while when you're used to a routine of early to bed and early to rise. Getting up in the dark at 5 A.M. in the morning to watch the sunrise, instead of your usual 7 A.M. wake-up time. Having a special snack at 3 A.M.

The point is that when we are bored and stuck, we often think first about trying a new activity, or a new job, or even trading in our old partner for a new one! By simply harnessing the power of chronos to alter aeon to shake up the stifling repetition of your life routines, by changing the temporal location of *when* you do the same old things with the same old person, you may find unexpected freshness, revitalization, and serendipitous opportunities.

The Meaningful Moment: Kairos

The ancient Greeks defined kairos as a moment in time experienced as a release from chronological time, the special and meaningful that is also fleeting and must be seized and utilized. Kairos is the source of the later Roman concept *carpe diem* (seize the day). Interestingly, in ancient Greek culture, the term kairos derived both from the art of archery—where it signified the opening or spatial tunnel through which an arrow had to pass forcefully in order to hit its target—and from the craft of weaving, in which the yarn must be pulled through an opening that appears in the cloth only momentarily as the loom operates.[24] Thus, it means a moment when a crack or portal momentarily opens up in the ongoing wall of time, providing new opportunities. Kairos moments are experienced as particularly influential times in our lives. They may be experienced as "time out of time," when even though the clock keeps ticking, we feel so focused on the moment that the action seems to have slowed down or become suspended.

This quality of time slowing down or standing still coupled with a high degree of positive emotional arousal and concentration is characteristic of what psychologist Mihály Csíkszentmihályi has called flow.[25] Many contemporary filmmakers like the Wachowski brothers (*The Matrix*) and Ang Lee (*Crouching Tiger, Hidden Dragon*) have utilized special effects in martial arts sequences to portray the unique, dramatically powerful experience of kairos, beautifully illustrating the experience of slowed time in a moment that actually passes extremely quickly. Such experiences in general, including those first encounters with a potential new lover, often have this sense of deep immersion, along with a sense of significance, of time out of time, of presenting a significant turning point, an opportunity to be seized. These encounters also often promise the possibility of erotic moments, which at their best also involve a heightened sense of presence and specialness, enhanced in good part by the love hormones coursing through our bodies.[26]

Think about a moment in your life that had heightened meaning and that represented a kind of turning point. It might have been associated with an important personal ritual or transition, such as a religious ceremony of arriving at manhood or womanhood, or a graduation, a wedding or commitment ceremony. Or kairos might have visited you during a powerful life event—a birth or a death, meeting a special person, a first kiss or first declaration of love, or a final goodbye to a friend or lover. Or a moment when you received special recognition at work, an important promotion, or a professional honor. Or when you got an unexpected opportunity to meet someone you greatly admire.

Or it might have been a moment when something completely seren-dipitous occurred that changed your life forever, in a positive way. Couples who report that their relationship was "love at first sight" often describe their first, unplanned encounter as having this quality.[27] Just think of Tony and Maria in *West Side Story*—they sight each other from across the room, surrounded by the members of their ethnic gangs and, as in a slow-motion dream, draw closer to one another—until rudely awakened by the protesta-tions of their friends and family members.

Sometimes, rather than being paired with an event that has "special" or "unique" written all over it from the start, we enter kairos's height-ened present-ness through seeing familiar things or people, but with fresh eyes and a deeper sense of appreciation, sometimes opening a new direc-tion for our lives. A central tenet of many religions and philosophies of life—whether the American Transcendentalist movement of Emerson, Thoreau, and Whitman, the European Existentialism of Kierkegaard, Sartre, Camus, and de Beauvoir, or Buddhism and other traditions that practice some form of mindfulness—directs us toward grasping with new or renewed wonder the common, the everyday, the familiar.

The key to a satisfying life, some say, is to infuse even the most mundane of moments with a sense of presence, preciousness, and possibility. The prominent American Buddhist Jack Kornfield titled one of his books *After the Ecstasy, the Laundry*.[28] He writes: "What happens when the Zen master returns home to spouse and children? What happens when the Christian mystic goes shopping? What is life after the ecstasy?" Rather than the orig-inal quest for nirvana (a more aeon-like state of unchanging bliss), contem-porary Buddhist practitioners are more likely to seek kairos moments of clarity and joy and bring those experiences back to regular life.

In the land of love, for some the moment of kairos occurs upon first meeting, for others it takes place down the road a bit. Rather than experi-encing love at first sight, for some the birth of their romantic relationship came after a period of knowing each other as colleagues or friends.[29] One couple I worked with had met as volunteers in a charity organization, and for months they were friendly and collegial but barely noticed each other. One day they happened to sit together for lunch, and looking into each others' eyes, sparks flew that grew into a full-fledged love.

Yet with this couple, as with many others when I first meet them in therapy, by the time they'd come to see me, they felt so ground down by the conflicts they'd experienced and by the boring routines of their lives, they had lost touch with what they felt was special about each other in the first place. With such couples, after hearing about the problems plaguing their lives in the present, I always ask them how they first met and what they each first found attractive about the other. Often, the serious, pained faces of each partner suddenly brighten as they recall that first meeting, or the first time they really took notice of each other. They often say things like: "She was the smartest woman I'd ever met, we just talked for hours, and I also found her incredibly beautiful"; and, "He was so kind and funny, he really made me laugh, and he didn't take himself so seriously like other guys I'd met."

Recalling these initial positive bonding experiences with our partners can restore a sense of hope and excitement, essential for bringing us together to create changes in how we spend our time together.

Of course, events that we hoped would feel special—like that first meeting of your future partner, or the moment when, at least for one of you, the relationship shifted from "just friends" to "object of desire"—can be experienced with a range of feelings that would make them distinctively unlike kairos. A first kiss with a new partner might have been awkward or disappointing (if not downright repellant), rather than transporting. One might be consumed with anxiety while going through one's wedding, and afterward feel like it was all an unpleasant blur.

When couples describe their first meeting or the early weeks of their relationship as bland, uninspiring, or even unpleasant, or when they have difficulty identifying any moment in their history when they experienced really falling in love, I encourage them to locate any points in their joint history when things improved, when they started to feel, even if fleetingly, a sense of specialness about one another. Sometimes those moments occurred but by now are buried under years of bitterness and resentment. I ask such couples to recall together the positive, peak experiences they've shared up until now. It could be a moment during a first vacation together, the time when they started to feel really in sync sexually, the birth of their first child—even meeting the in-laws for the first time! Sometimes when an event that we predict won't go well defies our expectations, we can experience it with that sense of specialness characteristic of kairos.

In addition, although some contemporary writing on kairos pairs it exclusively with positive emotion, the traditional usage of the term suggests that such experiences can be either positive or negative. Opportunities for kairos often occur in moments of crisis or conflict, such as in a near-fatal accident, in response to a death or an attack. Sometimes it is these sorts of events that stand out in a couple's history as particularly intense and as life-changing—getting caught in a dangerous storm at sea in a small boat, being mugged, surviving a car crash, having a miscarriage, and the death of a child.

These sorts of events typically either bring a couple together or present rifts that can drive them apart. If an event holds special significance for one but not the other, it is crucial that the couple revisit the event so that the one deeply affected can express her (or his) feelings, as well as her (or his) hurt and loneliness at having experienced the event seemingly alone. Sometimes, the one who seems unaffected has consciously or unconsciously squelched his (or her) feelings as a way of trying to help the most affected partner cope, and as a way for both of them to move on from the painful event. Unfortunately, this strategy may set off a polarizing pattern in which one partner feels stuck holding the memories and emotions associated with the powerful past experience while the other insists on letting it go. The more one attempts to move on, the more the other holds on to the event and its associated feelings. Talking about the event and about how each partner felt about it can allow the one holding on to finally lessen his or her psychological grip on the event. It can also allow the other finally to experience suppressed emotions about it. They can then bridge the chasm created by the different positions they took toward this significant moment in time and can move on together, putting that event in it's proper place in their shared history.

Similarities and Differences Among the Three Times

There is overlap between the experience of aeon and the experience of kairos. Both involve a sense of release from the passage of chronological time, both involve deep immersion in the present. Yet while the promise of aeon (whether in this life or, in the view of most major religions, in an afterlife) is of an ongoing immersion in the endless now, kairos seems by definition more fleeting, a kind of briefer, peak, intense experience. And while by definition, immersion in eternity means time stops and there is no more future or past, the now of kairos powerfully shifts one's direction into the future.

Although the experiences of time in chronos and kairos are qualitatively different, there's also an interesting overlap in how they operate in our lives. One consequence of a meaningful kairos experience is that it affects our path into the future, often by shifting our life direction in previously unplanned and unanticipated ways. It is a moment of realization, of novel, heightened experience, of more acute awareness of our selves in the world, that may have consequences for how we choose to live our lives and construct our future. And conversely, we must make time in our schedule in order to experience kairos—or at least, we must stay attuned and open to the possibility of such a moment so that we can shift from the everyday flow of time across clock and calendar and experience the unique moments that characterize kairos.

How to Use the Three Types of Time

You needn't be locked into just one type of time—especially if you are, like most people, stuck in the all-pervasive chronos. Being aware of the three types of time will allow you to recognize when you've had too much of one and not enough of the others. Awareness of the three textures of time is the first step in your ability to shift your relationship to time. When you need a break from the grinding mill (or, at times, the exciting forward movement) of chronos, you can seek out experiences that create a sense of endless, peaceful, and eternal aeon. When you want to shake things up a bit, want to break out of your rut, there's kairos to the rescue to help you experience your life moments as special and unique. As I described, you can also use chronos—small changes in the timing of your daily, weekly, monthly, or yearly life events—to shake up a life in which everything feels too predictable. And if life feels just too darned meaningful, precious, and intense all the time, you can even move from kairos to chronos, reimmersing yourself in the sometimes comforting mundane of the everyday. When we've had a series of significant events happen one after another, either positive, negative, or both, we can long for a sense of regularity, even a bit of boredom in how we spend our time.

Resolving Time Type Differences

Your relationship is affected by how in sync you are with your partner in the type of time you value, seek, and predominately inhabit. It can be a problem when each partner seeks and inhabits a different one of these three types of time predominantly or exclusively.

For instance, John, a calm, logical CPA in his early 50s, loved the predictability of his daily routines and sought a sense of sameness day after day. In contrast, his wife, Eleanor, an emergency room nurse in her late 40s, was drawn to drama and saw deep meaning and significance in events that John didn't even notice. Their emotional conflicts largely centered on their profoundly different temporal orientations. John was a good example of someone who utilized chronos—keeping regular schedules—as a means to achieve aeon, a sense of life experiences as relatively unchanging, while Eleanor was an enthusiast of kairos. She was always trying to get a rise out of him and make him see the significance of small moments; he was always trying to calm her down and get her back to the regularly scheduled program, to a sense that things were essentially unchanged or, if anything, gradually changing in a positive direction. Our initial sessions typically began with my asking, "So, how was your week?" To which Eleanor would either reply "Wonderful!"—and then describe a moment between them that held great meaning for her and that John could barely remember—or "Horrible!"—and then describe an equally meaningful but unpleasant moment that she experienced as signifying the futility of their relationship and that John would also have initial difficulty recalling. In contrast, John's reply each time was, "Oh, it was a pretty good week, pretty much the same. I think things are generally getting better." On weekends, John preferred to follow a comfortable routine of sleeping a little late, reading the paper together over coffee, doing some shopping, making some dinner, making love. Eleanor, on the other hand, regularly checked Websites for upcoming concerts, especially by the famous aging rock bands of the 60s and 70s that they both enjoyed, arguing that "if we don't see them now, we may never have the chance again!" In other words, Eleanor, in true kairos style, sought to capture unique opportunities and seize the special meaning of their moments, whereas John generally preferred to create an aeon sameness to their life, smoothing out the ups and downs of particular moments into a relatively comfortable warm bath of chronos-driven routine.

To help Eleanor and John decrease their conflicts and bridge their differences, I applied my four-step method of Relationship Rhythms Analysis to resolve time-based problems and get couples in sync: Reveal, Revalue, Revise, and Rehearse.

First, I introduced them to the three types of time, *revealing* that underneath the specific contents of each of their fights were dramatic differences in how much they emphasized chronos, aeon, and kairos. We also explored the ways in which each had adopted and strengthened their respective time styles as a way to deal with challenges growing up in their respective families. John had grown up with an alcoholic father whose emotions and behavior ranged widely depending on whether he was drunk or not. The father's drinking also meant periods of job loss when the family struggled financially. John, blessed with a calm temperament, wanted nothing more than to have a safe, predictable life—the less change, the better. As a teen and adult, he refined his inborn calmness and created routines that led to a sense of stability. And by becoming an accountant and tax expert, he entered a profession in which he could obtain a steady income and help himself and others achieve financial security. Yet, sometimes he longed for a bit more excitement.

Eleanor, on the other hand, grew up in a family in which the routines and rituals were so regular as to feel stifling. Emotionally sensitive and temperamentally excitable from birth, she brought a higher level of energy and enthusiasm for life that her parents at times welcomed (nicknaming her "the fireball," not only for her temperament but her flaming red hair) and at others times tried to dampen. As a teenager refining her personality and distinguishing herself from her family, she became even more committed to her style of experiencing strong emotions, seeking out special moments that would evoke strong feelings. To that effect, she was drawn to nursing as a profession and found emergency medicine particularly exhilarating. Despite her determination to create an existence different from her family's routinized, emotionally even ambience, and after spending her 20s and 30s in a series of passionate but short-lived love affairs, she came to long for a more emotionally calm relationship through which she could settle down into a more predictable life.

Revealing their respective allegiances to fundamentally different time types, which were in turn connected to their respective lifelong attempts to create higher or lower emotional intensity and life predictability, provided Eleanor and John a new and interesting way of thinking about their mutual frustrations. This view of their relationship struggles as based on fundamentally different time orientations allowed them to step back from the intensity of the specific conflicts and see one another and themselves with greater understanding and compassion.

We then explored the history of how they met and what attracted each to the other. John initially loved how Eleanor could seemingly make any moment special, generating excitement when his predictability edged into boredom, and Eleanor originally felt calmed by John's steadiness and predictability, reminding her of the positive side of her overly monotonous family life. Recognizing how their disparate time types played into their mutual attraction helped them *revalue* these differences. I helped them see that the problem wasn't the differences per se, but that over the years, the "time roles" they took in their relationship had become increasingly extreme and polarized, as each felt responsible for holding up their end of the implicit time balance in the relationship. The more Eleanor pointed out to John the implications for their marriage's future of certain experiences—especially the negative ones—the more John tried to minimize the importance of these moments and convince Eleanor that they were doing fine overall. The more Eleanor searched for potential "one-of-a-kind" experiences to savor on the weekend, the more John suggested they stick to the known and familiar. I joked with them that the ancient Greek gods of Chronos, Aeon, and Kairos were in constant battle for control of the time orientation of their marriage, and they laughed.

As an exercise in grasping each other's perspective and *revising* their respective time roles to create greater flexibility in their approach to time, for two weeks I had each one deliberately adopt the role usually taken by the other. Each day, John had to point out an interaction that might portend either a positive or quite negative meaning for their lives together, and Eleanor had to reassure him that overall, they were doing fine, and things were likely going to work out well. John also took responsibility for finding and suggesting unique, "limited-time-only" activities for them to do, while Eleanor had to assert the importance of keeping to their regular routines. Not surprisingly, this seemingly simple exercise was challenging for them both, but it had the intended effect of shaking up and depolarizing their time positions. Just as any successful negotiation occurs when competing positions are distinguished from the persons who initially held them,[30] separating each time type from the partner who usually advocated it freed them to become more flexible.

As they *rehearsed* trading time roles over a few weeks, John and Eleanor were able to see how their conflicting time styles could be combined. They learned that they could have a life that recognized the comfort of regular routines as well as the excitement of seeking the new and unique. The gods Chronos, Aeon, and Kairos could sit at the same table.

Time is what we make of it. Time is not out there, a purely objective feature of our life and world, just chugging along down a one-way track like a train traveling the route of our destiny, with our progress marked by the digital clicks of the clock and the boxes of the calendar. That view of time certainly dominates our world these days, and it's got great usefulness, but we can tune into other ways of experiencing time that provide an important counterbalance to the somewhat relentless nature of chronos. Recognizing the availability of aeon—the sense of suspended, peaceful timelessness—and kairos—the opportune, special moments of heightened experience—allows us to shift among three time types as needed. We associate each with different states of emotion—although you and your partner may differ greatly in how each type of time feels to you and whether each provides primarily positive or negative feelings. Each time type, if lived to the exclusion of the others, can feel limiting. Each time type can become a trap or a door. All have wonderful things to offer a time-full life.

Furthermore, *recognizing* that you and your partner may each favor one time orientation over another can help you identify the temporal basis of your conflicts. Many of your struggles about how to spend your time—or your seemingly discrepant emphases on work versus play, predictability versus novelty, change versus continuity, excitement versus calm—may be rooted in your different degrees of allegiance to one of these basic time orientations over the others. *Revaluing* the different time orientations you each have come to represent and the role those different time orientations played in your initial attraction to one another; *revising* the balance of these orientations in your day-to-day lives, thereby reducing the polarization in who takes responsibility for representing the usefulness of each time type; and *rehearsing* these new patterns—these four steps can provide you with a fuller, less conflicted, and greatly revitalized relationship. Ferreting out the hidden influence of the Five Myths of Relationship Time will provide you the freedom to create successful rhythms of relationship that guarantee sufficient time for pleasure while avoiding needless blame and guilt for somehow not managing your schedule perfectly. And, you may get the chores done more quickly and painlessly.

As we will explore throughout the rest of this book, the quantity, pace, flow, and patterning of time are largely under your control. We can take charge of our couple time. Realizing this central truth about time is a key to making practical changes in our lives, both in relationship to time and in the time of our relationships.

The Tortoise and the Hare: Making Peace with Pace Differences

"I CAN'T KEEP UP the pace! I'm always rushing around. It feels like the world's moving too fast, and no matter how hard I try, I'm always falling behind!" How often do we hear, or utter, these words to describe our experience of time? I'm sure when you read the title of this chapter, you assumed it would be a litany about our fast-paced lives and tips on how to keep on top of the tempo or find peace and tranquility in a jacked-up world. The solutions to dealing with today's hyper-speed pace offered by most books fall into three categories of advice:

1. Get organized—for example, the book, *Time Management from the Inside Out.*[1]
2. Harness speed as a powerful means to influence others and obtain desired outcomes—for example, the book *It's Not the BIG that Eat the SMALL... It's the FAST that Eat the SLOW: How to Use Speed as a Competitive Tool in Business* (CAPS in the original!).[2] Or another business book, titled *A Sense of Urgency.*[3]
3. Resist the pull of pace, drop out of the race, or at least simplify, and slow down—as in the books *Slow is Beautiful*[4] and *In Praise of Slowness.*[5]

All three of these perspectives offer useful strategies for living in our fast-paced world. I will draw upon them as resources as we explore the most effective ways to manage and best utilize the pace of life today.

Often partners conflict because their paces differ. The metaphor of two ships passing in the night doesn't apply. Rather, the problem of partner pace differences is more akin to ships trying to sail side by side in a two-boat flotilla but finding themselves sailing at widely different knots. Sailing through life at different speeds, couples find it hard to connect, to communicate, or to coordinate their activities and efforts to build and maintain a life together.

Let's recognize that our fast pace is often not of our choosing. At work we're expected to produce more and faster. The daycare hours for our kids extend to just after work hours so we have to rush to meet them. There is little time in the evening for dinner and homework, and we're again forced to move at breakneck speed just to not fall behind. It's an aspect of human nature known as the availability bias to assume that others accomplish their tasks with less effort than you do, that things come easier to them. So we grow envious and want to know why our partners can't help us achieve and maintain the Jones's pace. The Fast One in a relationship moans to her partner, the Slow One, "Everyone else I know gets things done faster than you, wants to fit as much as possible into the weekend, and likes the idea of snowmobiling through the Alaskan tundra at high speed…how did I end up with such a slug?" On the other hand, for persons who like to take a stand and go against the tide, the fast pace of contemporary life provides the perfect foil for what's wrong with the world, and the target for their rebel yell can move from society at large to their fast-moving partners. The Slower One asks, "Why are you such a conformist? Why do you want to stay in the rat race? Don't you want to 'go your own way,' be your own woman? Plus, you're so uptight all the time—doesn't look like fun for you, and it sure isn't fun being around you!"

Personal pace runs (or walks) deep. Research on temperament in child development shows that the ways our parents responded to our in-born temperament affects whom we're drawn to as our intimate partner. If we were trained or encouraged early on to develop our innate energetic and excitable side, we bring that emotion style, along with its associated speediness, to the mating market. If instead we were trained or encouraged early on to bring out our capacity for calmness and slowness, that emotion/pace combo style is part of what others perceive about us and find either appealing or a turn-off.

The startling discovery I've made in studying and helping couples with pace differences is that the partner's pace and the role it plays in how they handle emotions is one of the key attractants early in the relationship, and we often pick persons whose pace is the opposite of ours. We unconsciously look to our partner to either speed us up (and energize us) or slow us down (and calm us). But somewhere along the journey we get tired of having our partner rush us (if we are slower) or drag us down (if we are temperamentally faster). And there's the rub that leads to couple conflict. The interesting thing is that most couples don't realize the root problem of their conflict is the difference in their pace—they complain of "communication difficulties," "arguments about getting things done," "different energy levels." The slow partner describes the fast partner as "neurotic," "restless," or "anxious," while the fast one assesses the slow one as "boring," "uninspired," "unmotivated," or "depressed." Yet, like the other elements of personal time, deep-seated pace differences manifest in surface issues such as communication breakdowns, unsatisfying sexual intimacy, and overall daily irritation about just feeling constantly out of sync.

Let's start by putting you on the pace map. You and your partner will create a "pace profile" by answering some questions that will help you identify your individual overall paces and how much these differences have affected your relationship.

Where Are You in Time? Assessing Your and Your Partner's Paces

To assess your pace and your partner's pace and the degree of difference between the two of you, use the brief form of my Life Pace Questionnaire. (For the complete questionnaire, go to my Web site: www.syncyourrelation ship.com.)

Question 1 asks you to rate yourselves on a scale that ranges from 1 (extremely slowly) to 8 (extremely quickly) for twelve everyday behaviors. To determine the overall similarity or difference between your and your partner's paces, subtract the lower total from the higher total score. The larger the difference in your total scores the higher the degree of pace difference.

Keep in mind, however, that even when partners are quite well matched in their paces on most activities, a large difference on one or two everyday activities can create conflict. For instance, you and your partner may have a similar pace of walking, talking, and completing your morning bathroom routines. But you may differ greatly in your speed of eating—maybe you wolf it down while he slowly picks at his food, or vice versa. Or perhaps you are well matched on getting things done around the house, waking up, and getting dressed, but when you're out walking together he always seems to run down the sidewalk while you prefer a more leisurely, measured pace. Periodically when he realizes you're not at his side, he turns to give you that "Come on!" glare; or you shout out to him (as my wife does when I

Life Pace Questionnaire
(brief version)

1. **Individual Life Pace:** Persons can differ in the speed or pace at which they do various life activities. Each of the scales below describes activities that can be done at different speeds or paces. Using the following 8-point scale, enter the number in the space provided that best describes your pace *in general*.

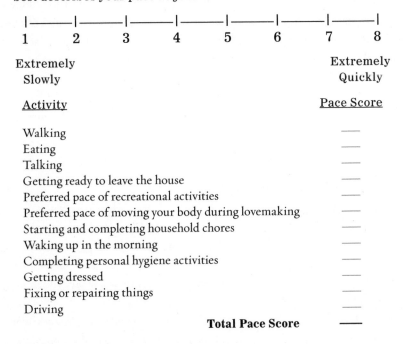

Activity	Pace Score
Walking	——
Eating	——
Talking	——
Getting ready to leave the house	——
Preferred pace of recreational activities	——
Preferred pace of moving your body during lovemaking	——
Starting and completing household chores	——
Waking up in the morning	——
Completing personal hygiene activities	——
Getting dressed	——
Fixing or repairing things	——
Driving	——
Total Pace Score	——

2. **Perception of life pace match:** How similar do you feel your life pace is with that of your partner? Circle a number.

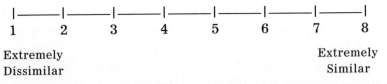

3. **Satisfaction with life pace match:** How satisfied are you with the degree of match between your life pace and your partner's life pace? Circle a number.

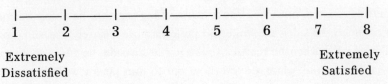

4. **Most influential life pace:** Whose life pace has more of an effect on your time together—your life pace, or your partner's? Circle a number.

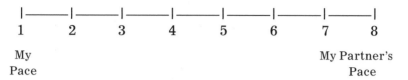

My
Pace

My Partner's
Pace

5. **Frequency of conflict around life pace:** How frequently do disagreements, arguments, or fights between you and your partner revolve around life pace issues? Circle a number.

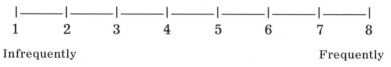

Infrequently   Frequently

unwittingly propel myself away from her because of my lifelong tendency to walk quickly), "It's not a race!"

So, after you've looked at your overall pace difference score, review your answers for each activity and see if any differ by at least 3 scale points. Talk together about how that discrepancy affects you—does it pop up as a frequent point of irritation, blow up as a major issue, or is it barely notable? No couple is the same, and no research to date (not mine or anyone else's) has established that relationship distress or happiness is tied to a specific, objective degree of difference in pace. For some, a slight difference creates that sense of being out of sync; for others, the differences only become noticeable when they are more extreme.

Instead, it seems that each partner's *perception* of the degree of match is more important than the objective overall (or specific behavioral) degree of similarity or difference in pace. By "perception" I simply mean how it seems or appears to you. There are numerous scientific studies showing that our perception of whether time is moving slowly or quickly is different under different circumstances.[6] The clock keeps ticking along at the same old pace, but on some occasions time seems to pass quickly, and on others those same tick-tocks seem to last forever. The same goes for how we view our own pace and that of our partner. You may think your partner is a speed demon, yet he sees his pace as totally normal. He may feel there's a huge difference between your respective paces of doing the morning ablutions, while you don't see it that way. With that in mind, use Question 2 to rate your perceptions about the degree of pace match or similarity between you and your partner. Do you have similar or different perceptions? If different, talk more about how you view one another, and see if you can come to a greater consensus about the degree of similarity or difference of your paces. Developing this shared appraisal is the first step toward resolving difficulties that arise from pace differences.

Your discussion about similarity or difference in life pace likely moved into Question 3: How satisfied is each of you with the degree of match in your respective life paces? A person could have a pace quite different from that of his or her partner but still consider it to be a good match. What about you? What about your partner? Do you agree? Disagree? Talk about it.

Question 4 probes whose life pace has more of an effect on your time together—your life pace or your partner's? If your paces are different, do you and your partner share control over the speed at which you walk, eat meals, make love, start and finish tasks? Or is one of you always speeding things up while the other really wants to slow down? Conversely, is one of you always asserting a slower speed while the other wants things to move more quickly? One of the major areas of conflict between partners centers on whether one or the other sets the pace of their lives together. When one partner feels pushed around by the other's pace, it can lead to resentment and conflict. What's true for you and your partner? Do you agree? Disagree? Talk about it.

Compared to other aspects of your relationship, how important is the issue of life pace? Once couples start thinking about it, they are often surprised at how much of an issue differences in their paces present. Think about the other issues you may deal with—disagreements about how to handle money, difficulties in communication, differing attitudes about spending time with in-laws or friends versus with each other. How do these common issues compare to your struggles around the general speed of your life? Your responses to Question 5 can guide a discussion about how frequently disagreements, arguments, or fights between you and your partner revolve around life pace issues. This conversation can set the stage for taking action to revise your pace differences to create less conflict.

Several permutations of a couple's paces may land them in trouble—one slow and the other operating at breakneck speed, or maybe two slowpokes or two speedsters. You might both be full-fledged members of the Speed Society and, like most people enamored of the fast lane, at times you crash and burn. You complain about having no time for quiet and calm. Creating a more balanced life rhythm in which you preserve, on a regular daily or at least weekly basis, time to decompress and slow down together can provide much needed diversity in your pace profile.

Conversely, you may be a couple that suffers at times from your both being too slow. You may both be folks that have difficulty keeping up with the fast pace of life humming all around you in work or other areas of endeavor. And although your relationship may feel cozy and relaxed when you're off-task and are not confronting life challenges, maybe at times even the pace of leisure activities feels sluggish and time together lacks excitement.

It would be unfair to discuss couples' temporal rates without admitting that our lives are stressed by outside factors.

The Speed Society

In his 1999 book *Faster: The Acceleration of Just about Everything*, James Gleick[7] compiled a startling list of everything that has sped up. And just think—that was 1999! In 1999 an Intel microprocessor operated at 1,350 MIPS (million instructions per second), and by 2010 it had increased 109 times over, to 147,600 MIPS! In 1970, a general practice doctor had an average of 30 minutes to hear your complaints and make an initial diagnosis. Today, the average is 7 minutes! The number of cuts in an action film (shifts between angles and characters' viewpoints) have steadily increased over the history of film: now when you watch a fight scene, the speed of the movement between fighters' perspectives rivets your nervous system and attention,[8] and watching the film can feel like you're receiving a 1-2 punch.

Everywhere are messages that we should pick up the pace if we want a life of excitement, success, wealth, and belonging. Ever since the personal computer and the Internet blasted into our lives in the mid-1990s, I've made a hobby of collecting magazine advertisements and taken photos of those full-body ads on bus stop billboards for computers with faster and faster processor speed and speedier Internet connectivity. My favorite ad for a high-speed modem says, in big, ominous black letters on a devil-red background, "Waiting for Data Is a Sin," then in smaller letters touts the product's speed-demon rate of connectivity. Another favorite of my speed-tech ads is for mobile phones: a photo with stylish-looking young executive types tobogganing down a long marble staircase, all smiles, with ties and pearl necklaces whipping back in the wind, cell phones at their ears. Another: a tech mag cover that declares "The Speed Issue" with a bird-winged laptop flying into cyber-space. It would all be funny if it didn't signal a fundamentally flawed prem-ise of our cultural zeitgeist: faster is always better, and we must jack up our nervous systems to match the pace of our ever-faster technological servants. Indeed, we may wonder who is the master and who is the servant in the human-tech relationship, as we respond simultaneously to our jangling cell phones, an incoming fax, our daily dose of 100 e-mails (many marked with a little red "urgent!" exclamation point), while also sending a quick response to someone else who just *must* reach us even faster, barging into our visual space via IM (for those of you uninitiated, Instant Messaging).

Then, of course, there's the urgency with which we struggle to fix or replace computers, phones, and online connections when they break down. There's nothing quite like the contemporary panic of having your hard drive crash—especially when you haven't backed it up in a while. So sym-biotically linked are most of us to our computers that when they malfunc-tion, we feel as if we've just had a seizure or incurred a lesion in our own brains (since many of our visual and auditory memories, notes, schedules, and ideas are stored in that slim, squarish slab of plastic, flickering little multicolored LCD lights, and metal). Life seems to go on hold, or goes on but in relative slow motion. Until we're up and online again, we're lost, moving in a viscous liquid while others continue to race by, sending and receiving, receiving and sending. Dropping and smashing or losing a cell phone leads to the same panic—how will anyone reach us? What if we miss a text from a friend or a crucial client call?

Sure, there are still places we can go to temporarily get off the high-tempo track, but in most of those places, the fast tempo life is all around, like the winds of a tornado whipping around a calm center. In Brazilia, Brazil, the city borders on the rainforest. In Nairobi, Kenya, the city sky-line can be seen from a neighboring wild game reserve. Walk a few blocks outside the old sections of cities across the world—beautiful, history-laden, far-flung metropolises like San Juan, Puerto Rico, New Orleans, Louisiana, Kyoto, Japan, Florence, Italy, Iraklion, Crete, Buenos Aires, Argentina, or Istanbul, Turkey—and in literally just a few steps you leave an era of a slower, more human-scale tempo that existed for hundreds or even thousands of years and are jettisoned in time into a world where let-ters take seconds rather than weeks to travel to distant corners of the globe, where a journey from New York to Hong Kong that would have taken weeks by ship can be accomplished in 19 hours, where instead of a leisurely one-to-two-hour lunch and a nap, families rarely eat lunch together during the work week and spend an average of 14 minutes eating dinner when they eat together at all.

Ours is the Speed Society. Peter Whybrow, a psychiatrist and head of the Semel Institute for Neuroscience and Human Behavior at UCLA, describes American culture as a kind of mania—we're moving faster and faster, and when we inevitably reach a block that forces us to slow down and adjust our expectations, we experience depression.[9]

This bipolar fallout of the high-speed life is experienced at the broader socioeconomic level as well as on an individual, personal level in couples and families. Arlene and Jim, a high-flying couple on the fast track in the New York corporate world, came to see me because they were miserable. Getting their first jobs on Wall Street right after college, each rose quickly in their respective companies. By their late twenties when they met at a party, each was earning six figures and the future looked bright. They started dating, and were married a year later. Now nearing their first anniversary, Arlene was angry at Jim all the time, and was on antidepressant medication. Jim, intimidated by her rages, had begun to withdraw, and sometimes stayed out late and overindulged in alcohol at business dinners, coming home roaring drunk, which angered Arlene further. They described their problem as "communication issues," but on hearing the details of their weeks and weekends, I suspected a temporal root to their problem.

Like many folks on the career fast track, each was beginning to show the signs of burnout. Symptoms include a state of emotional, mental, and physical exhaustion caused by excessive and prolonged stress, reduced energy, feelings of helplessness, hopelessness, cynicism, resentment, lowered self-worth and self-efficacy, and reduced productivity. Arlene flat-out hated her job and dreaded going to work each morning. Jim found himself less compassionate with his supervisees, more distant—similar to how he was responding to his wife. Their weeks were overstuffed with Jim's business dinners and Arlene's business trips. On weekends, Arlene tended to set a packed agenda of chores and social engagements that Jim felt helpless to resist.

The couple loved to travel and, with no kids yet, had the time and money to do so. But a recent week-long trip to Italy involved running to every ancient site in Rome and breezing through three museums in Florence, never lingering on any one painting or sculpture. By the time they returned, they were more exhausted than when they left. "Rome was just so hectic, we didn't really like it," Jim assessed. "We would have enjoyed a beach better." "Yeah, now we need a vacation from our vacation," Arlene sighed defeatedly.

I asked: "Was it Rome itself that was so hectic, or you that were too hectic taking in Rome?" The two simultaneously raised their eyebrows as if this was a big insight—and for them, it was. My question launched them into a process of learning to cut back, slow down, and attempt less but enjoy life more.

I encouraged them to substitute regular "do nothing" weekends for their typical "pile-ons," as they called them, during which they could just hang out. Each evening, they turned off cell phones and laptops after 9 P.M., to spend quality time together. Rather than wolfing down take-out food, they started cooking leisurely meals. Each got back into exercising regularly, which decreased their overall work-stress levels. And the next vacation they scheduled was to a laid-back beach in the Caribbean. As a result of all this slowing down, their sex life improved markedly, they recovered the sense of humor that had bonded them in the early days, and their mutual bitterness vanished. They had relearned how to connect and play at a more relaxing pace.

Being Slow in a Fast-Fast World?

Although this jacked-up tempo of life might be fine for some whose temperament fits the fast lane, what's a natural-born slowpoke to do? Despite the overall speediness of society, not everyone feels comfortable with it.

Slower-moving folks can feel out of step with the dominant tempo trends of our increasingly global culture. And even naturally fast-paced persons will unexpectedly smash up against the rocks of life's fast-moving river from time to time (or, for many of my hard-driving but depleted clients, on a daily basis), after being borne along by the rapid currents of their lives.

Rebecca and Matt were one such couple. Matt was an untenured professor of medieval studies, Rebecca co-owned a small bookstore specializing in photography. On weekends, they shared enjoyment of slow days spent sleeping late, pouring over old and rare texts, taking leisurely walks. They preferred a simple, nonmaterialistic life, took pride in distinguishing themselves from their more ambitious, hard-driving colleagues and friends, and neither had grand aspirations to make vast incomes. But after four years together and each on the cusp of 40, they'd come to feel a bit bored with the slow pace of their routine. Rebecca noted wryly, "We're like a couple of overeducated, bookish couch potatoes." They both wanted to have a child, but both were afraid of how busy and "chaotic" there lives would become. They found it difficult to talk about this topic or any other that might lead to a sense of urgency. Another of these topics was Matt's upcoming tenure year—he needed to produce more publications and quickly. Time pressure was definitely not their cup of tea.

To help them break out of their state of stuck-ness and entropy, I first noted how their relationship and lifestyle was built around valuing slowness. Their understanding of what drew them together had always centered on their shared hobbies, similar vocations and values, particularly their rejection of the "money-making rat race." But naming slow pace as the underlying basis of their bond was a new idea for them. Both noted that they were described by their parents as somewhat fearful, shy babies, and it seemed their adoption of a slow-paced existence was in part a way to avoid situations that would feel overwhelming and too arousing to their sensitive nervous systems.

Agreeing that we might try some activities to broaden their pace range, I suggested that they start in the area of pleasure, rather than addressing their more serious life issues, by varying the pace of their leisure activities. One assignment was to get up early, rent a couple of bikes and zoom around the city. Another was to dine at a hectic, noisy restaurant instead of their usual quiet spots. I knew they were making progress when they shyly reported that they'd gone to a local amusement park and gone on the rollercoaster—three times in a row!

To get Matt in higher gear for his writing, I suggested he engage a writing coach who set deadlines for him and helped him review his drafts. He made excellent progress once he had someone besides himself to push him a little. The couple decided to start trying to have a child, and in short order Rebecca was pregnant. I counseled them that, while life certainly gets a bit busier with a baby, it takes a few years for the pace of child-rearing to really pick up. With their continued experiments in upping the pace, by the time the child required more speed on their parts, they'd be well prepared. For now, their natural slow pace would be an asset in creating a soothing environment for their infant.

In sum, this couple profited from the useful side of speed, breaking them out of a sluggishness that was not serving them well, while at the same time affirming the wonderful aspects of their shared preference for a slow pace.

The problems couples experience when both are fast or both are slow can be challenging, but at least they are on the same "pace page." When there are dramatic pace differences between couple partners, they can feel out of step and out of sync with one another, and as we'll see, lots of problems can grow from that fundamental couple arrhythmia.

A Couple in Two Tempos

Mary-Lou and Bill were one of the first couples that got me thinking about pace and intimate relationships. Bill was a 40-year-old postal investigator, and Mary Lou, 38, an accountant. They had been living together for 14 months, had recently bought a small weekend house in the country, and were planning marriage, the second for both. Yet they were starting to question making a life together because they fought constantly about how they approached getting things done. Housework, repairs, finances—just about everything having to do with maintaining a life was an opportunity for conflict. Take a typical Sunday. After breakfast, they'd delve into various projects around their country house, which they'd bought for a great price as it needed a fair amount of work. Bill had been working on building some new cabinets for the kitchen. He carefully measured and remeasured the space, looked into different types of wood, carefully studied the variety of possibilities for hinges and knobs. Mary-Lou was growing impatient. "Let's just get it done!" With a mix of hurt and frustration on his face, Bill protested: "They aren't near the same quality as what I can make myself. Anyway, what's your rush? I thought we were going to make this our dream house?" Mary-Lou sighed, "Yes, Bill, but I don't want to die before we reach the dream!"

In contrast, Mary-Lou's approach to all tasks was rapid and highly efficient. At meals she typically wolfed down her food while he lingered over every bite. Armed with scrubber, sponge, and soap, she'd fly into the kitchen pots and over the countertops with an intensity that got Bill's heart pounding just watching. When they went shopping together, Mary-Lou came prepared with her list and barreled along with her cart so fast, Bill could scarcely keep up. "She needs a license to drive a shopping cart at the speed she goes!," he complained to me. Bill preferred to take his time, sometimes checking out new products and comparing labels and prices. "Come ON!" Mary-Lou would hiss; Bill would coolly retort, "Chill out."

Although initially Bill admired Mary-Lou's efficiency and Mary-Lou appreciated Bill's care and thoughtfulness, now they saw each other's paces mostly negatively, as a sign of a lack of commitment to doing the task at hand well. Bill saw Mary-Lou's speediness as reflecting an attempt to get things done as quickly as possible, irrespective of the quality of her work; Mary-Lou saw Bill as a "tinkerer" who dragged things out interminably.

Interestingly, despite their pervasive pace differences that went well beyond chores and getting things done—they were different in their speed of eating, drinking, walking, talking, driving, making decisions—neither had ever concluded that their fundamental problem was this marked difference in pace. Like most couples I've worked with, they focused on their specific areas of conflict—fixing, cleaning, filing, and buying things—without ever recognizing and naming their dramatic pace discrepancy as the unifying source of their conflict in all these more specific areas of daily life. When I observed that this might be their fundamental difficulty, it seemed to switch on a light of recognition in them both. The evidence was all in front of them; they just didn't have the language of time to help them connect the dots. As often happens when I suggest that underlying time differences may be the root of a couple's problems, the mood in the room softened considerably. Mary-Lou and Bill looked at each other with gentleness and even a wisp of warmth that I'd not seen until then. It was as if they suddenly saw each other again as people as opposed to seeing each other primarily as problems to be managed.

As we launched into an early version of what I now call my Relationship Rhythm Analysis method of identifying time problems, they quickly recalled that it was precisely these pace differences that each found so attractive about the other. Once we *revealed* their pervasive pace differences more formally using my Life Pace Questionnaire, they spontaneously began the next step—*revaluing* those differences. They recalled together that when they first met, Mary-Lou loved Bill's laid-back pace, and Bill was thrilled with the fast-paced excitement Mary-Lou brought to their lives. In their previous marriages, both had partnered with persons more similar to their own paces. Mary-Lou recalled, "My ex and I were both so fast, it was like a competition to see who could get to the finish line first. I loved that Bill didn't move at that pace. Plus, I found his easygoing ways much sexier." Bill smiled and said, "Yeah, and if you think I'm slow, you should've met *my* ex. She'd never get around to doing anything. When I met Mary-Lou, I found her 'can-do' attitude so refreshing, and her energy was, and still is, amazing. Yeah, it drives me crazy sometimes, just like I guess I drive you crazy, but I wouldn't want to be around another slow-poke again." Mary-Lou smiled in agreement.

I then shifted the mutual appreciation focus to the present. I asked, "How about now? Even though your pace differences often annoy each of you and put you out of sync, are there ways that these differences still work for you?" Mary-Lou to Bill: "There's definitely times when I feel you are a grounding presence in my life. I mean, I can get pretty spun out with all my rushing around and multitasking." Bill to Mary-Lou: "I still admire your efficiency, you get a lot done for both of us, and I still like your high energy—sometimes! Sometimes I want to chill, that's all."

I then asked them about their paces as children. Their stories confirmed my hunch that they operated at these speeds from childhood. I nodded in recognition of a pattern I've now heard from hundreds of couples. Not just their striking differences in pace, but in how those pace differences are linked to a fundamental aspect of their personalities—what psychologists call "temperament."

Pace Runs Deep: Tempo and Emotional Temperament

Temperament is an inborn and influential aspect of our core personality that determines how quickly, for how long, and how strongly our nervous systems respond to stimulation either from inside our bodies (changes in our thoughts, memories, feelings, physical sensations), or stimulation from outside our bodies that we pick up through the five senses. Like time, temperament is such a fundamental, noticeable aspect of our lives that ancient scientist-philosophers had a lot to say about it. Hippocrates and later Aristotle developed the theory of the four humors, a comprehensive categorization of personality types that were also linked to particular forms of illness. Persons were described as predominantly "sanguine," "choleric," "melancholic," or "phlegmatic." Sanguine types were viewed as sensation-seekers but calm at their core, not quickly aroused; easygoing and outgoing, loving, cheerful, optimistic, and sometimes irresponsible in their search for adventure and novelty.

Like sanguines, melancholics—the ancient term for what we'd now call mild depression or at least a brooding, poetic soul—were also described as having a high threshold for stimulation. It took a lot of energy to get a person of melancholic temperament going—but rather than the sanguine's style of being positive, cheerful, and seeking stimulation from outside, they were viewed as inward-oriented, reflective, often sad, and sentimental.

In contrast, cholerics were those persons highly reactive to even low levels of stimulation, and hot tempered, even violent at times, edgy, and ambitious. Like cholerics, phlegmatics were described as basically hyper-sensitive and easily stimulated, but rather than responding with anger or other outward expressions of energy, they were dominated by fearfulness and described as inward-oriented, slow moving, even sluggish, and withdrawn, a strategy for protecting themselves from overstimulation.

Matt and Rebecca, the slow-poke couple just described, are a good example of people with fundamentally phlegmatic temperaments.

This theory was refined further in the Arab world as well as in the Roman world by the Greek physician Galen, and persisted through the early modern period. Eastern medicine had quite similar taxonomies that continue to form the basis of traditional Chinese medicine as practiced today.

Today, technology can identify what parts of the brain are associated with particular clusters of behavior to paint a new picture of temperament, which, remarkably, has confirmed many of the original observations on how different persons respond to stimulation. (Although the old terms for the four temperament types are not used in current scientific research, I use them here more informally in describing some of the couples I've worked with to capture the general feel of each partner's temperament.) Current developmental research has found that infants and the adults they grow into vary noticeably in their quickness to anger and frustration, or quickness and intensity of fear, and in how intensely they feel these emotions. They also vary in the intensity and duration of positive emotions such as interest, excitement, and joy, and in their curiosity about desirable objects such as toys. And they vary in their level of extraversion. As they get older and their brains mature (especially the frontal lobes, responsible for developing self-control, planning, focus, and choice), children vary in terms of how readily and how long they can focus their attention.[10]

Temperament appears to be shaped both by one's genes and social environment—especially in our early years, how our parents respond to our temperament.[11] The child's ability to increase or decrease his or her level of emotional arousal to adapt to the social and task requirements of the moment is a core aspect of psychological functioning, termed by psychologists "emotion regulation."[12]

Of course, sometimes there's a great match between a child's temperament and a parent's temperament, and the parent has the patience and skills to respond to the difficult aspects of the child's temperament in a way that helps the child modulate and reduce those less-adaptive aspects. But sometimes there's not such a great match, and a struggle ensues that leaves them each depleted, frustrated, and stuck. And sometimes the struggles between parent and child result in unresolved conflicts that the child carries forward into adulthood.

So what does all this information about temperament and the early parent-child relationship have to do with pace and partners? It's to show that we often seek a partner who in some way plays the role our parents played when they were managing our temperament. And as I've described, a major aspect of our emotional temperament is our overall life pace. Our parents worked to get us energized, moving, and focused if we tended typically to be sluggish, spacey, too slow; or they strived to slow and calm us down if we tended to be edgy, fearful, impulsive, moving at and through the world too fast. After the childhood relationship with our parents, the intimate relationship with our adult partners is our most intense attachment relationship.[13] We look to our partners for safety, security, support, and soothing, just as we sought security and soothing from our parents. And a fundamental conduit through which we obtain that security and soothing from parents, and later from partners, is how they respond to our emotions. So, we unconsciously seek and select a partner who helps us manage our temperament as our parents did—or as we needed our parents to do but perhaps couldn't because of lack of fit between their temperament and parenting skills and our particular temperamental style. So we are either looking for our partners to step into the role our parents played in regulating our emotions and our pace, or we are still searching for someone who can take on the role we needed our parents to play but didn't.

And just as we likely struggled with the control our parents attempted to exert on our level and quality of emotional arousal and pace, we often end up resisting the control that we unconsciously recruit our partners to exert on the intensity and style of our emotional arousal and pace!

Barbara and Ted, a couple I worked with a few years ago, perfectly illustrate how we may gravitate toward a person with a different pace and emotional energy, engage them to balance out and regulate our emotional style and pace, then resent and resist their attempts at controlling us. Barbara, 43, was a high-level administrator in human resources at a hospital, and Ted, 41, was president of a family furniture-manufacturing business. After a year of fertility treatment, they had a son, Kevin, now 2 years old. Married 4 years, they came to couple therapy because they were increasingly irritated with each other, fought about how to spend their weekends and whether to have another child. Barbara desperately wanted another, even though it would involve time, effort, and the cost of in-vitro fertilization with a donor egg. Although Ted wanted Barbara to be happy, he felt their lives were already overwhelmingly full and did not want another child. In addition to his discomfort with the idea of a donor egg, he mostly felt that having another child would put their lives under tremendous pressure. He said, "I have trouble keeping up the pace at times—I thought having kids would be easier than it turned out to be. And the fact is, we're both working full time and long hours, and seeing Kevin only at night and on the weekends."

Barbara agreed that their lives were busy and that the process of getting pregnant and having another child would potentially tax their energy reserves. She noted, "I've been afraid to acknowledge Ted's point, because I didn't want to give him ammunition to shoot the whole pregnancy project down."

What became clear in our first session was that the disagreement about whether or not to have another child had revealed fundamental personality differences between them, differences that we were then able to trace as the root of all their other conflicts: Namely, as Barbara said, "we've got big differences in temperament and pace." (Trust me, this is a quote, and I did not feed them these lines!)

Unlike the many couples I've worked with who do not recognize the impact of their underlying temporal and temperamental differences, Ted and Barbara had the concepts and language to describe this fundamental source of their difficulties. Barbara described herself as "high energy. I want to go out, meet people; he's OK staying home with a book." Ted added: "She's always pushing, pushing, pushing, trying to keep up with friends and family, trying to be the perfect mother, have the perfect career. I'm always trying to slow us down. On the weekends, she wants to fit in too many things, and we end up rushing around and completely exhausted."

Using the ancient language of temperament types, we could describe Barbara as a mix of sanguine and choleric, whereas Ted fit the profile of a phlegmatic and sometimes a bit of a melancholic. As a phlegmatic type, he preferred lots of time in his own head, reading, fishing, watching sports on TV, or just "spacing out." But when put under prolonged pressure and high stimulation—as he'd been feeling since Kevin's birth, doubly so since Barbara started insisting on having a second child—he could become a bit brooding and melancholy, which only slowed his pace further. To which Barbara would of course respond by trying to get him moving faster. He'd experience that as overstimulating, leading him to put the brakes on whatever they were doing, resulting in a frustrating struggle over pace. As Barbara put it, "our different styles become magnified when life is lived by a clock, when every moment is chock full with work, commuting, child care, and there's no time for ourselves, to work out or to spend much time alone with each other."

Clearly, here was a case of opposites attract. When she first met Ted, Barbara found it "fun to draw him out. Now it feels like a chore." Ted countered, "At first, I liked that Barbara seemed to appreciate that I could help her slow her down and take it easier. It made me feel useful, manly, like her protector. But now," he said as he turned his gaze from me to Barbara, "I feel tired of always being the anchor, the guy holding the kite string while you're the kite, the one who has to remind you how much you complain about being stressed and overworked and too busy and tired."

In examining their respective families growing up, it became even clearer how Barbara and Ted had come to choose each other. Barbara's father was intense and fast-paced—qualities she admired and emulated— her mother was "passive, sweet, loyal, shy, loving, steady and dependable." Her father was more fun to be with—"but he always had three things to do before getting to me." In addition, his stimulation-seeking had led him to have an affair that, when revealed, caused great embarrassment to the family, as he was a local politician. With my line of questioning leading the way, Barbara could quickly see the parallels—she had relied on her mother to soothe her, calm her, and contain her, and in Ted, she'd picked a partner to do the same. Yet, just as her father consistently resisted her mother's attempts to rein him in and slow him down, Barbara fought Ted's attempts to do the same for her.

For his part, Ted had a mother similar to Barbara's, but his father was also slow and deliberate. Everything was planned carefully—house projects, vacations, weekends, and recreational activities (gardening, camping, fly fishing, the activities Ted now longed for)—and tended to involve long periods of time, "more time than we ever seem to get on weekends." Although Ted still liked his family's temperament, something about Barbara's energy appealed to him powerfully. And he liked that the calmness he'd inherited and honed in his family at least initially made him so attractive to her.

After revealing the extent of their fundamental pace and temperament differences and how these made it difficult to coordinate their lives in time, we returned to the pressing issue of whether or not to try for another baby. If my emerging theory about them was correct, their pace and temperament discrepancies might also contribute to this issue.

I reasoned aloud that each had completely opposite ways of responding to anxiety, whether at work or in their personal life. Barbara's approach was to add on more, and pick up the pace to get it all done. But that often left her overwhelmed, frantic, and exhausted. In contrast, when Ted felt anxious, he immediately looked for ways to slow down and do less. When life got busier after Kevin's birth and each began to sense their growing disconnection, each got anxious about the relationship and went into their typical coping mode. Given that she acknowledged Ted's points about how busy and stressed they already were with one child and how much pressure trying for another might produce, and given that she hadn't provided any other reason for her relentless insistence on having another child (having worked with many couples on this choice, I was familiar with a wide range of reasons typically offered), I wondered if it was at least in part just another example of her tendency to add more to her life when stressed. And of course, true to form, Ted would try to rein her in, try to convince her to reduce their challenges.

From their wide-eyed expression of startled recognition, it seemed like a light went on for them both with my suggestion. Barbara noted, a bit tearfully, "I'd been feeling our differences might be insurmountable—so I guess I thought if we got busy trying to have another child, it might save our marriage." Ted was startled to hear that Barbara had been feeling that shaky about their relationship. But he surprised her when he said, gently, "You know, Barbara, I don't want to feel pressured to have another kid, or that if I say 'No' that it will ruin your life, our life together. But on the other hand, it's your emotional intensity and your desire to have a child that attracted me to you in the first place. I just want us to slow the pace enough to have a real, open discussion about it. I'm not ruling it out, I just can't make a decision that quickly." Barbara nodded appreciatively; and they embraced.

After this rather dramatic session in which we *revealed* the power of their pace discrepancies and how these both expressed and fed fundamental differences in their emotional temperament, we followed the other steps in the Four R's of addressing time challenges.

Reveal your couple rhythms
Revalue the rhythms that work
Revise the rhythms that need changing
Rehearse new rhythms

This session and others that followed helped them start to *revalue* their pace and emotional differences, remembering that these were a primary aspect of their initial and continued attraction to one another. By recognizing how Barbara unconsciously recruited Ted to help her slow and calm down, and how Ted relied on Barbara to get him energized and excited, they came to view this pace and "energy management" difference as one of their core assets as a couple—but a difference that had become too extreme and polarized. Simply by becoming aware of this subtext of their everyday life and interactions, by getting in tune with their different tempos, they became more appreciative and less judgmental of one another.

We also experimented with *revising* how they brought their respective tempos to the table: by being more deliberate about balancing whose pace would dominate in certain activities, and by using these moments to learn from one another more actively and expand their joint repertoire of speed. For instance, with my encouragement, the couple instituted a weekend dinner ritual in which each got to be the chef one night and the other had to be the sous-chef, taking orders and working at the other's chosen tempo. This ritual became a model that they used in other activities (gardening, deciding how busy to make their weekends in general), in which each got to take turns leading and following, eliminating much of the power struggle between them that often got enacted around pace. It also brought out their sense of humor—when taking orders from her in the kitchen, Ted might say "Yes, chef, right away!" with a playful smirk, and if Barbara sensed Ted was speeding up in his preparations, she might tease him with, "Are you sure we shouldn't roast that duck just a little longer? Maybe a double-cooked duck?"

As Ted and Barbara experimented with immersing in and adapting to each other's pace, they gradually moved toward a common tempo in their joint activities, in which neither felt the need to push or pull on the other's pace. They no longer felt fundamentally incompatible and reaffirmed their desire to be together. As Barbara started to slow down, and as she learned to face and talk about her anxieties rather than to add on new, distracting activities, she came to recognize more fully just how stressed and exhausted she already was. She began to reconsider the plan to pursue having another child through in-vitro and donor egg. I had suggested a few weeks before that somehow, despite the felt urgency of this decision, the couple needed to create a temporary period of less time pressure about it so that they could have a full conversation about their feelings, pro and con. Both responded well to this idea of a temporary "no pressure zone." As Ted sensed that Barbara was taking the time pressure off, he came forward by expressing empathy about her longing for another child. In fact, he surprised her by revealing, with tears, that he shared that longing. But he had great concerns about the stress this would add to their lives—especially if, due to fertility procedures, they ended up with twins. He also had strong negative feelings about the prospect that the child would have only half their genetic material.

As the couple got better at soothing each other emotionally about this issue and in general, they decided to give up the plan of having another child. This led to a period of mourning, especially for Barbara, for the child that might have been. It was paired with a deeper recognition and appreciation of the fullness of their present life, which they learned to enjoy together more completely. They maintained their tendency toward different paces, and the different emotional temperaments from which those paces emerged, but could now appreciate and deliberately utilize their differences in tempo and temperament to balance one another, rather than being problematically polarized by pace.

~

Applying the Four R's to Your Relationship Pace Problems

Now that you've seen how I helped other couples with their pace differences, and having completed the Life Pace Questionnaire and compared your answers, use the Relationship Rhythms Analysis Worksheet to guide yourselves through the steps of the Four R's: *revealing* your problematic pace differences, *revaluing* aspects of your pace differences that work for you, *revising* pace differences that are too extreme, and *rehearsing* new pace patterns. As an example, check out the one that I filled out with Bill and Mary-Lou to summarize their pace issues and their plan.

Having used these techniques and exercises, you should emerge from this chapter knowing how to identify and alter the negative effects of pace differences underlying your couple conflicts. You will also have practiced a systematic, four-step method of identifying and changing pace differences that can be applied to other time problems covered in subsequent chapters.

Although every couple must find their own creative solutions to pace problems, here's a general menu of solutions to get you started:

Surface Conflicts (common areas of conflict):
Couple Pace Pattern (Check One):
__Fast-Fast__Slow-Slow__Faster-Slower

REVEAL
What are the pace problems under
your surface conflicts?

REVALUE
What does each of you appreciate
about the other's pace?
How were your individual paces
part of your initial attraction to one
another?
How do your respective paces
(either similarities or differences)
still help the relationship?

REVISE
What can you change to make your
paces more compatible, less stressful, and more enjoyable?

REHEARSE
What's your practice plan? Make
a commitment to specific activities you will do on a daily, weekly,
monthly, and yearly basis to change
and/or better align your paces.

Flex Time: Activities to Expand Your Pace Range

As we've seen through the examples in this chapter, how we inhabit time
involves simultaneously our thoughts, emotions, physiology, and behaviors.
Being in time is a full body-mind, holistic experience. That's why time, in this
case pace, is so powerful! The exercises below are designed to help you learn to
be more flexible in pace—both for your own sake and so that you're better able
to sync up with your differently paced partner. You can practice these exercises alone or with a partner. Although I've described how our pace is linked

Surface Conflicts (common areas of conflict): Arguments about getting the housework and repairs completed; annoying differences in speed of eating and walking

Couple Pace Pattern (Check One):
__Fast-Fast__Slow-Slow__Faster-Slower

REVEAL What are the pace problems under your surface conflicts?	Bill slow-paced, Mary-Lou fast-paced
REVALUE What does each of you appreciate about the other's pace? How were your individual paces part of your initial attraction to one another? How do your respective paces still help the relationship?	Bill: likes Mary-Lou's fast pace because "exciting" Mary-Lou: likes Bill's slower pace because "calming"
REVISE What can you change to make your paces more compatible, less stressful, and more enjoyable?	1. Bill pick up the pace a bit, Mary-Lou slow down a bit 2. Tease each other with affectionate names when pace getting extreme (Bill = "Slowpoke", Mary-Lou = "Speedy Gonzalez") 3. Remembering the positive aspects of our pace differences—don't get on each other's case so much!
REHEARSE What's your practice plan? Make a commitment to specific activities you will do on a daily, weekly, monthly, and yearly basis to change and/or better align your paces.	Try this new rhythm out whenever we have chores and housework to do (at least weekly)

TABLE 3.1

Couple Pace Type	Sample Solutions to Pace Problems
Faster—Slower	1. Revalue and stay mindful of the specific positive effects on your relationship of your pace differences. 2. Trade off taking charge of the pace in walking, eating, cooking, household tasks, leisure activities. 3. Find and practice activities in which your paces are similar. 4. Use humorous pace-based nicknames to remind each other when your pace is getting extreme; bring the paces closer to center.
Fast—Fast	1. Revalue the specific positive effects on your relationship of your shared penchant for speed. 2. Create regular times for slowness at the end of the day, week, month, and year. See the decompression chamber activity described in chapter 8. 3. Get a good book, CD, or DVD on mindful living, meditation, and slowing down. 4. Give a humorous, descriptive nickname to your shared tendency to move into overdrive, and use it to signal each other to downshift: the Cyclone, Mark V, Speed Racer are some examples.
Slow—Slow	1. Revalue the specific positive effects on your relationship of your shared affinity for slowness. 2. Experiment with fast-paced fun activities. If you can first play faster, you might be able to "task faster." 3. Get a good book on getting organized. See the endnotes of this chapter for some suggestions. 4. Give a humorous, descriptive nickname to your shared tendency to move into the slug zone, and use it to signal each other to upshift: the Big Drag, Slothlife, Slacker City are some examples

to our basic emotional temperament and how that temperament is largely an inborn characteristic, like all other aspects of our personality, we can evolve, adapt, and modulate how we express and even how we experience the levels of energy and emotional/physiological arousal associated with temperament. With those changes in how we handle our temperament, we can shift our pace. And, vice-versa: *Shifting and controlling our pace* is one of the most effective ways to manage and modulate our temperament. We may be naturally a bit hypersensitive, overreactive, quick to anger, and fast moving, but by practicing slowing down, we can learn to calm and soothe our choleric tendencies. We may be naturally a bit phlegmatic, but by practicing speeding up, we may generate more internal energy and bring more zest to our relationships.

Slowing Down

Mindful Breathing:
Whether you take the fast or slow track through life, or through particular moments in your life, mindful breathing should be an essential companion on your journey to keep you centered and calm. Many people who successfully manage high speed use slow, steady breathing as a tool to keep them relaxed and focused. Philip Glass, the famous contemporary composer known for the shimmering, rapid patterns of his music, describes himself as "moving fast on the outside, but calm and slow on the inside." As a professional drummer, I've learned that in order to maintain a relaxed state even at up-tempos, it's critical to breathe slowly even as my hands are moving rapidly.[14] Professional athletes whose success depends on consistently operating at high speeds and on pushing the envelope to set new records—race car drivers, slalom skiers, sprint and marathon runners—learn early on to control the rate of their breath. Inside, they often experience themselves as moving slowly, even though they are actually moving extremely fast. There's a scene in the 1998 film *Without Limits,* about the legendary long-distance runner Steve Prefontaine (played by Billy Crudup), which shifts from the actual race to a view of it from inside his head, and it's all in slow motion, and when it shifts back to the actual high speed of his running, it's startling.

And of course, mindful breathing is the centerpiece of any meditative practice designed to help you slow down.

Try this—

Sit in a comfortable position. You can sit in a chair, with back straight and your weight on the sit bones of your buttocks, feet planted fully and firmly on the floor. Or you can sit on a cushion on the floor in the lotus position (back straight, legs crossed with one ankle over the other, hands resting gently on your knees, or in your lap, or in the traditional Buddhist position of tips of thumbs touching tips of index fingers and the backs of hands resting on your upper thigh just above the knee). Or you can stand, feet firmly planted on the ground, shoulders' width apart, your tailbone curved in just a bit to give you extra stability.

Breathe in through your nostrils (to stay concentrated, it works better to take slow nostril breaths rather than breathing through your mouth), fill your lungs, and slowly release the air through your nostrils. Notice the cool-ness of the air coming in through your nostrils, and the warmth of the air as it leaves your nostrils. Focusing on the cool-warm cycle is one way to turn your attention more fully to your breath. Notice also how your belly rises slightly as you breathe in and falls as you breathe out. To help sense this, place one hand gently over your belly, the other hand resting gently on top of the first hand. Let's accentuate that belly movement. Imagine your belly is the handle of a bellows—if you've never seen a bellows, it's an old fireplace tool that fills with air as you separate the handles, and pushes out air as you close the handles together. As you breathe in, you deliberately accentuate the rising of your belly, and as your breathe out, pull your belly in. In doing so, you will be moving your diaphragm up and down. Diaphragmatic belly-breathing takes practice.

Most of us are used to taking short, rapid breaths by moving our chest up and down. Actually, most of us go through our stressful days unaware of how we breathe, or even *that* we breathe! You'll get deeper breaths with dia-phragmatic breathing than breathing from the chest. Notice how you feel after three or four of these deep, slow breaths. Hopefully, you're beginning to feel a bit more settled, a bit more focused, a bit more relaxed even with these few breaths. As you get better at breathing, you will find you can cre-ate a sense of deep relaxation and calm with just a few breaths, especially if you remember to breathe deeply and deliberately throughout your day, even during fast-paced and stressful activities—rather than only once at the end of the day when you sigh or yawn from exhaustion!

Once you've gotten a feel for basic diaphragmatic breathing, there are a few variations that will help you train your breath and help you focus.

Breathe in to the count of four; hold the breath for three seconds, then breathe out to the count of seven. Repeat for three cycles. Research has shown (as has thousands of years of pranayama, the ancient Hindu tra-dition of breath control) that the slow exhale is most directly related to increasing relaxation. The slow out-breath activates the parasympathetic, calming side of your autonomic nervous system.

While breathing in, in your mind's voice, think to yourself the words, "I know I am breathing in." While breathing out, think to yourself, "I know I am breathing out." Think of this as the breathing version of Descartes's famous dictum, "I think, therefore I am." This practice of linking one's subvocal mind and thoughts to breathing was refined by the venerable Thich Nhat Hanh, the Vietnamese Buddhist leader and one of the great-est translators of Buddhist practices for a contemporary audience.[15] Also excellent are the books and audiotapes by leading American mindfulness researcher Jon Kabat-Zinn.[16]

Mindful Walking:

Again, this ancient practice of linking the breath to the simple act of walking is well described by Thich Nhat Hanh, and as I can attest to from many personal experiences with my wife and children, it is a central activity of mindfulness retreats that he and the monks and nuns of Plum Village conduct. And believe it or not, kids enjoy it just as much as grownups! You can do mindful walking around your apartment, around your block, or in a favorite setting (beach, woods, city street—although you may feel self-conscious doing it where others will inevitably stare). You can walk in a circle, or in a straight line. You choose!

As you breathe in, step forward with your right foot (whether you start with right or left makes no difference—but we've got to start somewhere!). Feel your heel planting on the ground, then shift your weight forward until you feel your entire foot firmly planted. As you breathe out, step forward with your left foot. Again, plant the heel first, then roll forward onto the rest of the foot. Repeat this pattern of breathing in with the right step and breathing out with the left step for at least 3 minutes. To help you focus, you can again use the thought, "I know I am breathing in, I know I am breathing out" along with your steps and breath.

Now start experimenting with increasing your speed while maintaining mindfulness and slow breath. Double up on the steps and double the pace for each breath—take two steps (right, left) per each in breath, and two per out breath. After a couple of minutes of this, quadruple the number of steps and pace for each breath: four per in breath (right, left, right, left), four per out breath. This simple, powerful exercise trains you to remain calm at the core even while you are moving quickly through the world. Now you are equipped to whip down a city street, running a little late for an appointment, but breathing and walking mindfully so that you remain (at least relatively) calm through the journey and arrive at your destination focused and relaxed, rather than out of breath and a mess of jangled nerves.

Please don't dismiss this incredibly powerful practice if Buddhism is not your thing. Just like the act of deep, mindful breathing, mindful walking and mindful movement in general is by no means limited to Buddhism. Every major world religion practices some form of coordinating breathing with focused, rhythmic walking or other simple movements. The ancient Christian tradition of labyrinth walking, the Muslim tradition of reciting prayers in a rhythmic fashion, the Jewish tradition of davening—all provide calming, focusing practices that link rhythmic body movement with slow breathing, designed to assist practitioners in reaching higher states of concentration, awareness, and spiritual joy. And plenty of secular physical activities—such as hiking, running, swimming, aerobics, pilates, karate, singing, playing the saxophone, even drumming—provide opportunities to calm our minds by linking rhythmic physical movement with rhythmic breath.

Slow Sex:

As a therapist, I naturally work with many couples to improve their boring, unsatisfying, or nonexistent sex lives. There are many issues that contribute to sexual difficulties and I will not catalogue them all, as much has been written on sex and couples.[17] But time and again, I've found that a root cause of partners' sexual incompatibilities are their different fantasies, expectations, images, and behaviors regarding the *pace* of sex—in every step, from the pace of moving from a romantic dinner to getting naked and into bed to the pace of the moving body parts (penises, labia, tongues, fingers, lips) during sex, and everything in between.

One woman told me, with lip-curled disgust, about how her partner would enter the bedroom, efficiently take off his clothes, go under the covers, and wait for her to do the same. "It was like he was undressing for a medical exam!" she moaned. Another complained of how her partner would move too quickly from kissing and fondling to inserting his penis in her, and then would start pumping away "like he was in a porno flick, expecting me just to come the faster he moved." It may be a stereotype or an aspect of male and female sexual function, but in heterosexual couples, the fast one is often the male and the one wanting slower sex is often female. Just think of the Pointer Sisters' classic tune *Slow Hand,* with the lyric, "I want a man with a slow hand…somebody who will spend some time…." But the sex-pace-gender pattern certainly can and does go in the opposite direction. And in my work with lesbian women and gay men, I've also found differences in partners' desired sexual pace.

The ancient Indian tradition of Tantric sex provides a guide to pairing slow breathing with extremely slow sexual touch. You might want to check out a course at your local alternative education workshop or meditation center (in New York and most major cities, there are several such centers that offer courses in a wide range of mindful practices, including Tantrism), or you may want to read or watch videos on Tantric sex.[18] But here are a few simple things you can do, without getting into the details of Tantrism, that will help you and your partner experiment with the pleasures of slow sex.

Approach sex as play, not as work. You are off the clock, out of the calendar. One fact that many folks don't know is that even though it is exciting, sexual arousal as a physiological response mostly involves the parasympathetic nervous system—that part of the nervous system that is activated when we are digesting food, sleeping, calming down. The opposite, sympathetic branch of the nervous system is the part that is activated when we are facing a danger, an unpleasant challenge, overload at work—it is the fight-or-flight response that many of us spend much of our days immersed in. Many diagnosable sexual dysfunctions—male impotence, premature ejaculation, retarded ejaculation, dyspareunia, vaginismus—involve anxiety either as a root cause or as a result of experiencing symptoms due to other medical causes. Decreasing anxiety about sex, in part by following the steps described below, can go a long way toward solving these problems for many people. (However, it is always worth checking with a physician if you experience persistent difficulty or pain with your genitals.)

Create a physical setting for sex that is erotic and sensual for both of you. You may have some big differences about these aesthetic dimensions, and now is the time to talk about them and find some consensus. Although the stereotype formula suggested in couple sex self-help guides is candles, incense, and soft, gentle music, that doesn't work for everyone. Pick the kinds of settings, smells, sights, and sounds that turn you both on. I knew a biker couple (I mean, motorcycles, not 10-speeds) that loved to pull off on the side of a hot highway in the desert, find a secret spot behind some sagebrush, lay down a big rug, turn on a little tape deck with bluesman Stevie Ray Vaughn laying down some rockin' grooves, and spend the afternoon slowly doing it.

Try standing up and undressing each other, very, very slowly. Kiss or stroke the part(s) of the body that you've just revealed. Then put that piece of clothing (shirt shoulder, bra strap, underwear band, stocking) *back on* your partner, and repeat. Then move on to other clothing items.

Stroke each other's hair. Look in each other's eyes, look away, and look back. Don't stare—that feels weird for most people—just look, and smile, maybe a bit mischievously, or lovingly, or both.

Kiss each other—on the lips, elsewhere. Kiss simultaneously, or take turns initiating and receiving (a one-way kiss on the lips can be surprisingly erotic). Encourage your partner to let you know what feels good and what doesn't. Simple signals like moaning "um hmm!" for "yes" or "ungh" for "no" are often sufficient; if not, you might want to speak in words, or before having sex in this way to talk about the places you like to be kissed and touched, and the quality of contact you like. Some like a firm touch, some like a gentle touch; some like a wet kiss, some hate it and prefer a drier one. The key is not to get defensive if you're not immediately doing what your partner likes (and as the receiver, not to get impatient). This is not a Hollywood movie! And if it was, you'd be getting plenty of direction and opportunity to rehearse anyway!

In oral sex and genital sex, try doing everything really, really slowly. See what happens when you barely move your tongue against your partner's genitals, and for men, when you barely move your penis inside your partner. Go slow and breathe. This kind of sex can be unbelievably and surprisingly intense—often much more erotic and arousing than fast-paced movement.

After immersing in this slow-motion sex, try speeding things up and slowing things down. Stay in tune with your breath and your partner's breath. Keep the groove with each other, make small pace calibrations to keep up with where your partner is.

Once you both reach orgasm (and don't make simultaneous orgasm the holy grail or sine qua non of great sex—if it happens, great; if not, relax, it will happen another time!), take time to linger. For goodness sake, don't pop out of bed and check your e-mail!

Speeding Up

Several of the above exercises involve starting slow and speeding up. But here's a few further exercises to help you stay calm and centered while absorbing stimulation or moving at a faster pace. They offer great, focused practice in dealing with speed, the skills and spirit of which you can transfer to more real-life moments.

Speed Watching:

Typically, as we shift our attention increasingly rapidly among different things, our breath gets more shallow, and we become tense and sometimes overstimulated. This ten-minute exercise directly trains you to stay calm and centered when confronted with a number of stimuli. The experiential lessons learned can be applied to such diverse situations as when you are searching for something lost among a pile of items; moving quickly down a city street surrounded by lots of people and moving vehicles; being confronted with a number of messages, or sources of messages, at work or at home (simultaneously ringing of cell phone and landline phone and urgent e-mail message); or trying to attend to a crying baby while the doorbell is ringing.

Sit in a setting where there are a number of things to look at. This could be in a garden, at a zoo, in a museum, on a park bench, or on the front stoop of your apartment building or house. First, do some mindful breathing (see instructions above) to settle into your body. Now look at one thing—a flower, a squirrel, a stone, a person, a storefront, a painting. Breathe in to the count of four, and out to the count of four, and experience the calmness of focusing on one thing. Do this for two minutes.

Now, add one more thing to look at in alternation with the original thing. Every four seconds, shift your focus from one thing to another; breathe in to the count of four as you take in one thing, and out to the count of four as you take in another. Do this for two minutes.

Add two more things to look at with the other two (for a total of four things), and for each one, focus for one second, moving your eyes in sequence among the four objects, breathing in to the count of four. Now reverse the order in which you look at the objects, and breathe out to the count of four. Do this for two minutes.

Now go back to alternating between two objects, breathing in to the count of four as you take in one thing, and out to the count of four as you take in another. Do this for two minutes.

Finally, return to the initial step. Focus on one thing, breathe in to the count of four, and out to the count of four. Do this for two minutes.

Speed vs. Slow Cooking: A Tale of Two Sauces
Pick a cuisine or style of food you like to cook. Almost all have fast recipes and slow recipes. On one night, try a fast recipe; on another, a slow recipe. Bring your mindful breathing into the act of cooking. Personally, I cook a lot of Italian. One fast sauce recipe is oil, garlic, salt, pepper, with a little grated parmesan and chopped parsley on top. Done in five minutes (boiling the pasta takes longer). A slow recipe is creamy zucchini sauce. Takes about 40 minutes to prepare. The point of this? For those of you who have no time to cook, or always feel rushed cooking, try some different recipes!

Drumming:
As a professional drummer as well as a psychologist, I can't resist "laying on you" (as we musicians say) one drum-related exercise for staying calm while enjoying speed. (In one workshop on time that I did in Germany for couples and families, it turns out most of them were there not to get my psychological wisdom, but because they'd seen on the flyer prepared by the host institute that I would be teaching attendees how to play a rock n' roll beat!).

Get a pair of drum sticks or use two wooden spoons. With your dominant hand, slowly count out loud and play along with the following beat: "1 and 2 and 3 and 4 and." Tap your foot (the same side as your dominant hand—right foot if you're using your right hand, left foot if you're using your left hand) just on the count of 4: "1, 2, 3, 4." In other words, your hand will play double the number of beats as your foot, but it should all hang together. Repeat over and over until you are comfortable keeping a steady beat. This is your basic rock cymbal beat with bass drum. (If you can get a-hold of a drum set, by all means, knock yourself out!)

Now, with your nondominant hand (left if you are a righty, right if you are a lefty), now add a beat on 2 and 4, to go along with your basic rock cymbal beat. This is your basic snare drum beat, what we call the "back beat," which gives rock (and funk, and country) its basic syncopated kick. I've put in bold the 2 and 4 indicated where that snare drum beat coincides with the cymbal: "1 and **2** and 3 and **4** and."

Now speed it up gradually and keep breathing. When you're starting to strain, steadily slow down, reestablish a slower groove, then try speeding up again. Over time, as your muscles learn this movement, you will be able to go faster. The key is to stay relaxed as you increase your speed. A tight drummer makes everyone uptight. Just as in sexual arousal, for the drummer's beat to move people, it has to be loose and relaxed, even when fast.

Hope you had fun learning the essence of rock drumming. Now, think about this activity as a motion metaphor for the other things you need to learn, master, and do at different paces, including quickly. How do you coordinate all the parts? What's the virtue of starting slowly and then practicing speeding up? How do you stay relaxed even as you operate at high speed?

In this chapter, you've learned how pace differences underlie many couples' conflicts, how pace differences are one of the things that probably attracted you to your partner in the first place, and how those differences can become one of your greatest assets as a couple. Pace differences become a problem only when they are not recognized and valued, when they become extreme and polarizing. You've learned how pace is an outgrowth and expression of one of the most influential and well-researched aspects of our psychological selves: temperament. You've seen how changing your pace can help you modify your temperament. And you've learned some practical tools for slowing down and speeding up.

Just as we'd get bored if our musical diet were restricted only to slow ballads or fast rock and roll (or if you're a classical fan, largo movements or scherzo movements in concertos and symphonies), life as a couple gets boring when all our activities move super-slowly, and overwhelming when every aspect of our lives move super-fast. Use the ideas and practical tips in this chapter to develop a broader repertoire of paces in your activities. Enjoy the full range of tempos that life and love have to offer.

Syncing Your Relationship Rhythms

"It don't mean a thing, if it ain't got that swing."
—Duke Ellington and Billy Strayhorn

THE GREAT JAZZ COMPOSER and band leader Duke Ellington and his co-composer Billy Strayhorn got it right—rhythm forms the basic time structure of our lives and the foundation of our ongoing, intimate relationships. Humans, like other animals and plants, are creatures of habit in need of regularity in their daily lives, and those habits of how we use time are what I call life rhythms. Regular rhythms determine when, how often, and in what sequence the many activities of life occur on a daily, weekly, monthly, and yearly basis. Our lives swing along with less effort when we've got good rhythms. The great jazz drummer Shelly Manne put it this way: "The time (meaning the basic jazz cymbal rhythm) is so important because if you have the time feeling—the swinging feeling—you can become as free as you want as long as that basic element is there."[1] Without regular joint rhythms between partners, we feel we're always starting and stopping again, renegotiating and reestablishing the basic patterns of our lives. Couples that constantly need to reset their joint rhythms inevitably suffer wear and tear. It's difficult to manage the multiple responsibilities of a life together, let alone finding regular time for pleasurable intimacy, when you're constantly having to reset your couple rhythms. If rhythm is the "vehicle through which the forward movement of time is structured,"[2] then shared rhythms structure the temporal foundation and forward movement of intimate relationships.

Surprisingly, although the crucial role of rhythm is obvious to musicians and dancers, psychologists and other social scientists have had relatively little to say about the role of rhythms. In the early 1980s, anthropologist Albert Scheflen, who pioneered the study of rhythms of interaction, reasoned this was due to the primary focus on individuals and their perceptions of interaction, rather than actual observation of the microsequences of persons interacting. He wrote:

> It is striking how belatedly we have discovered the obvious. Any dancer or musician could have told us that we must share a common rhythm to sing or play or dance together. So could any athlete who plays on a team. And privately we have always known that a common rhythmicity is essential to consummate sexual union....Are scientists always the last to know what artists and others have known all along?[3]

The few researchers who've turned their attention to interaction rhythms over the past three decades have convincingly documented the fundamental power of rhythm in determining the quality of relationships. Most research has focused on mothers and infants. Pioneering researcher Beatrice Beebe and her colleagues have amassed substantial evidence showing that the degree to which mothers are sensitive to and match the rhythms of their infants' changing facial expressions, body movements, and vocalizations strongly predicts the quality of the babies' attachment style years later.[4]

From the micro to the more macro level, the great musiciologist and anthropologist Alan Lomax found relationships between a culture's musical and speech rhythms, patterns of child rearing, economic development, and social structures. His ethnographic research documented the ways that rhythms ensure the smooth flow of interaction between individuals. Lomax wrote: "Rhythmic patterns facilitate the co-activity of groups and aid their members in coordinating energies and resources in work, nurturance, defense, social discourse, rites of passage, interchange of information, and above all, expressive acts."[5]

Several theorists have identified the general importance of rhythms in determining the quality of couple, and especially family, relationships.[6] However, much of the research has been vague about the processes by which couple partners establish these rhythms and stay in sync, and the impact on the relationship of being out of rhythm. Without "banging my own drum" too loudly, I am one of the few psychologists who have examined the details of couple rhythms described in this chapter.[7]

So what exactly do I mean by rhythm? As applied to human behavior, I've defined rhythm as a patterned sequence of behavior that repeats at regular, predictable intervals, and at regular times, in which the elements of the sequence follow one another at a fairly uniform tempo or speed.[8] More simply, Merriam-Webster defines rhythm as "a movement or activity in which some action or element recurs regularly."

Here's a simple example: like you, I have a morning routine. Most weekday mornings I'm up at 6:45 A.M. to catch a little breakfast with my wife and kids before the kids leave for school at 7:00. I stretch a little, take a shower and get dressed, leave the house by 7:30, hop in the car for a 5-minute downhill slalom to the train station, park, walk briskly to the train platform with about 5 minutes to spare before the 7:50 shuttles me off to the city. If any element of the sequence takes longer (leave the house just 5 minutes later and I run the risk of getting stuck behind a school bus that stops at every other driveway on the block), or if I need to add additional activities to the sequence, the whole rhythm collapses. On most days, that's okay—flexibly adapting to fluctuations in rhythm caused by unforeseen factors is a cornerstone of coping with challenges and stress. And sometimes I engineer a change in my morning rhythm—Fridays, after a long week of late hours, I try to sleep in a little and I work at home. It's a welcome relief from the grind of the rest of the week. If rhythms never vary, they can feel constraining and boring. On the other hand, if I had to decide each day when to get up, which train to take, which route to traverse to the station, I'd be exerting way more energy than my brain could handle first thing in the morning. At their best, rhythms lock into place decisions we've made about what works best for us in maximizing pleasure and productivity and avoiding stressors.

But how do two people's individual rhythms coalesce into a joint rhythm? What are the symptoms and the effects of couple arrhythmia? In this chapter I'll elucidate different ways that two people interact in time, how two individuals can come together and become more than the sum of their parts, and what to do when partners lose their groove.

When we meet someone for the first time, we usually run a quick test on whether we can get into a conversational groove with them. It is one of the green lights that determine if we will pursue forming a relationship with them—whether that's a professional relationship, a friendship, or a romantic relationship. We feel our internal yellow light flashing ("proceed with caution!") when the conversation feels rhythmically awkward, and the red light blazes ("get out of here!") if we feel strikingly out of sync. Have you ever had the jarring experience of meeting someone at a party and finding that each time you speak, the other immediately speaks over you? You then stop to let her finish, you try again, and instead of the normal give and take of a conversation, she talks over you again? You feel you can't get a word in edgewise. Pretty soon, unless you're forced to stick with this conversation to be polite, you'll give up and move onto someone else. Or perhaps you've experienced the opposite pattern—you speak, and then rather than responding immediately, your conversation partner pauses for a second or two or three before he speaks. Within a minute of such an awkward give and take, you start wondering what's up with him—is he arrogant? Stoned? Extremely shy? The point is, the awkward, odd rhythm of your verbal encounter with this man signals to you, within seconds, that something is off. The conversation likely ends there, as you politely extricate yourself, mumbling that you need to get a drink or use the restroom.

Research shows that, normally, persons who've just met automatically and unconsciously adjust their speech rhythms to create a joint rhythm that allows the conversation to flow. When that doesn't happen, the conversation feels extremely awkward and is likely to be brief.[9]

Likewise, once you've entered into a relationship with someone, you might have assumed that you would just get along and your interactions would flow relatively smoothly. But differences between you and your partner in personal rhythms may have persisted, making it difficult to establish a joint rhythm, a sense of easy togetherness. You probably have a gut sense of when you're not in the groove with your partner. The relationship feels out of sync, but you don't yet have the concept of rhythms to understand why. Instead, you may notice that you feel cut off, disconnected, frustrated, lonely. As the months and years go by, your arguments may center on housework, or bill paying, or other aspects of maintaining a life together. You may blame one another for your all-but-absent sex life, or that it's been weeks or months since you went out for a really fun evening (and blame each other for not initiating one). Or you may believe that your partner dislikes your parents because he seems never to want to spend time with them, while he counters that you don't like his, because when it comes to planning the holidays, you always prioritize time with your folks.

So you talk endlessly (or at least ruminate privately) about your unhappy feelings, or you fight over and over again about whose needs matter most, or who initiates things most, and who feels pushed around by the other's initiative. But like most couples, you don't realize that, beneath these common signs and centers of conflict, the fundamental problem is often the lack of clear, mutually satisfying rhythms that would create a more predictable flow in your lives. As a result, the problem you try to fix does not address the core issue: your couple arrhythmias. Yet, once you come to some agreements about how regularly, how often, for how long, and in what sequence to arrange some activities in your lives, conflict may fade—you will have found your groove, your couple rhythm.

When you take a few beats to think about it, it's not surprising that rhythms form the basic structure of togetherness, whether in couples, families, communities, or companies. Look at an obvious example—a group of musicians. Any musician, no matter what style of music, knows that rhythm is the foundation that holds the ensemble together. Rhythm provides the steady pulse of energy that fuels the rest of the music and keeps the ensemble united, even as they play their separate instruments and fulfill their different musical roles, take solos, and support each other's individuality and creativity. Although it can also be refreshing and beautiful to have portions of a musical piece, or entire pieces, with little or no obvious beat, with instrumentalists interacting freely and spontaneously, eventually they will lock back into a shared groove. Even in the freest forms of jazz, musicians respond to each other's rhythmic offerings and begin to weave a spontaneous tapestry that typically culminates in synchrony.

Rhythm provides the essential time structure in which the melodies and harmonies reside. And rhythms also greatly determine how others—listeners, dancers—respond to the musicians. That is, rhythm provides the basis for one group of people to connect and coordinate with another group of people, to join their bodies and minds even when not physically touching.

Rhythm catches our attention not only for its importance in music, but for the huge role it plays in our sense of physical well-being. Truth is, we only notice our bodily rhythms when they're off. A regular heartbeat is the foundation of physical health. An irregular one is a sure sign of an acute or chronic medical condition and must be treated immediately. The lungs bring fresh oxygen into our system and expel carbon monoxide through the rhythm of the breath. If this happens arrhythmically, the heart cannot keep up its job of infusing blood cells with fresh oxygen, and the other organs that rely upon that steady supply of oxygen immediately suffer. The body is a well-timed clock.[10] As former National Institute of Mental Health writer Gay Gaer Luce noted, "Not knowing that one has a time structure is like not knowing that one has a heart or lungs. In every aspect of our physiology and lives, it becomes clear that we are made of the order we call time."[11]

If we conceive of a couple as a kind of organism, just like the human body with its multiple organs and systems, the functioning of this "couple organism" depends on whether they create well-functioning rhythms that help promote their goals and efforts. In other words, the degree to which you as a couple can attain the good things we all want out of a relationship—clear and empathic communication, emotional closeness, sexual intimacy, leisure, relationships with friends and extended family, successfully meeting the challenges of work, maintaining a home, and financial and material support—depends on placing these activities into a workable rhythm.

Our Rhythmic Selves

Much of our life is anchored by the rhythms of our bodies. Chronobiologists trace three major duration cycles, or periodicities, of bodily rhythms, including those of the brain, that affect our reasoning and emotions.[12] They distinguish between the *ultradian* rhythms, patterns repeating at frequencies shorter than a day, often within seconds or minutes—our heartbeat, breathing, and the well-documented 90-120 minute cycle between maximum alertness and a need for rest (which we constantly ignore by pumping ourselves full of caffeine or other stimulants);[13] the *circadian* rhythms—from the Latin *circa* (about) and *dia* (day)—patterns repeating at a frequency of roughly once every 24 hours, such as waking up and going to sleep; and the *infradian* rhythms, patterns that repeat across days, weeks, months, or years, like the monthly female fertility-menstrual cycle, and the wholesale replacement of human skin cells that occurs every three to five weeks.

There's even a profound link between our biological rhythms and our cultures' spiritual and religious beliefs, in that this fundamental rhythm is the "first act" in most religions' stories about the world's creation. In the Judeo-Christian traditions, God's first act was to divide time into a rhythm of night and day. In Hinduism, before time began, the great Lord Vishnu was watched over by a serpent while he slept. Then the night ended, dawn broke, and he awoke, producing a lotus flower from his navel, and then gave his newly born servant Brahma the command to begin splitting the lotus flower into spatial distinctions—heavens, earth, and sky. In both of these and many other creation stories, the structuring of time from some version of timelessness (as we discussed in chapter 2, the Greeks called this aeon) into a cycle and flow of partitioned time (some version of what the Greeks called chronos) precedes the increasingly detailed structuring and differentiation of space, of beings and of objects in space. The flow of time—the sense of time moving along, creating a past, a present, and future—is the necessary first step to make rhythms possible.

Whether or not we subscribe to a particular religion and its creation story, most of us live in some measure of synchrony with the physical reality of the rising and setting of the sun. Most of us are awake and active during the day, resting and asleep at night (or at least, some portion of the night, in our electric-light, up-all-night world). One of the first goals new parents set for their infants is to get them onto a regular schedule—awake in the day and asleep in the night.

The daily rhythm of natural light and darkness represents the most basic natural form of what chronobiologists call *zeitgebern*—literally translated from German as "time givers."[14] When we push the boundaries of wakefulness into the night, our bodies react. Sometimes it's exciting, elected, and desired—woo-hoo! we're up late!—and sometimes it's forced upon us and unpleasant, and we're exhausted. When our schedules or our partners' schedules are opposite—up at night and asleep in the day—it's a significant deviation from the expected norm, and we note it by saying we work the night shift. And most who work that shift aspire eventually to get onto the day shift. That's because while people can and do adapt to being on the night shift, it is often with some cost to psychological and marital functioning.[15]

When we consider the contemporary rhythm of work and rest across the seven days of the week, we see the link between the secular world of work and religious beliefs about the beginning of time. In Genesis, it is said that after six days of hard work, God created a day of rest—the weekly Sabbath. Religious scholar Abraham Herschel poetically calls the Sabbath "an architecture of time"—emphasizing how sturdy and real a temporal structure can become, just like a building—and notes that it is one of the most enduring rhythms in cultural history, one that forms the basis for our contemporary distinction between the work week and the weekend.[16]

We also have activities that reoccur on a weekly, monthly, yearly, or multiyear periodicity. These include dental and medical checkups or yearly submissions to the Internal Revenue Service or renewals every ten years of driving licenses and passports. Then there are celebrations or commemorations that carry much more emotional significance and meaning-laden symbolism—anniversaries, holidays, reunions, vacation traditions, yearly memorial services for the deceased. When circumstances prevail that force us to miss these mundane, festive, or solemnly significant occasions, when we accidentally overlook them, or even when we purposefully avoid them, we often fret about it and feel strangely unmoored from an anchor of our lives. Many studies have documented the importance of routines (such as regular meals together, times set aside for leisure, homework times, regular wake-up and bedtimes) and rituals for couples and families, as well as for larger social groups and whole societies, in creating a sense of stability, predictability, connection, cohesion, and identity.[17]

What biologists, psychologists, sociologists, and anthropologists have learned by studying the rhythms in, between, and all around us is that we are not as fully free to be who we want to be and do what we want to do as we might think. Our biological and social rhythms direct our lives much more than we often recognize or wish to believe. This science of rhythms is simply rediscovering and reaffirming ancient knowledge.

Before white Europeans arrived with their mistaken belief in a fully autonomous and free-willed individual, the First Nations and Native Americans who populated these lands lived by a wholly different philosophy. Human beings were viewed as an integral part of nature, not armed with a God-given mandate to rule the planet. And family and tribe were viewed as the essential unit of social being, with individual members being the manifold expressions of that unity. African culture and, to a great extent, the African American culture that developed from Africans brought to the United States as slaves, similarly regards the person as an integral part of the group. In contrast to the individualistic first premise of existence, "I think therefore I am," African and African American cultures are founded on the collectivist principle, "I am because we are."[18] Much of the world outside of the United States—even many of those societies that have adopted greater American-style emphasis on individualism over collectivism—continues to assume that a person's thoughts, emotions, actions, and life course are intimately tied to the relationships within which she or he is imbedded and to the evolving roles of the person in those relationships.

And one of the most defining aspects of a self in context—whether it's the intimate context of one's romantic partnership, family, peers, workplace, the religious or community group to which one belongs, or the society at large—is the nature of the social rhythms of that context. Our daily, weekly, monthly, and yearly rhythms greatly structure our lives with a force of obligation that is difficult to resist. We are rhythmic beings, connected to our bodies and each other through the force of multiple, overlapping rhythms.

What this means is that couples and families are governed by rhythmic patterns of connection and influence that determine the behavior of each member. Parents typically set and enforce explicit rules about waking times, mealtimes, homework time, playtime, bath time, and bedtime. When families lack clear temporal patterns, they often seem chaotic and disorganized—not only about time but in how and whether they achieve important daily life functions such as feeding, bathing, sleeping, socializing, studying, and working.[19] They also may have difficulty managing strong emotions—the skill I described in chapter 3 as "emotion regulation."[20] When children and adults have a sense of the regular pattern of activities in their days and weeks, they know when to gear up their level of general emotional arousal (for instance, in the morning, getting ready for school and work; later, during playtime) and when to gear down (for dinner and bed). When basic life activities occur irregularly in time, family members cannot develop more automatic fluctuations of arousal, and parents may then spend an inordinate amount of time getting their children energized or calmed, depending on the energy requirements for the next activity. Interestingly, I've found the same to be true with my adult clients.

Millie was a 60-year-old graphic artist whose husband died 14 years earlier. He'd been the one to say when it was time to go to bed, and he set the alarm clock for waking. When he died, Millie's days and nights blended into one another in chaotic ways. She developed a sleep disorder that led to exhaustion and, by the time she was referred to me, extreme anxiety, especially in the morning. She would awaken in panic at whether she should have gotten up earlier to get more done, or whether she should go back to bed for a few more hours. Every morning she grappled with the same question. At night, she often found herself up way beyond the 12 midnight bedtime she and her husband had adhered to for 20 years, or she would crash at 10 P.M. She'd tried a host of anti-anxiety and sleep meds, with minimal effect. Once I pointed out the irregularity of her sleep and wake rhythm and her obsessive worries about it, and I described the way that this basic rhythm entrains our general arousal levels, she gradually moved to a regular sleep-wake rhythm, dramatically decreasing her anxiety. And she cried—for the first time since her husband died—when I suggested that she may have avoided keeping the sleep-wake rhythm established with and enforced by her husband because to do so would be another reminder that he was gone.

Decades of hard biological and social science findings support what I have observed as a couple therapist. When two partners are out of sync in their rhythms, distress almost always follows. Arrhythmia in intimate relationships may set off a danger signal deep in our brains, because rhythmic alignment between intimates starts early, in infancy. As I noted earlier, the degree to which a mother and baby coordinate their interaction rhythms largely influences whether or not an infant forms a secure attachment.[21] Similarly, in our adult relationships, if we feel uncoordinated with our partners, it may set off anxiety about whether we can feel emotionally secure with them.

Talk to your partner about these two rhythms of life questions:

- What are some of the regularly occurring activities and events in your life that you rely on for a sense of stability and meaning?
- What are some of the most important rhythms in your couple life?

Taking Charge of Your Relationship Rhythms

Now it's time to dig into the details of relationship rhythms, so that you know exactly what's happening when you feel out of sync, and what needs to change to get in sync.

Rhythms weave together three essential components of time:

- Frequency: *how often* we wish to engage in particular activities like making love, talking about the relationship, taking trips, going out, staying in, seeing relatives, cleaning house, reviewing finances, and other sublime and mundane aspects of a life together
- Sequence: the *order* of activities—at the end of the work day deciding whether to catch up with one another before or after spending a little chill time alone; or on the weekend, whether to make love before or after tackling onerous housework chores; or on the scale of years, whether to establish a career and secure a particular level of financial status before having children versus having children while building a career and financial stability
- Temporal Location: decisions about *when* activities happen on the clock and on the calendar—for instance, one partner prefers to make love in the morning while the other prefers it in the evening; one craves physical contact during the week while the other can only get into it on the weekend; one partner wants to take vacations only during the summer while the other strongly prefers a winter holiday

These three time components are like atoms, and rhythms are like molecules, locking these components into regular patterns. And, just as many molecules link together to create all the matter in the universe, the sum total of our rhythms makes up the matter of our lives.

In long-term, intimate relationships, couples often find that fun, pleasure, and sexuality occur irregularly, only after one or the other partner is troubled enough by the absence of such contact to initiate it or complain about its absence. Although "date night" has become hackneyed advice in magazine relationship columns, couple therapists insist on its importance.

Without deliberate planning, couples will let their special time together lapse to last on the list after work, kids, house, and other obligations. Preserving regular together time is an antidote to potentially deeper emotional rifts. Instead of warmly turning to our partners and saying, "Honey, I miss you— let's make some time," we're far more likely to silently nurse feeling rejected and neglected, wondering why she doesn't reach out anymore—even as he wonders the same and waits for *you* to initiate contact.

When couples in my practice engage in mutual criticisms, I wonder aloud whether these common complaints become painful because the pair has so little regular time together and that, perhaps, they miss each other and are lonely. Amazing how such a simple observation goes to the heart of the matter and results in a longing gaze at one another in a moment of mutual recognition. Noting how common this pattern is in contemporary couples, I typically will explain further that unless they create a rhythm of regular time together, the only way they'll likely make time is when they return to this kind of frustrated state, a crisis of mutual neglect.

Of course, then they explain about being too exhausted to carve out regular time together. I then note that by *institutionalizing* this slot of time it will become the thing they do, not an expendable leisure activity they can axe when work picks up. They may even find that they start to conserve energy in other places in order to bring more to this new and essential event. And I also typically note that the pleasure energy they gain from one another will likely benefit all the other activities of their lives. And they will save energy that they previously wasted on arguments.

A historian of engineering, Henry Petroski, writes that frustration, disappointment irritation, and failure, rather than necessity, are the mothers of invention.[22] Feeling sad and upset and hurt about not getting enough time with one's partner can be a useful irritant that stimulates the invention of a regular rhythm of couple time. But if couples fail to act on their milder levels of irritation to institute this rhythm, they continually cycle between irritation and renewed attempts to spend time. Unfortunately, though, the cycle becomes a downward emotional spiral, with irritation and temporary loneliness growing into deep hurt, anger, and alienation, creating greater emotional hurdles and less incentive for making and enjoying time together. Couples that, early on in their relationship, establish a rhythm of time together can save themselves a lot of suffering and create a bank account of pleasure and good feeling they can draw upon when facing life's inevitable challenges. And there are scores of research studies to support this.

Research shows that instituting regular leisure time is a critical predictor of couple satisfaction and longevity.[23] And importantly, it turns out that satisfying regular leisure time—whether it's a weekly movie, dinner, sex, a walk in the woods or by the beach, or just reading together—impacts a marriage much more than the less frequent but sometimes more lavish (and usually, more expensive) yearly vacation.[24] Indeed, several studies have shown that, although any particular couple may of course benefit greatly from a vacation—even if they agree on where they want to go, what they want to do, travel well together, and avoid contact with work or even negative thoughts about work—overall, vacations have little effect on relationship stress.[25] It's the regular time together during the regular grind of life that matters most in preserving positive feelings and preventing relationship distress.

I have found it is far more important that a pleasurable joint activity occur regularly even if infrequently, than having it occur more frequently but irregularly and, as described earlier, usually only after a fight about the prolonged absence of time together. It seems to create more of a positive shared couple narrative if you can say, "We don't go out to dinner as often as we used to, what with the kids, the cost of babysitting, and all, but we know we can count on going out once every two months, so it's still a part of our lives together, a part of who we are." This allows you to affirm your identity in terms of the rhythms of activities you do, and to say, "We are a couple that does ___, ___, and ___" (fill in the blanks with whatever are your particular passions and interests). It can truly be said that rhythms form a core basis of our identities as individuals and as couples. When we think about what we like and don't like about our lives, or when we talk to an old friend and answer the question "So how's it going?" much of what we reflect on or talk about is how we feel about our rhythms—although before you read this book, I'd guess, you never thought of it that way.

Needing the Second Half

Not only do we feel it on an emotional level when our natural rhythm is disrupted, we feel it most painfully when our partner creates the discord. Janet was a lively red-haired woman whose natural perkiness had mutated into bitter snappiness over the past several months with her husband, Wayne, who for his part seemed stunned at her hopelessness about the future of their three-kid, ten-year, big-house marriage and clueless about the source of her rage. In our first session, she rapidly laid out the catalogue of things she disliked about him. Mostly, she felt he didn't know how to pay attention to her in a way that made her feel attractive and loved. She found herself fantasizing about an ex-boyfriend who'd recently moved into town—a man who'd not been the best "marriage material" in terms of his career and earning power but who made her feel sexy and interesting. "Wayne and I've got three kids, so I'm not looking to break up our marriage, but it just seems hopeless—Wayne just doesn't know how to love someone, he's too self-centered." As an example, she noted that whenever they had time alone, Wayne would talk nonstop about himself and his ideas—his work, his thoughts about politics, on and on, never pausing to ask her what she was thinking about. Wayne seemed miffed but mostly puzzled; he did not realize how much he'd been dominating the airspace in their talk time.

At the end of the session, among other suggestions, I told them to try date night again, but this time Wayne was to spend the first half hour asking Janet about her day, her thoughts, her opinions, and not utter a word about himself. After that, he could speak about his experiences, ideas, and concerns for a couple of minutes, then he was to ask for her reactions (rather than barreling on in his typical monologue). Janet seemed lukewarm about this suggestion—mostly because she didn't believe such a simple change in speech rhythms could really change her pessimistic feelings about the relationship.

We broke for vacation and at our next session, things had changed dramatically. I saw her for an individual session (having seen him alone a few weeks before when she was out of town), and she looked bright, pleased, relaxed. Even I was surprised at the rapid positive shift. "Things are much better!" she said. I asked what had changed. "Wayne listened to *me*, he stopped *talking*, or at least stopped talking so much. Before this, 'Date Night' had become 'My Turn Night' with Wayne—I felt he would just pour out all this stuff, and very intensely, like a kid telling a story, with all the boring details. He never got a chance to do that as a kid. So with me, it felt weird, and so unsexy. I felt like his mom, not his wife. Now our conversation goes back and forth. It's not just that he takes more of an interest in me—that's great—but what made the difference was getting the back and forth going in how we talked. Before, it felt really off!"

Everywhere we look and listen we can see how rhythms bond people to each other and to other aspects of their contexts. I have distinguished between three levels or durations of interaction rhythms that are critical for coordinating partners' activities: the *micro* length of tenths of a second to several seconds, the *molar*[26] or midrange length of minutes to hours, and the *macro* length of days to months to years.[27] Just as I use these levels to aid me in assessing their rhythms when I counsel couples, these categories of rhythms can help you identify where your rhythms are "on" or "off" in your relationship.

Micro Rhythms

Communication between partners happens on many levels. We want our significant other to intuit our needs—when we're on a professional call and cooking pasta with the other hand, we want a partner who knows to pass us the sieve without our asking. I call this the *micro* level of interaction. This is especially poignant in the nonverbal physical interaction of sex. For example, one partner's climaxing might consistently outpace the other's readiness, or one partner tries to take charge of stimulating the other in a particular way and rhythm but the other responds by initiating some other rhythm on another part of the partner's body, leading to a sexual traffic jam.

In our individual session, Janet said she hoped that she and Wayne could improve their sex life. The same one-way robotic quality that had characterized Wayne's conversational style also typified his approach to sex. He'd plant kisses on her lips and body in a mechanical, rapid rhythm that provided little time to actually feel and absorb the kiss, never mind reciprocate. After about 10 minutes, he'd offer her oral sex, which, she noted, he would perform "quite competently." Yet it all felt too mechanical, too unvarying— his rhythm was *too* steady, too repetitive, and too uni-directional. When she would get aroused and he'd go inside her, he often came quickly, leaving him feeling embarrassed and her feeling frustrated. He'd return to oral sex to bring her to orgasm, but both felt they weren't really having sex together. She sighed and noted, "Look, he's an engineer—that's how he approaches tasks. Everyone calls him 'Mr. Activity.'" Sadly, as she viewed it anyway, sex had become another task for him rather than an opportunity for real pleasure and play.

When in our next couple session I asked about their sex life, Wayne was embarrassed but, to Janet's surprise, described accurately her frustration with his rhythm. Apparently, our breakthrough about his dominating speech rhythms and their seeming "miraculous" improvement when he changed how he conversed with her had got him thinking about other ways in which his anxiety led him to create rhythms of interaction that were stiff. I instructed them in the ways of slow sex (see chapter 3) and also gave Wayne some simple but effective exercises for slowing his pace to orgasm. One week later, as they sat down and faced me at the next session, they touched each other's thighs, grinned that bashful grin I've seen many times when couples have a sexual breakthrough, and Janet flushed red in the face. "Well, it worked," she said.

Midrange (Molar) Rhythms

At the midrange level, a rhythm that often goes askew is the "morning routine." A smooth-running rhythm might look like this: Partner A showers while Partner B makes breakfast; they eat; B showers while A dresses, waters the plants, and feeds the cats; B dresses; they leave for the train. (Add children to the morning routine and you've got a whole other level of complexity in action coordination.) The entire rhythm can be speeded up or slowed down as long as each component behavior adjusts in relative duration to the others. When one component takes longer than usual without adjustments in the duration of the other components (for example, Partner B takes longer to shower because of a broken arm, or just because he's tired that morning and is dragging his butt, but A has to leave at a certain time to catch a train), the rhythm will be disrupted. Or if A wakes up to find B is already in the shower, but hasn't made breakfast (change in sequence). Or the couple enters a phase of their life, perhaps because of changes in one or the other's work hours, in which they suddenly rarely share a morning routine, as one must leave the house before the other is barely out of the shower or not even awake. Rhythmic disruptions, especially if repeated frequently or not adjusted, can trigger annoyance and a sense of disconnection in one or both partners.

On the flip side, small changes in unsatisfying daily rhythms can have big effects on your relationship. Saul and Jessica were first-time parents of daughter, Sophie. For a couple of months, Jessica had stayed up late and woken at 3 A.M. to breast-feed while Saul, head of a large clothing company that was a family business, needed to get to sleep by midnight at the latest in order to get up at 6:30 A.M. for work. (For those women already gearing up to chop Saul's head off for not sharing the nighttime feedings—or mine for not insisting he do so—Jessica insisted on handling this responsibility alone, as it was important to correcting her earlier worries that she wouldn't be an adequate mother.) As a result of this asynchrony in sleep and wake times, Jessica and Saul had not gone to bed together for some weeks and had lost what Saul especially felt was important: "cuddle and connecting time." When two months into their baby's life he'd asked Jessica to consider coming to bed at 11:30 so they could have that half hour together, she had vehemently rejected the idea and felt he was being unsupportive and unappreciative of her breast-feeding responsibilities and her continued insecurities. Saul backed down, but unhappily. Even while other aspects of their relationship improved, their standoff about this bedtime asynchrony filled many of our sessions for several more months, causing flashfloods of acrimony. When she finally felt more secure in her connection to Sophie, and more understood and less pressured by Saul, Jessica finally made it to bed by 11:30. Saul was delighted, and, to her surprise, she was too. They were able to restore an important rhythm in their life of watching a late-night show while holding each other and quietly talking.

Macro Rhythms

At the macro level, partners may argue about how often and regularly to sit down with their finances (one wants a monthly routine, the other twice a year), how often to take vacations (one wants a yearly vacation, the other claims she'll lose her business if she takes more than a week off every two years), how often to make love, and how often to visit in-laws.

Tony, 52, a physician, and Theresa, 48, a medical records clerk, were verging on divorce after years of conflict. Most prominent of their disagreements was that Tony felt trapped by Theresa's insistence, from early in their marriage, that they have dinner every Sunday with her family. Both were from traditional Italian American backgrounds, but they differed in how much they identified with their ethnic traditions. While Theresa enjoyed her Italian American heritage and the ritual of Sunday dinners, Tony had a much more complicated, negative experience growing up in his family, which included members involved in Mafia activities about which he felt ashamed. He had worked hard to distance himself from his background, in part by attaining his medical degree and making a life in his professional community. Nevertheless, Tony insisted that he loved her family and wanted to spend time with them, but felt he and Theresa and their young son, Richie, had never established their own family unit as primary. He never wanted to be "just one big happy family" with her parents and siblings. He insisted that if they could cut the frequency of dinners with her family to once a month, it wouldn't feel "so regular, so relentless." However, Theresa believed that it was important for their son to get to know his aging grandparents and believed that having the dinners weekly was the best way. Ultimately, their inability to compromise on this rhythm—with its links to their culture of origin—was a major factor that led them to divorce.

Where Are You in Time? Assessing Your Couple Rhythms

Now that you've gotten oriented to the meaning and importance of rhythms, talk together about *your* couple rhythms. Start with the degree of match between your daily and weekly routines and schedules—are you mostly in sync or ships passing in the night (or day)? Sometimes couples have developed quite regular rhythms of *disconnection*, rhythms of going to bed and waking up, of leaving for work and coming home, that reliably keep them from encountering each other. To connect, your rhythms need to overlap in ways that bring you together. If your rhythms differ, what's the impact on your sense of closeness and connection?

Does one of you control the daily or weekly schedule (wake times and bedtimes, off-to-work and back-from-work times, meal times) more than the other? You may have highly synchronized rhythms that keep you in lockstep closeness, but if one of you enforces strict adherence to these rhythms and the other feels she or he must obey, synchrony can feel like a prison. In order for couple togetherness to feel satisfying and not oppressive, partners must share the power to co-create the rhythms, and to request flexibility and change.

Do your couple rhythms allow time for solitude, for aloneness? How much alone time do each of you need and desire? Do your rhythms allow for time doing activities with others apart from your partner? How important are those times for each of you? How satisfied are each of you with the amount of time together versus time apart?

How satisfied are you each with the frequency, amount, regularity, and temporal location (day of week, time of day) of your couple pleasure time—time for fun, for dates, for sex, for talking intimately as friends? How do you feel about the sequence of where pleasure times fit into the rest of your activities? If not satisfied with any aspect of couple connection time, what would need to change to make it better? What about your rhythms of vacations?

How happy are you with your rhythms of talking about relationship problems and challenges? Does one of you feel that the other never makes time to talk about issues?

How satisfied are you each with the rhythms (again—frequency, regularity, sequence, and temporal location on clock and calendar) of handling your responsibilities—the regularity with which you each do housework, chores, shopping, childcare, finances, health care appointments, vehicle care, and other aspects of life maintenance?

WORKSHEET 4.1 RELATIONSHIP RHYTHMS ANALYSIS (RRA): RHYTHMS AND REMEDIES

Pick one activity about which you have regular conflict: sex, communication, meals, vacations, time together, daily work schedules, chores and housework, childcare, visits with friends or in-laws, or other activities. Use this worksheet to identify the differences in the elements of your rhythms underlying this conflict and to brainstorm some possible solutions.

	Differences in Desired Frequency of Activity	Differences in Desired Sequence of Activity with Other Activities	Differences in Desired Time Location of Activity	Differences in Desired Regularity of Activity
REVEAL What are your rhythmic differences around this activity?				
REVALUE What can you appreciate about each other's rhythms and preferences? How do your differences help the relationship?				
REVISE What can you do in each of these elements of rhythm to bring you more in sync as a couple?				
REHEARSE What's your practice plan? Commit to specific activities you will do on a daily, weekly, monthly, and yearly basis to change and/or better align your rhythms.				

These discussions will help you assess the degree of match between you and your partner on all these aspects of rhythm and where you might be having difficulties that need some work. For a more detailed and systematic assessment of your couple rhythms, complete the Couple Rhythms Questionnaire, available at www.syncyourrelationship.com. Then, to summarize what you've learned about your rhythms and those of your partner and your plan for change, complete the Relationship Rhythms Analysis Worksheet.

Couples Out of Rhythm

To illustrate further the problems couples encounter when their rhythms are off or when they haven't created workable rhythms in the first place, and how to go about fixing couple arrhythmias, here are three short vignettes of couples I helped to set up grooves of togetherness and coordinated effort.

Remember Arlene and Jim from chapter 3? The young corporate couple that raced around Rome and felt exhausted rather than replenished by their vacation? Both had demanding corporate jobs, and their different routines for waking, working, and going to bed meant they barely connected on weekdays. Jim was up and out by 6:15 A.M. and at the office by 7:00 A.M., where he was immediately immersed in managing a team of 20 analysts in a Wall Street investment firm, just as Arlene was rising to get to the office by 9 A.M., where she spent most of her day alone with her computer in a cubicle. She typically got home by 7:00 P.M., lonely and ready for human contact. She'd change into sweats and read e-mails until Jim returned an hour later, depleted from his hectic day, craving an hour in his own head. He was ready for bed by 10:00 P.M., while she was good to go until 11:30 P.M. In the first few months of living together, Arlene would launch right into talking about her day while Jim gazed glassy-eyed at the TV, occasionally grunting to show he was listening. Eventually, Arlene backed off, resentful and even lonelier; Jim sensed that but felt unable to please her.

Although they were convinced they had reached the end of the road before their marital journey had really begun, I readily solved their problem by identifying and helping them to transform the temporal structure at the root of their disconnection. I noted that, although it might not seem this way to Arlene, Jim also wanted connection at the end of the day. I said I could completely understand if Arlene didn't believe it, but suggested that Jim's zoning out when he came home might just be his instinctive, physiologically driven attempt to decompress and revive his energy so as to be truly available to her. By getting home earlier, she'd already had a chance to decompress; Jim just needed to catch up.

Jim, who'd been looking deflated and hopeless about convincing Arlene out of her angry disappointment, lit up at this explanation, and affirmed, "That's absolutely true! I really *want* to spend time with you—I'm just wasted when I get home and need a little time." Arlene's expression softened just a bit; she seemed ready to consider this possibility or, at least, to give Jim the chance to prove it.

To help them see their struggles as shared by many if not most couples, I described some important information about how our bodies and our brains react to stress and what happens when we take the time to relax and emotionally regroup. I explained how the physiological arousal that accompanies much of our workdays is a function of the sympathetic branch of our autonomic nervous system—the fight-or-flight response to challenges. During the day you, like most people, probably experience varying levels of anxiety or frustration as you work to address problems and achieve goals. To recover from periods of sympathetic arousal, the calming, soothing side of the nervous system—the parasympathetic branch—needs to be activated.

Like most people, your workdays are probably filled with one challenge after another, with little time reserved for mini-chills, moments when you can take a deep breath, be off-task, and restore some balance to your nervous system. Instead, there's a steady climb over eight hours or more in sympathetic arousal, resulting in a fair degree of stress and exhaustion by day's end. When you return home to your partner, you may typically transport this stress right into your relationship. Research has shown that the greatest number of conflicts between couple partners occur at the end of the day, upon reuniting after being apart. Each partner has his or her own particular needs and preferred ways of restoring some degree of internal calm, and these often come into conflict.

Another couple I'd worked with years before needed just this kind of synchronizing in the transition from work to home at the end of the day. Tim, a lawyer, had a commute of 90 minutes each way to and from work, and Laura, a painter and graphic artist, had elected to be at home with their two-year-old daughter, Rose, occasionally doing part-time work at home. Although Tim had suggested they get a babysitter for a few hours each day to give Laura a breather, she felt strongly about being the "only mother figure in Rose's life." When Tim returned home, Laura wanted him to take Rose for a couple of hours so that she could take a walk by herself outside and get some work done. Although Tim respected Laura's need for time and wanted to spend time with Rose, he felt so tense from his work day and the stressful commute that he found it difficult to switch immediately to parenting. He'd tried to use the commuting time to decompress by listening to music and books on tape, but the oncoming traffic was distracting. He felt torn—on the one hand, he wanted to be there for his wife and daughter, on the other, his gut told him he needed to calm down before he'd be ready to be a responsive dad.

Although he knew this was unrealistic and unfair, his fantasy was to have two hours to chill out by playing his guitar. Laura felt impatient with Tim's needs for recovery time, noting that she needed private time as well, and Tim felt guilty for expressing his wish, and then angry at Laura for invalidating his needs. I suggested that Tim might find he could recover more quickly if he knew each night he'd get a certain amount of time to chill out, and if Laura knew that she'd have reliable nightly time for her work and to relax a bit alone.

Based on what they said would most help each of them de-stress, we devised a nightly decompression chamber routine, a technique you learned about in chapter 1. I settled on the metaphor of a "decompression chamber" to describe this process because it seemed to capture the experience of many people—that after a day of feeling like they've been in the deep water, 50 meters below sea level, with challenges of all sorts, they needed to regain a more relaxed state. For Laura and Tim, the first step in their decompression chamber routine was to greet each other warmly (there remained much affection between them despite this area of conflict). Then Tim would get 30 minutes to play his guitar alone in the bedroom, then he'd take Rose until her bedtime, while Laura got a chance to work and walk for 90 minutes. They'd reconvene to put Rose to bed and then spend 15 minutes catching up, while Tim washed dishes and Laura relaxed more at the kitchen table (having done more than her share of housework all day).

Despite his initial sense that his need for solitude was "endless," after one night of playing guitar alone in his room, Tim felt lonely and "weird" being by himself. He brought the guitar down to the living room, where Rose would make a game out of fitting herself into his guitar case, hopping in and out of it. Laura, who initially ran out the door with relief as soon as Tim took Rose, ended up hanging around for a little while, then longer, as Tim played songs that she loved. She still took time for herself, sometimes while Tim caught up with housework, but what had begun as a desperate sense from both partners for alone time spontaneously evolved into a rhythm of family time, which both felt provided the decompression they needed and the reconnection with one another they craved.

Back to Jim and Arlene. I suggested that they, too, needed to create a joint decompression chamber rhythm to make a better transition between the stresses of the workday and their evening time together. In this new nightly rhythm, Jim and Arlene first greeted each other affectionately when Jim arrived. Jim then got 30 minutes to space out (or in) so as to catch up with Arlene's earlier chill-time before they connected for dinner and caught up about the day. Bedtime was a mutually satisfactory compromise—10:30 P.M., with TV off and time to cuddle and connect. As the couple instituted this decompression rhythm, as had happened with Tim and Laura, it quickly became clear that Jim didn't need time quiet *alone*. He was more than happy to have Arlene there—in fact, he preferred it—watching TV together, and he was even happy to give her a foot rub, one of her greatest pleasures. He just couldn't engage verbally until he'd had a chance to let his nervous system move from its heightened state of sympathetic arousal to a parasympathetic, calm state. This new nightly joint rhythm worked great for them.

In this chapter, you learned about the pervasive influence of silent, hidden rhythms in our lives—in our bodies and in our relationships. And you learned that when partners feel out of sync, it may be due to mismatched rhythms. Equipped now with the specific concepts of rhythms of different lengths (micro, mid-range, and macro rhythms), and knowing the component parts of rhythms (an activity's frequency, sequence with other activities, and the temporal location or place in calendar or clock), you've got a powerful set of tools to reveal the sources of your couple arrhythmias and create shared rhythms that bring you together. And most important, you've learned how important it is to set rhythms of pleasure time in motion and preserve those rhythms.

Don't let yourselves lapse into laziness about keeping alive those rhythms of fun, friendship, and sensuality, for doing so is a sure formula for loneliness and alienation. And it need not come to that!

Time Perspective: Prioritizing the Past, Present, and Future

IN YOUR RELATIONSHIP, does one of you constantly try to corral your partner into carefully scheduling activities for the upcoming week and weekend, while the other wants to take it as it comes, be more spontaneous? Is one of you always trying to chart out your long-term life plan, while the other finds talk about long-term life planning constraining, boring, unrealistic, anxiety provoking, a distraction from enjoying what's going on in your lives in the present? Does one of you feel comforted by (and lost without) to-do lists, while the other feels those lists reduce life to a set of tasks rather than an adventure to be experienced? Does one of you advocate putting most of your money into long-term investments, while the other likes to keep more money available to spend to make life enjoyable in the present? Does one of you plan dinners and dates with friends way in advance, while the other prefers to invite folks over spontaneously?

Or are you a couple in which one of you likes to try new restaurants, or new vacation spots, or new clubs, while the other likes to return to places you've enjoyed before? Does one of you enjoy seeing films about the future, while the other is a history buff, resulting in disagreements every time you try to pick a movie? Does one of you enjoy reminiscing about your shared past, taking out the old photos and videos, saving souvenirs, and making scrapbooks, while the other gets annoyed with all this remembering and collecting, preferring to create new experiences in the now or plan adventures for the future? Does one like to stay in touch with and spend most social time with old friends from high school and college (or even elementary school), while the other likes to meet new people? Does one of you insist on preserving the family and cultural rituals of your childhood, while the other feels it's important to create new rituals that fit your current circumstances and lifestyle?

If so, like many couples, you and your partner may differ in your fundamental *time perspective*: the degree to which you think about, value, and determine your actions based on the past, present, or future. These differences in time perspective can lead partners to feel that they just can't get on the same page or exist in the same time zone, and that they don't share common interests and approaches to life. In fact, I've found that many couples with pervasive disparities in time perspective often summarize their problem with the same broad complaint: "We've got such huge lifestyle differences." It's not surprising that they see their discrepancies as reflecting a fundamental difference in lifestyle. One's dominant time perspective is a psychological organizing principle that can influence how one views what's most important in many aspects of life. But once partners recognize their underlying differences in time perspective and how these lead to conflicts about money, friends, vacations, sex, and many other topics, they can come to revalue those differences and combine their approaches in a way that creates a richer, more varied, and fulfilling lifestyle.

As we've seen with other aspects of time—like life pace—I've discovered that at first the differences appear small but become more extreme over the course of the relationship. It's as if one partner becomes the flag bearer for the need to enjoy the present, while the other becomes the representative of the need to plan for the future. The more he insists on spending money to enjoy life now, the more she feels she must rein him in and save to achieve their life plans. Or the more she tries to pin him down to some evening in the week when they *might* make love, the more he insists that love making is only genuine when it is sparked in the moment. Although both partners recognize the virtues of the other's point of view, it's likely that now they find themselves arguing vociferously for one side of the truth because they fear the other's seemingly extreme view will dominate and lead them into trouble.

Likewise, the more one partner insists on preserving his family's holiday rituals, the more the other rebels, and not because she prefers her family's traditions over his—she wants to dump *all* the old ways of celebrating entirely and create something new. Or the more he piles up the photos and the old concert programs and the trinkets from past trips, the more she wants to pull her hair out, crying "we've got too much stuff!"

Yet these differences also account for what brought you together. We are often initially attracted to our partners in part because the other's time perspective offers a useful or exciting complement to our own.

But we usually don't consciously realize that source of our attraction, or at least, we don't conceptualize it in these broad terms. Instead, she admires his planning and carefulness, while he loves her passionate spirit and spontaneity. She admires his respect for tradition, and he admires her desire to create meaningful celebratory occasions and not just passively accept established customs.

Prominent social psychologists and time researchers Philip Zimbardo and John Boyd define time perspective as "the often nonconscious process whereby the continual flows of personal and social experiences are assigned to temporal categories, or time frames, that help to give order, coherence, and meaning to those events."[1] This means that just as our brains automatically categorize experiences along the continuum of good/pleasant to bad/unpleasant, our thoughts, emotions, and behaviors are automatically and effortlessly categorized and organized in terms of the temporal categories of past, present, and future. We generally don't have a thought, feeling, or mental image and then have to stop and tell ourselves, "OK, that's a memory of the past," or "That's an experience going on right now," or "That's a daydream about the future." Rather, our brains automatically tag our mental contents in terms of whether they're about the past (memories), present (perceptions), or future (imaginings and fantasies). If one's brain is not functioning this way, one is likely to be under the influence of a hallucinogenic substance, which can blur the brain's ability to peg a mental image to the past, present, or future, or one may be experiencing a psychotic episode or a frightening flashback memory due to post-traumatic stress disorder (PTSD). A person with PTSD may literally hear voices, see images, experience smells and tastes that are from the past but believe that the events that gave rise to them are happening right now. These are terrifying moments of confusion, as distinguishing the past, present, and future is an essential aspect of how we orient ourselves to reality.

In order to process our world automatically in terms of time perspective, we assume unquestioningly that we have a past, a present, and a future, that these time zones are meaningful and real, even though, as Buddhists, medieval scholars, and contemporary physicists from Einstein onward have noted, time is a human construction that we cannot possess except as an idea. It was St. Augustine who in the fifth century famously captured the ineffable nature of these different time perspectives when he wrote in the *Confessions* that time was created by us to interpret the present, that the human mind shapes time's eternity through the filter of individual experiences. He showed that the moment we think we're in the present, it's already past, and when we think about the future, we can only do so in the present—the future doesn't exist, and as soon as we get there, it's past. Thinking about these things can be a bit like Alice falling down the rabbit hole in Wonderland, where nothing is as it seems to be!

Yet, despite compelling philosophic arguments for the fuzziness or even unreality of the distinctions between the past, present, and future, for most of us, at least in postindustrial societies around the world, these temporal perspectives fundamentally organize our activities, experiences, and self concepts. We are usually clear about what is in the past, the present, and the future. But we can differ markedly in the degree to which we *value* and *emphasize* the past, the present, or the future. That is what we mean by time perspective: the segment of the past-present-future continuum that you most value and organize your life around. And when two people come to their intimate relationship with widely divergent time perspectives, they're organizing their worlds in very different ways without even realizing it.

Let's look at what research has documented about the link between time perspectives and people's personalities and behavior. Then we'll explore further what happens when partners diverge in their time perspectives, and how to identify and resolve those differences, or at least, put them to use in strengthening the relationship.

Time Perspectives and Personality Styles

Some of us may be inclined toward focusing on the past or the present moment, but then there's the great future-focused leveler—the punishing, autocratic, to-the-minute schedules by which we abide. Catching the 5:28 train, arriving to work by 9, picking up the kids by 6, holding that important meeting on a Tuesday not a Wednesday. Yet despite the dominance of clock and calendar in our world, people can still differ strikingly in their respective focus on the three time frames. The past and the present (and those who love them) have not been totally eliminated, despite our era's bias toward planning and scheduling everything in advance. Based on numerous studies using their Zimbardo Time Perspective Inventory (ZTPI), Zimbardo and Boyd identified the existence of six time perspectives derived from the combination of the three major time frames and three other ways of experiencing oneself in the world: The degree to which one emphasizes positive versus negative experiences, the degree to which one prioritizes seeking pleasure (hedonism), and the degree to which one feels in control of one's life, an aspect of self referred to as personal agency. The six time perspectives types are:

- Past-positive
- Past-negative
- Present-hedonistic
- Present-fatalistic
- Future
- Transcendental-future

Here's a brief summary of each time perspective type, drawn closely from Zimbardo and Boyd's book, *The Time Paradox,* which summarizes their research. Before you read on, you might want to find out whether you mostly fit any of these time perspective types by completing and finding your score on the ZTPI, because once you read the general profiles of each time perspective type, your responses to the inventory might be influenced by what researchers call social desirability, that is, the degree to which you would prefer to fit one or another profile, or believe that one is better or healthier than another. To complete the ZTPI and learn how to determine your time perspective profile, go to Zimbardo and Boyd's Web site, www. thetimeparadox.com.

So—don't peek at these descriptions until you've completed and scored the scale!

Past-Positive

People high on this time perspective savor positive memories, which are often set off by present sensory perceptions (sights, smells, sounds). Past-positives describe their lives as filled with more good than bad experiences. They like telling stories about their lives, experience nostalgia about their childhoods, and enjoy repeating rituals and traditions learned in their families. Compared to people who score low on this time perspective, they tend to be less aggressive, are less anxious and depressed, are more emotionally stable and happy, have higher self-esteem and more energy, are less shy and friendlier, more conscientious, and more creative. If faced with unpleasant present situations or future circumstances, they can gain reassurance from their memories.

Past-Negative

Past-negative types tend to think a lot about how things have gone wrong in their lives, are consumed by regrets about the mistakes they've made or the positive opportunities they've missed, and focus on how they have been mistreated by others. When faced with the need for action in the present or future, they may be reluctant to act because they believe they have not succeeded with similar situations in the past. Compared to people who score low on this time perspective, they tend to be more aggressive and have stronger tempers, are more anxious, more depressed, more emotionally unstable and less happy, have lower self-esteem and less energy, exercise less often, are more shy and less friendly, less conscientious, less worried about the future, and are somewhat more impulsive (since they have a low sense of self-efficacy and control over life's outcomes).

Although past-positives and past-negatives differ on how they regard their pasts and the degree of pleasure they obtain in reflecting upon it, they share a tendency to prefer familiar routines, activities, and people over trying something new or meeting someone new. They are not adventurous and tend to be politically and religiously more conservative, and may be more prejudiced than other time perspective types. Interestingly, and sadly, past-negatives may even prefer the known but painful over the unknown but potentially more positive experiences. Yet they have a greater sense of continuity in their lives than present- and future-oriented persons.

Present-Hedonistic

As the name indicates, the chief characteristic of people high on the present-hedonistic scale is that they seek out the pleasures of the moment and avoid engaging in activities that diminish enjoyment or cause unpleasant feelings. They seek novelty and excitement, and do not gravitate to activities that require regularity or that demand perseverance in the face of boredom or anxiety in order to achieve a goal. Given the choice of delaying gratification for a reward later versus indulging in enjoyable activities in the here and now, they go for the present gratification. They tend not to study effectively, consistently, or enough, and compared to future-oriented or past-positive types, may not do as well in school or work that requires diligence and repetition. Nor are they very amenable to messages that instruct them to take better care of things now (health, finances, relationships) to avoid problems in the future. While not as high achieving in many areas, they can be more creative than persons who score low on this perspective, and may be particularly adept in activities and professions that require intense focus on present processes. Generally, and not surprisingly, they are happier than people who are lower in present-hedonism. At least they are having fun while it lasts!

Present-Fatalistic

Present-fatalistic types believe that there is little they can do to affect the course of their lives, so they accept the conditions of life as they find them each day. People can become fatalistic because of how they think about negative past experiences in which bad things happened to them over which they felt they couldn't exert much control. Growing up with limited economic and educational opportunities, they may have learned to adapt and adjust to these limitations, forgoing dreams of a better life.

Not all of you out there reading this book have had an economically and educationally privileged life in which the only challenge you had in attaining success was your own perseverance. It is important to note that negative social conditions can contribute significantly to demoralization and fatalism—that as with all personality styles, including one's dominant time perspective, these styles can be shaped by the social conditions one lives in, and the degree of oppression or privilege one has experienced. With the growing popularity of positive psychology,[2] we tend to underemphasize the effects of our circumstances, both positive and negative, on the degree to which we can achieve economic and career success, health, or relationship happiness.[3] At the same time, plenty of research worldwide shows that people born in dire circumstances can often rise above those circumstances, that dreams of a better future, rather than being deferred, can be realized.

Not surprisingly, research shows that present-fatalism is associated with higher levels of aggression, anxiety, and depression, lower energy and self-esteem, greater shyness, higher risk of suicide, less conscientiousness, greater impulsivity, less creativity, and lower grades. In a sense, these are people who have given up before even starting.

If you are a practitioner of meditation, mindfulness, or Buddhism, you may wonder where you fit into these descriptions of present-hedonists and present-fatalists. Buddhists and others who practice mindfulness focus greatly on the here and now and on accepting positive and negative emotions. They attempt to release themselves from attachments to hedonistic pleasures and worries about the future. Zimbardo and Boyd note that these people may fit into a category they call the Holistic-Present. They did not include questions in the ZPTI that would tap that time perspective, arguing that it is not as common in Western cultures as in Eastern cultures. I believe that had they developed the ZPTI in the last 10 years, they might have included such questions, as Eastern philosophies, religions, and mindfulness have been widely adopted in Western cultures, been heavily integrated into psychotherapy practice,[4] and even been subjected to Western empirical research on their effectiveness in reducing medical and psychological symptoms.[5]

Future

Those high on the future time perspective envision possibilities for their lives and then work to achieve them. Rather than being responsive to current opportunities for pleasure, or satisfied with what they've already experienced, future types use the present to arrange the circumstances for their goals and dreams to occur. They plan each day, week, month, and year, and they get started earlier on tasks than others do. They make to-do lists and prioritize meeting deadlines and getting work done even when more enjoyable options are available in the moment. Compared to people who score low on the future scale, they are less likely to be aggressive, anxious, or depressed, have higher self-esteem, more energy, are less likely to smoke, use recreational drugs or alcohol, are more conscientious and less oriented toward seeking sensations, prefer consistency over novelty, study harder, have better grades, and are less prone to lie. Dentists may be interested to know that futures floss more than others! On average, futures complete more education and make more money.

The downside of all this forward-looking achievement orientation is that futures are more likely to cut back on hobbies, time with family and friends, as well as time for fun and sex with their partners. They also sacrifice involvement with their religious community. And they may cut back on personally doing household tasks.

Transcendental-Future

Transcendental-futurists are primarily motivated not by the future of their current existence, but by their imagined life after physical death. Zimbardo and Boyd found that this orientation is associated with strong religious beliefs and high involvement in religious practice, especially within the Muslim and Christian traditions, although individual beliefs and traditions vary widely. Jews and Buddhists were not found high on this time perspective. Certain transcendental-futurists have been found to be highly empathic, generally happy, and of course, focused on future rewards. On the other hand, Zimbardo and Boyd have explained suicide bombing as facilitated by this time perspective, and have found this perspective particularly prevalent in persons who've experienced a great deal of social oppression.

Acquiring a Time Perspective

What determines how you gain your time perspective? Remember Cindy and Jerry from chapter 1? Both grew up in families that valued a future focus, but they felt differently about that legacy. If, like Jerry, you admired one or both of your parents' focus on future planning, you might be inclined to emulate it; but if, like Cindy, you came to regard their relentless planning as oppressively constraining, you might rebel and cultivate a focus on present pleasures. Attending a college-prep high school versus one in which everyone is more focused on partying could determine your path—more educated people tend to be more future oriented, because planning and detail orientation are necessary for academic success. Illness and psychological disorders such as depression can lead some younger persons to forgo much focus on the future. On the other hand, as was the case for Phil Zimbardo, who was severely ill for years as a child, illness or other present hardships can lead one to focus extensively on hopes and plans for a *better* future. As we age and perceive less of a future before us, we tend to focus more on the past and present, although chronological age alone is less important than our perception, real or imagined, of how much time we have left.[6]

Relatively few people fit one time perspective completely. Many may utilize a combination of several different perspectives. You may be great at future planning at your job, but when it comes to weekends, you want a release from all that scheduling and want to take things as they come. Or you may generally have a positive view of your past, but occasionally, when comparing yourself to others and what they've achieved in their lives through careful future planning and hard work, you may be filled with regrets about plans not made or completed. Zimbardo and Boyd recommend that a balance of time perspectives—emphasizing the emotionally positive versions—provides the most flexibility and fullest sense of life.

But they and other time perspective researchers have not addressed what happens when couple partners hold different time perspectives.

Couples and Time Perspective Differences

Let's look briefly at two examples of the kinds of conflicts couples can have when each partner emphasizes a different time perspective, and how, with my help, they broke out of their impasses. Do you see yourself in either of these examples?

A Future and Present-Hedonist Pair

Carla, an energetic, engaging, serious-looking woman in her early 40s, and Jim, a lively graying man in his late 50s whose jaunty gestures lent him a youthful quality, consulted me about their marriage. Carla declared that they were in "constant conflict, about everything." Jim agreed, adding with a touch of bitterness that he felt Carla blamed him for most of their problems because "I don't do things the way you want them done." She shrugged her shoulders and nodded grimly in agreement.

Carla directed a large, successful health clinic and structured almost every minute of her life with detailed to-do lists and her long-range planner. Incredibly organized at work, she wanted the same kind of structure at home. On Sunday, she planned the week's meals for the couple and their 10-year-old daughter, Sarah. She wanted Sarah to stick to a strict after-school routine (30 minutes of play, 30 minutes of homework, dinner, then 30 minutes of homework, followed by one TV show), scheduled the family's weekends well in advance with Sarah's play dates, music lessons, and sports activities, plus social events for her and Jim. In planning vacations, she liked to pore over guidebooks and schedule each day to take in as much as possible. The day after returning from a vacation, or sometimes on the plane coming home, she would try to engage Jim in planning next year's trip. She also frequently tried, with little success, to get Jim to talk about their "five-year life plan." She insisted on creating a budget and keeping careful track of expenditures.

Jim found all this detailed planning "ridiculously rigid," felt controlled and "choked" by it, arguing that there was no room for spontaneity in their lives. He noted, "I've never lived my life this way, and sure, I've made mistakes and had some disappointments as a result, but also, a lot less tension and worry than Carla." On the topic of home finances, Jim, a successful financial products salesman, felt it was enough to establish broad categories of spending and stay generally within those limits, so that there was room for that "in the moment splurge." Five-year planning? "I do enough of that at work—I don't want to run my life like a corporation." Vacations? He preferred to pick a destination a few months rather than a year ahead, to "see what we get inspired to do closer to the time," even if it meant having to scramble and pay more for flights and accommodations. Carla often had to work late, arriving after Sarah's dinnertime, and Jim—whose work schedule allowed him to be home when Sarah returned from school—would occasionally insert some flexibility into Sarah's after-school routines. He would sometimes let her play longer and delay starting homework until after dinner. Or on occasion, rather than cook the meal that Carla had planned for that day, he'd whip up some burgers and homemade fries. Or Jim would suggest that, instead of going to her swim team practice, she "blow it off" so the family could take advantage of an unusually warm, early spring day and go for a hike. These changes enraged Carla, who felt undermined and unappreciated for all the structure she attempted to create in their lives. She felt Jim was trying to team up with Sarah against her, making her seem like the rigid taskmaster, and Jim, the fun, flexible parent. She also noted the importance of teaching Sarah the virtues of discipline and focus. Jim insisted it was not his intent to undermine Carla or be Sarah's favored parent; he just wanted to "go with the flow" more, a capacity he believed equally important to teach a child.

Jim acknowledged that his high emphasis on pleasure and spontaneity had caused him some difficulties—he described some ill-fated career moves and a failed previous marriage driven by immediate passions with no thought to the long-term viability of the relationship. He recognized that in many instances, he would have profited from engaging more foresight and planning.

Carla and Jim were overwhelmed by the wide range of different topics about which they fought, leading them to feel somewhat hopeless about continuing to make a life together. But it was clear to me that all their issues emerged from a fundamental difference in their time perspectives: the degree to which they each focused on and valued the past, present, or future. Carla experienced much professional success following a "future code" and thought it would serve her and her family well in their personal lives. And in many ways, it did. Jim's focus on the present served him well in business— he was good at seeing and seizing sales opportunities as they arose in the moment, connecting with potential clients and responding to their present needs and individual styles. His vivacity and capacity for passionately enjoying life was infectious. Like Carla, Jim thought he made an important contribution to his marriage and family life. And in many ways, he did.

By applying the four Rs of my Relationship Rhythms Analysis approach to their time perspective struggles, I was confident that they could transform their struggles into one of their greatest assets. That is, I believed I could fairly quickly bring them relief if I could *reveal* their fundamental time perspective difference and show how it infused all their other specific problems; if I could help them *revalue* their time differences, and recognize how these had been a central point of attraction for each of them; if I could help them *revise* the ways they expressed these differences; and if I could inspire them to *rehearse* new patterns that would bring the best of their perspectives together in a complementary, rather than competing, fashion.

I explained the concept of time perspective, noted how Carla seemed mostly future focused while Jim seemed much more focused on the present. I showed how their arguments about how closely to stick to weekly meal plans, Sarah's after-school routine, how to spend their weekends, their different approaches to financial and vacation planning were all linked to their time perspective differences. They responded with immediate recognition, and relief—they each felt I had seen and explained something fundamental about them that they had not put a name to. We explored how events in their families growing up led them to adopt their particular time perspectives. Carla's father's frequent fluctuations in job success and failure led to major ups and downs in the family's economic fortunes, and prompted her desire for greater regularity and predictability in her life. Jim's father's severe alcoholism and occasional acts of violence toward his mother and toward Jim and his siblings meant he had to "take each day as it came," adapting to his father's changing moods. He learned to make the most of the good days and to "try to be scarce" on the bad days.

Then we explored what attracted Jim and Carla to one another when they first met, and as is so often the case, these differences in time perspective played a major part. Carla loved Jim's spontaneity, fun-loving side, and capacity for joy in the moment—"I felt he helped me loosen up." Jim admired Carla's discipline and hoped some of it might rub off on him. Having rediscovered the value to one another of their different time perspectives, we then thought together about how to decrease the polarization that had developed between them. The couple agreed to blend their approaches to the weekly dinner planning, where three out of five weekdays Jim would serve what Carla had set out, and two days he and Sarah would make whatever they got inspired in the moment to cook. Jim agreed to stick to Sarah's after-school homework and play schedule, especially since Sarah was still having some difficulty getting her work done. But Jim suggested, and Carla agreed, that it would be good for Sarah to have one day where she determined the routine, as a way of helping her take charge of her time.

The couple decided to plan out Saturdays (since Sarah's sports and music activities were all on that day), but to let Sunday be "spontaneity day," where they would decide in the morning how to spend it. Carla agreed that doing five-year planning for their personal lives wasn't necessary, but Jim agreed to stick with her tighter budget, as long as they could still occasionally agree to spend a bit more freely when the moment moved them. And Carla promised not to start next year's vacation planning before the current trip was even over, as long as Jim agreed to get started "getting inspired together" at least six months ahead, rather than cutting planning so close that they ended up in a stressful scramble, which then fell in her lap to resolve.

Bringing together the strengths of both of their time perspectives worked well for Carla and Jim. Their fights stopped as they felt more appreciated by one another, having regained the balance in time perspectives that attracted them in the first place. As a couple, they learned to enjoy the present moment and also to plan well for future present moments.

A Past-Negative and Past-Positive/Future Pair

Tova and Michael, an Orthodox Jewish couple in their 30s with three young children, were on the brink of divorce (which is why I mention that they were Orthodox Jews—it is a big deal to get divorced or even consider it in this branch of Judaism). Whereas Tova recalled with bitterness many of the times when she felt unsupported by Michael, Michael thought their marriage had overall been quite positive—except for the fact that Tova complained so much about the negative events of their lives. He had frequently apologized for the times when he did not help out enough with child rearing because he was working so many hours, but pointed to a year when he left his career to become a full-time father so that Tova could complete her doctoral research in archeology.

He noted, "I tend to try to emphasize the good stuff, put negative things behind, and move on from the past." Tova countered, "Yes, but I can't do that, that's why we're here, I can't move on. You see, for me, if it's history, that's what it's all about." To which Michael, an IT manager for a major company, retorted, "Yes, but your history is always made up of all the bad stuff, with all the extraneous good stuff thrown aside." She replied, "Given my historical method, and given the objective reality...." To which he quickly responded, "As if there is an objective reality."

We had a breakthrough when I suggested that each seemed to have become specialists in one view of their history: The more Tova insisted it was largely negative, the more Michael felt compelled to remind her of the positive, and the more he spoke only of the positive, the more she felt she had to reiterate the negative. What was interesting in this regard was that, even when I asked Michael to review the history and include a fuller account of the ways in which he had not come through for Tova, she insisted that she wanted also to hear his account of what *she* did wrong. I suggested further that for them to resolve this time perspective impasse that had locked them into this downward emotional spiral, each would need to be able to represent in their conversations both the positive and the negative aspects of their history—freeing them from their polarized roles, and thereby allowing them both to notice, hold, and discuss the positive and negative experiences in their present and future.

This was the turning point that unlocked their emotional standoff and ultimately saved their marriage. But their path toward sharing a more balanced view of their past wasn't without challenges. For Tova, as for some others who fit the profile of past-negative, it felt scary to let go of her negative view anchor and allow herself to embrace the positive and the possibility of a positive future: She had learned to protect herself by assuming the worst. Likewise, as Michael started to sit with his negative feelings, he occasionally felt panicky. I helped them learn some active ways of soothing themselves, and each other, as they gradually expanded their ability to immerse in different time perspectives.

Where Are You in Time? Assessing Your Time Perspectives

If you haven't done so already, each of you should complete the Zimbardo Time Perspective Inventory (ZPTI) to learn what time perspective you each emphasize (www.timeperspective.com). If you don't have time right now to complete the inventory, based on what you've learned in this chapter about the different time perspective types identified by Zimbardo and Boyd, which perspective type, or combination of types, best describes you?

Next, visit my website (www.syncyourrelationship.com) to complete the Couple Time Perspective Inventory (CTPI). It will help you identify how similarly or differently you view aspects of couple life related to time perspective.

Next, let's go through the four Rs of the Relationship Rhythms Analysis to help you understand and resolve difficulties emerging from discrepant time perspectives.

Reveal

Compare your time perspective profile on the ZPTI (or your general impressions of your time perspective type) with your partner's. Do you share a time perspective or are yours different? Are your results surprising, or do they confirm what you already perceived?

More specifically, in thinking about couple issues and lifestyle choices related to time perspective, discuss how much you agree or disagree with these sample questions from the CTPI about leisure time (they're numbered differently in the actual questionnaire):

1. As a couple it is important to plan how to spend your weekends as early in the week as possible rather than see what you feel like doing when the weekend comes.

2. When it comes to couple leisure time on the weekend, I think it's best to leave things open, not to plan things out too much in advance.

3. I'd much prefer to sit around with my partner looking at photographs of times we've spent together and talking about those experiences than doing new things or planning out what the next adventures will be.

If you highly agreed with question 1, you're likely more future-oriented when it comes to couple leisure time. If you highly agreed with question 2, you're likely more present-oriented. If you highly agreed with question 3, you're likely more past-oriented. If you found you each responded differently to these questions, discuss how these differences in thinking about leisure time have affected your relationship.

To further assess how similar or different you are in time perspective, you might also find it useful to reread the ten questions that opened this chapter. Each question describes a couple in which the partners differ in time perspective. Discuss how much these portrayals resemble your relationship.

What would each of you say about the general degree of conflict you experience about time perspective as a couple? Do you agree or disagree overall on how much time perspective has been a source of conflict in your relationship?

Revalue

If the inventories or the discussion questions revealed that you are quite similar in time perspective, discuss how this has been helpful to your relationship. How do your similarities in time perspective in general and on specific issues and activities make coordinating your lives easier?

If your scores or discussions revealed mild, moderate, or extreme differences, talk about any ways your difference in time perspective might have been a source of attraction to one another initially, or how that difference still represents a source of attraction. If you completed the CTPI, look at the questions on which you had different scores (different by 2 to 4 points). Talk about how your differences on those questions are helpful, or might be helpful, to your relationship. (If you've not yet completed the scale, just consider how you and your partner might utilize the following differences.) For instance, if you differ about whether to spend more time with old friends versus meeting and making new friends, consider how, by combining your past and present perspectives, you could both maintain continuity with old friends as well as venture out into new-friend territory. Or if one of you prefers to put money aside for the future rather than spending it on things that you could enjoy in the present, whereas the other prefers to spend more now, instead of fighting over which perspective on money is correct, you could find a compromise. You could regularly put money aside for a secure future but also create a monthly discretionary spending account reserved for a few impulse purchases or present quality of life purchases. You might agree that either of you can spend up to half that money without consulting one another (after all, some of those purchases might be gifts or surprises for one or the other—remember to save receipts for possible returns!), or you might feel more comfortable agreeing ahead of time on these purchases. Whenever you encounter differences in issues or preferences related to time perspective, try to remember Zimbardo and Boyd's suggestion that people with the capacity to utilize the past-positive, present-positive, and future perspectives in combination function most effectively. That goes for couples, too.

Revise and Rehearse

Now talk about whether there are any liabilities, limitations, or problems that come from having the *same or similar* scores on the CTPI. That's right. So far I've emphasized how differences in time perspective may result in conflict, but sometimes having the same perspective can be limiting to the couple in certain ways. For instance, if you both highly agree that it's more pleasurable to go to the same restaurants repeatedly than to try new places, how might your agreement on sticking with familiar restaurants keep you from having new dining adventures? Or, if you both "highly agree" on a preference for dreaming together about things you might do in the future rather than talking about things you've done in the past, might it be better to balance out your future focus with a bit more reminiscing? After all, without taking time to remember the experiences you planned, you may lose a storehouse of positive experiences that will be pleasurable to savor one day.

Now the more obvious consideration: How do you need to adjust to your *differences* in time perspective? If one of you thinks it's important to collect souvenirs and make scrapbooks, and the other wants to throw the

WORKSHEET 5.1   RELATIONSHIP RHYTHMS ANALYSIS: PROBLEMS IN TIME
PERSPECTIVE DIFFERENCES

What is each of your dominant time perspectives?

List briefly your surface conflicts (common issues of conflict for you):

REVEAL

How might your time
  perspective differences result
  in your specific issues or
  conflicts?

REVALUE

What does each of you
  appreciate about the other's
  time perspective?
How were your time
  perspectives part of your
  initial attraction to one
  another?
How do your respective
  time perspectives (either
  similarities or differences)
  still help the relationship?

REVISE

What can you change to make
  your time perspectives more
  compatible, less stressful, and
  more enjoyable?

REHEARSE

What's your practice plan?
  Make a commitment to
  specific activities you will do
  on a daily, weekly, monthly,
  and yearly basis to change
  and/or better align your time
  perspectives.

old stuff away to make room for new stuff and new experiences, can you find a compromise? Can one of you cut down on the amount of memorabilia hanging around the house and the other tolerate or even learn to appreciate the past-oriented collector's tendencies?

If one of you believes strongly that it's better to put aside sad or hurtful past relationship events and move on to make things go well in the here and now, can you set aside a regular time for talking about and resolving old hurts, and at the same time use those conversations, even if unfinished, to move toward doing what you think will most improve the relationship right now?

The ability of a couple to make such creative compromises will either make or break their relationship.

To summarize what you've learned about your respective time perspectives and your plan for change, complete the Relationship Rhythms Analysis Worksheet for Time Perspective.

Getting in Sync about the Future: Resolving Differences in Personal Timelines

As we've seen, partners' differences in their dominant time perspectives can result in a wide range of specific conflicts. And we've seen that by revaluing these differences and bringing them together, couples can create a more balanced life.

But whatever each partner's general emphasis on the past, present, and future, once the conversation turns to what each partner wants and expects life to include in the present and the future, and by when, serious difficulties may arise. Partners may differ greatly in their expectations about when they will finish their education, get employment, reach a certain level of job or career success, purchase an apartment or house, or have children, or may have other discrepancies in their desires about when they will achieve certain life goals. In my experience with hundreds of couples, this issue of synchronizing hopes and plans for the future can make or break a relationship more than any other time issue.

Remember Marcia and Fred from chapter 1? In their late 30s, Marcia wanted to try to have children, and Fred had started another round of grad school. Fred said he wanted to have kids, but he just wasn't ready to take on that adult responsibility. Marcia reminded him that her biological clock had been ticking for some time already, and she couldn't wait any longer if she was to possibly conceive a child. We explored and came to grasp with their underlying emotional issues: Fred's anxieties about moving on from being a student and becoming a working professional; and Marcia's earlier ambivalence about having a child, which may have led her to pick a man who from the beginning expressed ambivalence about marriage and fatherhood. But after all that increased understanding, they didn't make it as a couple, because they were not able to take the key step in resolving the discrepancy in their personal timelines.

Simon and Justine, both in their early 30s, met at a New York City nightclub, introduced to each other by mutual friends. They were immediately attracted to each other and began a passionate romance. Eight months later, Justine moved into Simon's apartment, and they began talking about marriage. But while Simon, a lawyer who worked long hours, saw their growing commitment as a signal that they should cut back on their busy nightlife, Justine, a part owner in a restaurant, continued to want to party into the wee hours of the morning. The more Simon insisted that Justine cut back, the more she felt constrained by him and determined to extend this "free time" in her life. Simon began to question whether they were really in the same place in the steps toward their future.

There are many factors that affect whether couple partners readily align themselves in their goals for the future. Of course, one is the degree to which they both emphasize the future time perspective—the focus on planning and goal setting. When one partner is generally oriented to planning the near and more distant tomorrow and views the present as a stepping-stone on the path toward future goals, while the other seeks to live for today, enjoy the moment for its own sake and let the future take care of itself, the couple may not even be able to have the conversations required to share their respective visions of the future.

This was initially the case with Simon and Justine. Although he enjoyed present pleasures, at his core Simon was highly focused on the future: He had strong aspirations in his career and wanted to realize his vision of having a stable family and children by his mid-30s. He had lots of early training in this future-focused approach to life. Through education and hard work, his father and mother had both risen from working-class backgrounds in Boston to establish themselves in business careers, and they had drilled into Simon and his sister the importance of occupational success and using their time wisely.

In contrast, Justine came from a small mountain village in Switzerland, where her family had for generations owned a successful hotel. Although Justine was also raised to value hard work, the family's success relied on staying put and sustaining the hotel's tradition, which in turn meant focusing mostly on keeping that tradition alive in each day's hosting. Given the family's generations of business success, they could reasonably argue that the future will take care of itself if you take care of the present. In her own way, Justine was, like Simon, future focused, and had created for herself an image of a future quite different from that envisioned for her by her parents. Justine's move to New York was viewed unfavorably by her parents, who counted on her and her brothers to take over running the hotel once they retired. Yet, Justine had always dreamt of life in a big city, and she hoped to use her hotelier and cooking skills to create a successful restaurant career in New York.

As we came to understand it, when they first met, both were escaping somewhat constricting families. Their shared enjoyment of the New York City nightlife was a welcome respite from a total focus on serious pursuits, especially for Simon. Ironically, although Justine certainly enjoyed the freedom of staying out late and meeting lots of people, these activities were actually related to her work aspirations and quite similar to the role she would have played had she stayed in Switzerland as the hostess in her family's hotel, entertaining guests and creating a lively atmosphere. What appeared to Simon as her relentless partying was, Justine explained, a central activity of her business: networking to create a buzz about her bar and restaurant. Yes, she wanted to marry Simon and start a family, but felt she needed another year to firmly establish her restaurant. Then she could step back from all the networking. Once Simon understood the relationship between Justine's nightlife excursions and her goals for the future, and once Justine agreed to limit the late nights to three nights a week so that they could have more couple time at home, they were able to establish a clearer sense of a future together, and went forward to get engaged and, later, married.

There are two key steps that determine whether couples can link their personal timelines. First, can you agree on *what* you want to achieve? If one of you doesn't want children and the other does, and even after much discussion and exploration of feelings neither of your positions have changed, then the one who wants to have a child will need to decide whether she or he wants a child more than they want to stay in the relationship. Conversely, the one of you who doesn't want a child needs to decide whether he or she is willing to sacrifice the relationship and let the other go to pursue the dream of having a child. Similarly, if one wants to move back to his homeland and the other does not, or cannot move because he or she wouldn't be able to maintain his or her career and make a decent living in that land, they may need to part. These decisions never feel fair to either party, and each of you is likely to feel the other is being controlling, selfish, and stubborn. Or, maybe you can, less in anger and more with sadness, just realize that your lives are unavoidably, inescapably diverging, wish each other well, and move on.

But if you can agree on the *what* of your lives, then it may be possible to find a compromise about *when* to achieve that *what*. Using the effective, research-tested speaker-listener communication technique and the ABCs of problem solving from the PREP® program that I will describe in chapter 9, you will be able to talk about what a particular goal means to you, why you want it to occur when you do, and then work out a compromise. Remember, research shows that a certain degree of sacrifice and compromise is not only normal for any long-term relationship: it's essential.[7] So can you sacrifice some or even greatly on the *when* of the *what*—stretching yourself to accommodate your partner, without severely compromising your integrity?[8]

Where Are You in Your Personal Timelines?

One method of gauging how much you and your partner agree on your life goals and of charting their timing is to map them. Get a roll of brown wrapping paper and lay out on a long table or on the floor a piece of the paper that is at least 144 inches (12 feet) long. Draw two parallel lines across the length of the paper, one for each of you, separating the lines by at least 12 inches, to allow space for writing on the bottom line. Divide the lines into two-inch segments. Each two-inch segment represents one year, creating a total of 72 years each in length (make the sheets longer or shorter as you desire, depending on how long you hope to live). At the left-hand edge of the paper, on your respective lines, each of you should write your respective date of birth. Counting forward in years, make a vertical mark on each of your lines for the month, day, and year you met. Mark and indicate the year for any goals or other important activities that you had achieved before meeting each other—finishing some aspect or all of your education; getting launched or established in your line of work; having a child (by a previous relationship or other means); breaking up with a previous partner (or getting divorced if you were married); taking a long-desired trip; winning a piano competition, cook-off or bake-a-thon, fly fishing contest, Nobel prize, or gold medal at the Olympics; watching every rerun episode of *Seinfeld* or *Star Trek.*, climbing all 46 mountains above 5,000 feet in the Adirondack range of New York, or hiking the entire Appalachian Trail—whatever's been an important goal for you.

Now, on the timelines going forward from the point where you met one another, write when you hope to achieve further separate and joint life goals. Readers of this book will be starting from all sorts of different places in their lives and their relationships: some of you may have just met each other, some have been together a few months, a few years, some for decades. Some of you met when you were young—I've worked with several couples who met when they were in high school, and they're now in their mid-30s or even older, so they achieved several of their life goals (graduate education, career, world travel, getting married) while growing up together. Other couples I've worked with met in their late 40s or early 50s, had long ago finished their education and become established in their work lives, and one or both may have been married and divorced and had children. So for some of you, many of your life goals will occur going forward from the point at which you've met. For others, you will have achieved quite a number of your life goals by the time you met.

Everyone has different goals, but common goals in the life cycle of an individual and a couple include: completing some level of education and occupational training, getting established in some form of employment or career, getting married or establishing some other form of committed relationship, having or adopting children, reaching a certain level of financial and material attainment or success, developing a circle of friends or joining and participating in a community (religious/spiritual or secular), travel. Mark out the year(s) when you hope to achieve these or other goals. Now compare your time lines and goals. Do you agree pretty much on the *whats* of your life but disagree on one or more of the *whens?* Talk about it, using the structure of the speaker-listener technique if you anticipate that the conversation might get heated.

By each of you identifying your dominant time perspective; by seeing how your time perspectives influence your beliefs, priorities, desires, and actions; by seeing where your differences in perspective might lead to specific conflicts about money, sex, friends, weekly leisure time, travel, and other things; and by seeing even where your similarity in time perspective (if you were similar) might lead to limitations, you've acquired a powerful tool to create the compromises that will make your relationship more satisfying. And by getting clearer about each of your life goals and when you want to achieve them, you can either save yourselves a lot of grief by realizing now rather than later that you just won't be able to make a life together, or you can make some compromises and get your futures in sync.

Resolving Struggles about Punctuality

IF YOU WANT TO get a quick fix on the nature of the closeness and power dynamics between you and your partner, just look at your struggles about time. So far we have seen how couples might struggle when one partner is focused on an orientation to time that centers on the clock and calendar while the other wants to cultivate the sense of time standing still. We saw how partners can feel pushed around by each others' paces: the fast one feels dragged down by the slow one, the slow one feels rushed by the fast one. We've met couples battling over their daily, weekly, monthly, and yearly rhythms: fighting about everything from when to wake up or go to sleep; when, for how long, and how regularly to make love; or when and how often to visit the in-laws or to take vacations. And we've encountered couples in which one partner sets a priority on preparing for the future, while the other seeks to enjoy the present or finds it important to review the past.

But nowhere are differences and power struggles around time more overt than in partners' approaches to punctuality. Discrepancies in partners' time orientations, paces, rhythms, and time perspectives are often the hidden cause of other more obvious problems: poor communication, unfulfilling sexual and emotional intimacy, conflicts about when and how to complete household chores, disagreements about what to do in the evenings and on weekends. We've seen how once we identify and shift the underlying time patterns, couples can rapidly resolve those surface problems.

When it comes to punctuality, there's nothing hidden about it. The problem is right out there in front of your face. These struggles are so evident because they come down to a moment in time, as implied by punctuality's etymology, the Latin word *pūnctum* for "point." You're either on time or you're not. And when one partner is time sensitive and the other casual about the clock, each can feel pushed around by the other. The prompt partner feels he is always waiting for the other; the late-inclined partner feels she is being controlled. Each can feel hurt, disrespected, and neglected, all because of differences in being on time.

We might assume that, as a concept, punctuality is easy to define but, for a range of reasons we'll explore, couples often differ about how they define what it means to be prompt and how high to value it.

Personality and Punctuality

The struggle about punctuality may be particularly intense because some cultures associate it with the values of conscientiousness and agreeableness, the latter of which includes being considerate of others and the desire to please them. So central are these values that they are two of the so-called Big Five (the others are neuroticism, openness, and extraversion), the most-studied dimensions of personality. Conscientious people have habits compatible with work that is results oriented and follows a timetable. According to three German personality researchers, people high on the trait of conscientiousness "actively manage their goals, and are organized, dependable, dutiful, orderly, self-confident, self-disciplined, and deliberate."[1] Likewise, they find highly agreeable folks embody lots of wonderful traits—trustworthiness, straightforwardness, cooperativeness, modesty, tender-mindedness, altruism." Not surprisingly, their research shows that persons who score high on conscientiousness and agreeableness are more likely to be on time than those who score lower on these personality dimensions.

In distressed couples, I've found that generally punctual partners often deride their rarely punctual partners (hereafter referred to as GPP and RPP, respectively)[2] precisely for the personality flaws their lateness seems to reveal. The GPPs use such descriptions as disorganized, undependable, undisciplined (e.g., not conscientious), untrustworthy, deliberately uncooperative, arrogant, self-centered, uncaring, or too noncompliant for their own or the relationship's good (e.g., not agreeable).

What does the RPP say in self-defense? The chronically late partner may simply cry "uncle!," agree with the GPP's assessment, feel ashamed, incompetent, and apologetic for the lateness, and vow to be more on time in the future. When the late partner again fails to be on time, the two may reenact the pattern of one criticizing and the other apologizing, which

creates an imbalance of power. This is one version of a common dysfunctional and polarizing couple pattern called the blamer-placater.

The blamer-placater pattern can center on other issues, such as money,
in-laws, or children, with the criticized partner accepting the full blame,
even if they are only partly or not at all responsible, just to avoid conflict.[3]
On the other hand, the behaviors named by the blamer are often global
and open to interpretation—for instance, "You are spoiling our children,"
"Your unfriendliness is the reason my mother never wants to visit us,"
"Your spending habits are ruining us financially"—such that the blamed
partner may challenge the other's assessment and reject the blame. But
because punctuality is so hard to contest—again, you're either on time, or
you're not—and because it's associated with positive traits, it's often hard
for the placater, once the placater gets up the gumption, to challenge the
GPP's righteous indignation and break the blamer-placater pattern.

In response to the RPP's attempts to loosen the taboo against lateness
in some cases (to a party, to dinner at home when work takes precedence),
the GPP may curl his or her lip with disdain, and say something like, "How
can you possibly argue that it's fine to be late?" RPP may withdraw back
into the "guilty as charged" position, and the power dynamic remains in
place. Over time this blamer-placater pattern, while on the surface keeping
the peace, results in emotional distance and disaffection between partners.
In some relationships the GPP seeks the position of greater influence, but
I've more often found that the punctual, conscientious partner feels burdened and resents being more powerful.

Some RPPs refuse to recognize that prompt is right and cast GPPs'
traits in a negative light. They might use such descriptions as uptight,
obsessive, overly concerned with rules, driven by a massive superego and
anxiety, nothing but a well-socialized robot in a postindustrial, clock-
tethered, Matrix-like world. In fact, some research indicates that highly
punctual persons have a higher sense of time urgency, a component of the
famous Type A personality.[4] Research also suggests that those folks at the
more extreme end of concern with punctuality (that is, those who insist on
being early) are associated with one of the most negative collection of traits
identified in personality research: neuroticism, the third of the Big Five.
Inhabiting the negative end of the emotional stability continuum, people
who score high on neuroticism tend to be overly sensitive, anxious, depressive, unsure of themselves, impulsive, vulnerable, nervous, and irritable.[5]

The only problem with the RPP using this description of the GPP is
that it may be a case of the pot calling the kettle black. Another behavior

sometimes associated with chronic lateness is procrastination, which is occasionally linked to neuroticism, depression, and anxiety. So worried are these individuals about the tasks they need to complete, they avoid and avoid until the last minute, and may then incur big consequences for their lateness.[6]

Yet recent research shows that procrastination is a way to induce inspiration for some people. They become effective with an imposed deadline and deliberately plan to start projects later in order to create the optimal level of arousal.[7]

RPPs may view themselves as free spirits, unbridled by social conventions and open to new ideas and experiences, or as extroverts, so busy interacting with others and taking in the world of sensations that they lose track of time. They refuse to worry about a trivial minute here and there. One rarely punctual client I counseled saw her behavior as a reflection of her independence, and her principled refusal to adhere to the promptness practices she'd learned from her parents. However, from a research point of view, this self-description by the RPP doesn't have much merit as an explanation for lack of punctuality, because openness and being an extrovert appear to have no relation to whether one is early, late, or on time.[8]

The personality styles of people, whether they are typically punctual or typically late, can vary quite a bit. The person who is punctual because she is highly responsible and organized may be a different personality type than the on-time person who is concerned about others and doesn't want to inconvenience them. Both types are likely quite different than the person who is punctual or even insists on being early because he is highly anxious and wants to avoid the additional agitation triggered when he's late. Likewise, the person who is often late may be a bit disorganized about time but still a reasonably caring and trustworthy person—it's just that her lack of organization ends up temporally trumping her level of agreeableness. And both the timely and the late partners may be similarly high on the dimension of neuroticism—anxious, depressed, and irritable—but for one it drives his punctuality, while for the other it's the basis of her lateness.

In sum, although research provides some clues about the personality styles that drive punctuality and its opposite, there is no simple profile of the characteristically punctual or the chronically late. Yet, when partners quarrel about being on time, they tend to develop simplistic negative theories about what drives the other, theories that deepen the conflict and degrade the quality of the relationship.[9] Each partner comes to believe that the other's punctuality behavior is a sign of the other's negative traits and reflects the other's negative feelings about the partner.

Punctuality and Personality in Couples

Although there's been no study to date to measure directly the effect of punctuality on the quality of relationships, some of the personality traits associated with level of promptness do play a role in initial mating and the level of long-term marital satisfaction. Studies have found that partners that differ in their level of conscientiousness are less happy together than those well matched on conscientiousness.[10] Interestingly, though, both for couples who said they fell in love at first sight and for those who said they were friends before they became lovers, being well matched in agreeableness didn't seem to play a part in their initial decision to be with one another. The match on other characteristics, like how much they both enjoyed company, their emotional stability or negativity, and their level of autonomy or independence did play a part for those who transformed a friendship into love, while raw passion seemed to be the deciding factor for those who fell in love at first sight. Yet those drawn together primarily by passion but who discovered over time that they differed in conscientiousness found that passion, intimacy, and commitment dimmed.

Whatever brings partners together initially plays a major part in their satisfaction in the relationship over time. Not surprisingly, there is evidence that more durable, long-lasting pairings have individuals better matched in conscientiousness and agreeableness.[11] And since one of the major ways these personality traits are expressed is in terms of promptness or lateness, for some couples the differences in the durability of their relationship may in good part be due to whether they struggle or get in sync over punctuality.

That was certainly the challenge facing Carl and Trisha when they came to see me.

Punctuality and the Struggle for Connection

Carl, 51, and Trisha, 42, were both native New Yorkers (he, Jewish American, she, Irish American). They married a year after they met, attracted by each other's shy, gentle demeanors. Eighteen months later, they came to see me on the brink of divorce. The main issue was that he was perfectly punctual and she constantly late. Carl was quite conscientious, careful, organized, and responsible in his work as an IT specialist in an investment bank. He was also fundamentally an agreeable fellow, trustworthy and dependable. His unerring punctuality was driven both by a strong sense of responsibility and, in his close personal relationships with family, friends, and a previous girlfriend, by a desire to give and get a secure, dependable connection.

Unfortunately, over time, as he continued to try to get Trisha to be punctual and she continued to be late, he'd also come to resemble someone who might fit another punctuality-related personality style, that of neuroticism. He'd become testy, depressed, negative, and anxious, but only in regard to their relationship. At work, at least as he reported it, he was his usual, more easygoing self.

For her part, Trisha's personality seemed at first more characteristic of a punctual person. At work she was never late. She was a high-level administrative assistant for a top banking executive, extremely conscientious, at times "a bit scattered" because of all the things she had to manage, but unfailingly punctual. Like Carl, she was also quite an agreeable type, friendly, approachable, and caring about others' feelings. She noted, modestly, that she was a competent, supportive supervisor of junior colleagues. But when it came to her social relationships, especially intimate ones with men, she sometimes seemed irresponsible and disorganized, forgetting to follow through with promises and, especially, being chronically late. Although her female buddies accepted her "flakiness" about time in light of her other great qualities as a friend, her previous boyfriends had, like Carl, become frustrated with her temporal unpredictability, contributing in part to the break-ups.

Trisha had been married once before in her early twenties to a man in the navy, who was often at sea for months at a time. Although when her husband was away she had little pressure to arrive home at any particular time, she became too lonely and eventually divorced him, desiring a relationship with someone who would "really be around." Now she had Carl, who was around every night, waiting for her, but she rarely made it home in time.

As they struggled over and over about punctuality, Carl had become a blamer, and Trisha a placater. He described feeling deeply hurt, rejected, and eventually angry when she arrived late to dinner or to movie dates. Trisha was always deeply apologetic and would promise to be prompt the next time, yet for the very next date she would arrive late. As we delved into their family histories, their particular personality-punctuality puzzle started to fall into place.

The first step in helping this couple break out of their painful punctuality standoff was to *reveal* the sources of their approach to promptness.

Carl came from an extremely close family in which everyone always knew where everyone else was all the time and what they were doing, and lateness was viewed as unacceptable separation from the family nucleus. Every day of his childhood, his father arrived home promptly at 5 P.M. and the family would eat dinner exactly at 6 P.M. He initially described this with a sort of unquestioning pride, unable to acknowledge that this tradition was at all unusual in current urban life. In contrast, Trisha came from a family that had rarely shared meals or other daily activities together, and she felt her parents couldn't have cared less whether she showed up on time or at all. She recounted, in a matter-of-fact way with little apparent emotion, that "everyone took care of themselves."

For Carl, Trisha's lateness meant she didn't love him or want to be with him. Given her family history of no one expecting her to show up at any particular time, she literally seemed unable to comprehend that someone cared whether or not she was on time. And having essentially lived alone her entire life, she felt Carl's insistence on her being punctual was controlling. For his part, Carl felt that Trisha held all the power—the power to keep him hanging, waiting for her.

As we explored further their family histories with punctuality, Carl came to see that the standards his family maintained were unusually high and perhaps unreasonable to impose on others. He even came to acknowledge that he sometimes felt "locked down" in his family's all-for-one-and-one-for-all style. Ironically, his family's extreme closeness resulted in him being unable to sustain an intimate adult relationship: Frustrated with his partner's lateness or other displays of lack of conscientiousness, after a few months he'd break things off and end up alone again. When he met Trisha, even though she was always late, he thought he'd better try to work things out with her or he'd end up alone forever. For her part, Trisha eventually became quite emotional in our sessions as she reflected on how her family's complete lack of punctuality and togetherness left her feeling completely abandoned.

My next step with this couple was to help them *revalue* their differences. Even though it was their major source of conflict and now threatened the future of their relationship, we thought about how their radically different orientations to punctuality might have attracted them to one another. We realized that Trisha saw in Carl a chance to be with someone who, unlike her family, really cared if she was there or not. Despite his frustration with her, Carl could see that initially he was drawn to her independence, her more relaxed demeanor as reflected in her behavior about time, her seeming comfort being on her own, accountable to no one, an independence he'd been unable to assert growing up in his family. They came to see that, by valuing, utilizing, and learning from their punctuality differences, they had an opportunity to help each other grow emotionally and to have a satisfying marriage. By responding to Carl's request that she be punctual, rather than feeling she was acceding to his control, Trisha could feel loved; in loosening up his standards, Carl could learn to relax, rather than feeling thwarted and hurt. This change in their understanding of the meaning of each other's punctuality behavior enabled them to *revise* their respective responses. As they *rehearsed* the new patterns, their relationship radically transformed from a rigid standoff bound for divorce into their first true experiences of adult intimacy and trust.

Culture and Punctuality

Cultures differ dramatically in how they define punctuality and lateness or how they cast either personality type. And they differ in beliefs about who has the power to be late and who must be punctual.

In his book *A Geography of Time,*[12] social psychologist Robert Levine notes that in the United States, we gauge the severity of lateness in units of five minutes, with each increment of five minutes indicating greater tardiness. The significance of one's lateness depends on what one is late *for*—late to a dinner date with an old friend or five minutes late to a job interview. Arab cultures measure lateness in fifteen-minute increments; running 30 minutes behind is therefore just a little late, the equivalent of running ten minutes behind in the States. An American businessman might express dismay at his Saudi host's arrival 25 minutes late, but he'll be greeted with counter-indignation since for the host this is normal. Levine found that in Mexico, the slowest among the 31 countries he tested, it is *expected* that you will arrive late (operating on "hora Mexicana"), and if one arrives on time, one might get laughed at.[13]

In such far-flung places as Burundi, Indonesia, Syria, or El Salvador, people gather for events based on much broader segments of time, such as the morning, afternoon, or evening. Clearly, punctuality is of less significance in these societies. You show up when you show up, and when the people meant to be there arrive, the event begins. The event ends when participants are ready for it to end, not at a set, predetermined hour and minute. Levine reports many examples of persons from clock-based societies visiting event-based societies for business or pleasure, and amusing or downright offending locals with their irritation about appointments starting "late."

Most of the northern hemisphere is made up of clock-oriented societies, where being on time is expected and highly valued. Thus, in the United States, Germany, Switzerland, and England, punctuality is an expected asset of successful and agreeable types. But for the most part, in countries with warmer climes, less industrialization and economic development, and more concentration of wealth among an elite upper class, being late is associated with prized personality attributes. For instance, in Brazil, according to Levine's research, people who were frequently late were viewed as more successful and also as "more relaxed, happy, and likeable."

In countries and cultures where lateness is a way of life, being on time is still expected of servants, those lowest in the pecking order. Indeed, Levine found that across all cultures, whether they value being on time or being late, the richer you are and the more powerful you are in the workplace, the more you can get away with lateness, the more you can proffer negative judgments about others' punctuality, and the more you can expect promptness from those lower in rank. Thus, no matter where you go, at the bottom rungs of economic and social status, you must be on time, at least when you're relating to those higher up. This finding underlines the link between social power and punctuality: Those with more power can keep others waiting.

Social research helps us understand how punctuality and power get linked in couples, and how demands for promptness by one partner and consistent resistance to those demands by the other partner escalate into make-or-break moments in relationships. So let's look at how punctuality differences can play out and sometimes wreak havoc in intimate cross-cultural relationships.

A Simple Case of Cultural Differences?

At first glance, Allen and Claudia's punctuality differences seemed nothing more than a simple reflection of their cultural roots. Both in their late 50s, Allen was born and bred in New York City; Claudia was raised in Rio de Janeiro. Allen fit one of the classic New York white, upper-middle class, male profiles—anxious, irritable, driven, overly serious, and exceedingly punctual. He took offense if anyone, especially Claudia, was even five minutes late to a meeting or dinner engagement. He exemplified the earlier-cited research that linked punctuality to high levels on the dimension of neuroticism. Being punctual (and typically early) was a core strategy for reducing his level of irritability and anxiety.

Once again, my first step was to *reveal* the deeper reasons and meanings for each partner's approach to timeliness. Even though on the surface, this couple looked quite similar to Carl and Trisha—another punctual, uptight guy, another laid-back chronically late gal—the underlying reasons for Allen's and Claudia's approaches to punctuality couldn't have been more different than those of the prior couple. When Allen was a young boy, his father developed a severe bipolar disorder. When he was depressed, he seemed to move in slow motion and be late for work or for family dinners. Allen had to find and urge his father to get to the dinner table, or to get ready to go to work, or to leave the home for a family outing. When the father was in his manic phase, he was always rushing everyone to do a million things, but because he tried to overstuff the family's schedule, they were constantly late to each activity. Allen had learned to be extremely vigilant about his father's moods and punctuality.

To compensate for this anxious upbringing, as a teen he developed the habit of always being a little early, if not right on time; this helped him feel that his world could be an orderly place. His standards for punctuality were so high, he found himself imposing the same kind of hypervigilance and criticality on others—especially Claudia, who was rarely on time.

Claudia's reluctance to adhere to strict punctuality had an equally interesting family history. Her parents had emigrated from Germany to Brazil as Nazism was on the rise in the late 1930s. As liberal Germans, they could not abide by the racism and anti-Semitism that was gaining hold, and they feared their acts of political resistance would result in imprisonment and possibly death. Claudia and her brother were born in Rio. Although her parents enjoyed many of the aspects of their adopted homeland—the weather, food, music, and the general friendliness of the Brazilians, the one quality they found impossible to adjust to was the relaxed attitude about punctuality. They found this behavior annoying and rude, and talked about punctuality as one of the remaining sources of pride for them as Germans.

As a teenager, Claudia started to verbalize her distaste for what she felt were her parents' ethnic slurs about Brazilians—a comment her parents found upsetting, given that their own liberal values had prompted them to leave Germany. Claudia began to come late to her own family's dinners and other events, deliberately differentiating herself from them around the practice of punctuality—behavior which led to great conflict and eventually led Claudia to leave home. She wound up in New York.

So why did Allen and Claudia end up together? After all, we might expect Allen to have gravitated toward an equally punctual mate, while Claudia might have been expected to be happiest with a temporally laid-back guy. Asked if they'd ever dated someone more similar to them on the dimension of punctuality, each readily reported, "Yes." And as we've heard with couples differing drastically on other temporal dimensions, Allen and Claudia each uttered the single adjective I've come to expect when asking people why they didn't choose to be with someone more like them in time—those others were "boring."

I shared with them the hunch that at an unconscious level, Allen and Claudia were drawn to one another in part because each provided the other with an opportunity to grow. With one another they could struggle with but learn from one another's approach to punctuality, and resolve and move beyond nagging old painful conflicts from their families of origin. Helping them *revalue* their differences softened their struggle and moved them from a head-to-head contest of wills to a side-by-side collaboration in which they could *revise* their respective behaviors and *rehearse* new punctuality patterns. I suggested that if Allen could loosen up his standards a bit, Claudia could meet him halfway, move out of her continued "teen rebellion" about punctuality, and the couple could end their constant conflict.

This new way of thinking about how each could help the other become more flexible by respecting the positive aspects of each other's approach to punctuality appealed to Claudia and Allen. Now better informed about the role punctuality played in their respective families, each felt more sympathetic to the other's style and less inclined to engage in power struggles about being on time.

Allen and Claudia's case is a great example of how individuals' reasons for being early, on time, or late are rarely reducible solely to such simple cultural stereotypes as "Germans and Americans are punctual" and "Brazilians are late." Often, there are multiple aspects of one's culture that combine to determine whether one is punctual or late, and those in turn are filtered through one's family experiences, emotional strengths, and psychological challenges.

Culture Meets Personality

Another couple I worked with illustrates yet again the unique combination of culture, personality styles, and psychological issues that can be associated with struggles about punctuality. Reggie was a highly conscientious, 27-year-old,

Chinese American man. He worked long hours in a tech-development firm. He was a highly responsible son, who helped with the family business, and was also pursuing an acting career with some success. It was through his acting that he met Jane, 30, a theater company administrator. Jane was a white woman whose family had been in the United States for several generations. Like Reggie she was highly conscientious, but she struggled for years with depression and anxiety, especially feeling insecure about whether others truly loved her. Their mutual physical attraction and shared interests in the arts, as well as their sense that they were both responsible persons, formed the basis of their bond and belief that they had found their life partner. But one year later, they were in therapy with me. Frustrated with Reggie's constant lateness for their time together due to his working late on another deadline or his responding to his mother's needs, and after repeated pleas that he be on time or at least call her to say if he'd be late, Jane had a brief affair with a mutual friend. Reggie was shocked that she would betray him this way, especially because Jane knew his father had maintained a secret affair with another woman during much of Reggie's childhood. Yet Jane had felt equally "betrayed" by Reggie prioritizing his work and his mother over her.

As we came to *reveal* and understand the childhood family dynamics that shaped their current approaches to time and to punctuality in particular, we learned that Reggie's father had been largely absent from his life, which highlighted the significance of his father's advice to him. "Don't be lazy," he urged his son, "finish strong." Although Reggie resented his father's assessment—"who does he think he is, he doesn't know me, he's not involved in my life, really," the father's assessment stuck with him. As a result, he felt compelled to complete work assignments in as timely a way as possible. And with a steady stream of new assignments, he often found himself torn between his work and his genuine desire to "kick back" with Jane.

Likewise, in part because of Chinese cultural traditions centered on loyalty and deference to one's elders, Reggie found it difficult not to respond to his mother's requests for assistance, even if he had other things planned with Jane. The only way he found to resist his mother's requests was to not show up at all. His mother would never mention these incidents. They'd just carry on as if nothing had happened.

For her part, Jane largely felt unwanted and ignored in her family. Told that she was "an accident" as the unplanned fourth child, she longed for someone to show consistent affection and commitment to her. Although Reggie was plenty affectionate, he did not come through for her in the consistency department.

Through our work together, Reggie came to recognize that Jane's insistence that he prioritize punctuality for their relationship time provided Reggie a powerful opportunity to take a stand for what he really wanted and to move away from the obedient-boy stance of his youth. And Jane came to realize that as long as Reggie let her know what was going on when he would be late (rather than transferring to their relationship his habit of just not showing up at his mother's), she could be alone and not revisit the panic she often felt as a child of being invisible and uncared for. Their struggles over punctuality virtually vanished with this greater mutual understanding of each other's stance and behavior about lateness, with Reggie being on time more often and with Jane not experiencing Reggie's lateness as a sign that she was unimportant to him.

With yet another couple, the punctuality issue came down to a matter of transportation and a psychological condition. The Anglo American man coped with his severe attention deficit hyperactivity disorder by being careful about punctuality; his Mexican American partner frequently ran late because her job required her to take two subways and two buses in each direction, from home to work and back. As a Latina woman socialized to take on all the couple's chores uncomplainingly (a belief called "marianismo"), she had too much to manage.[14]

As these vignettes of cross-cultural couples demonstrate, although there are broad cultural trends in adherence to clock time and the importance of punctuality, no one is simply a temporal archetype (or stereotype) of one's culture. A wide variety of personality differences, power differences due to gender, family backgrounds, psychological and physical disorders, work roles and pressures, as well as concrete issues such as the availability, reliability, and speed of transportation can all affect whether one is generally punctual or not.

So, as we've seen in dealing with other conflicts about time, one of the most important things couples can *do* (and my first job as a couple therapist in helping them) is to *develop greater understanding* for each partner's beliefs and behaviors about punctuality, and to examine how their behaviors may unconsciously lock together and create distress. Revealing these deeper reasons for the seemingly surface, basic behaviors of being on time or late, developing this greater understanding of what makes one person care a great deal about being punctual and the other less so, or what might lead the late person to recoil from being on time is the key to softening each partner's stance toward the other and to correcting mistaken negative attributions. From there, spurred on by a greater sensitivity to each other's feelings and actual motivations, partners can start to *revalue* their differences, and *revise* their patterns by making the kinds of conscious compromises and adaptations that are at the core of relationship harmony.[15]

Where Are You in Time? Punctuality

Here's a step-by-step approach to identifying and resolving the punctuality problems in your relationship. These questions are drawn from my detailed Relationship Punctuality Questionnaire (RPQ), which you can find on the Web site www.syncyourrelationship.com.

Step 1: Quiz Yourselves on Punctuality. You and your partner might begin by asking yourselves four series of questions (all from my RPQ), the first about how punctual you are individually for certain activities (rate your answers on a scale of 1 to 5, where 1 is never, 2 is rarely, 3 is sometimes, 4 is often, and 5 is extremely often) and the second about how important you each think it is to be punctual for that activity (on a scale of 1 to 5, where 1 is not important and 5 is extremely important). Here are some activities to consider: getting to work or classes; getting to work-related meetings; finishing work or assignments by deadline; leaving work for home; getting to social events with friends on time; getting to dinner with partner or family; paying bills; returning books or videos; arriving at cultural or sporting events; getting to medical appointments; responding to e-mails or phone calls. You can pick a few or rate yourself on all of these activities, but make sure that if you will be comparing your answers to your partner's, that you pick the same activities, otherwise the scores won't be comparable!

Next, consider how often you use certain reasons for being late (here too you could rate your answers on a scale of 1 to 5, with 1 indicating never and 5 for always). Some reasons I often hear that you may have heard yourselves giving: too much to do; not enough help; difficulty managing time; unexpected demands from boss, employees, students; falling off schedule because of lateness of others; responsibilities to other family members who move slower, like aging parents or young children; transportation; illness or disability; losing track of time; cultural background; something about your personality; not wanting to arrive at the place you're supposed to get to; simply not concerned with being on time.

Now, ask yourselves some questions about your perceptions of attitudes and feelings about punctuality—your own and your partners'. (Again, rate these on a scale of 1 to 5 if you wish, with 1 being never/not at all and 5 being always/a lot.) In this series, you might consider: how punctual are you, and how punctual is your partner; how important is punctuality to you, and to your partner; do you feel anxious when you are late, and when your partner is late; how much do you feel you try to change your partner's punctuality, and how much pressure for change flows from your partner to you; how much do you believe your degree of punctuality is a source of conflict in your relationship, and how much do you think your partner believes that your differences in punctuality create conflict?

You and your partner should answer these questions separately, so that you do not influence each other's responses. Again, make sure you answer the same questions so that you can accurately compare your answers. And if you want a more structured format for moving through the questions, go to the Web site and complete the entire questionnaire.

If punctuality has been a problem for you at work, in managing responsibilities, or in other aspects of your social life (family, friends), focus on questions in section I of the RPQ that deal with those issues to pinpoint areas that you want to improve.

Step 2: Review Your Answers Together. You can use the scores you obtain to identify and discuss with each other your punctuality differences and problems, and to generate solutions. Arrange a time to talk about what you discovered about your individual proneness to be late or early and your impressions of your partner's punctuality style. (If you sense the conversation could get too hot to be productive, use the PREP® communication skills described in chapter 9 to structure the conversation so that you avoid escalation, criticism, and other hurtful language.)

Here are a few discussion points to guide you. How much does each of you view punctuality as a source of conflict in your relationship? Just agreeing that punctuality is an issue, even if a pretty big one, often smooths the way toward making changes. So if you find you've both rated the importance of punctuality as a 4 or a 5, be happy that at least you agree! If one thinks punctuality is a problem and the other doesn't, don't despair—the point of this process is to help you understand each other's punctuality perspectives and what contributes to lateness (if one of you tends to be late generally or to specific activities), so that you can resolve these struggles in a way that works for both of you.

A look at the overall difference in your scores on each series of questions may reveal what contributes most to your conflict about punctuality. You can also focus on particular items that may cause conflict—for instance, if you frequently attribute your lateness to overload at work and your partner thinks you need to get a handle on the workload so that you can make it home in time for dinner.

You may view each other as fairly similar in how much you *value* punctuality (the "how important" question), but you may be quite different in your actual punctuality behavior. (As you saw, there are all sorts of reasons for being late, most of which have nothing to do with whether or not we believe it's important to be on time.) Your focus as a couple will be to discuss in more detail what's led you to perceive each other's actual behavior so differently and to figure out how to come to agreements about changing perceptions and/or behaviors so that you are more aligned in your punctuality and in your perceptions of one another. Combing through your responses about punctuality for specific activities and reasons for lateness will help you do that.

On the other hand, if the difference in your scores on punctuality are relatively low but the differences on the importance of punctuality are high, that suggests your arguments most likely center on the value of punctuality. But given that you don't perceive each other to be terribly different in your actual punctuality behaviors, this also suggests that one of you is already accommodating the other by adopting his or her standards for punctuality, thus overriding your own beliefs about punctuality to adhere more closely to your partner's preferences. And that in turn may signal a power struggle around punctuality in which one partner is exerting a lot of effort to control the other's behavior, and the other is acceding, perhaps unhappily, to these efforts.

Does one of you attempt to exert more control over the other's promptness and beliefs about promptness? Is there generally a power struggle going on about punctuality? How do you each feel about this? As you saw in several of the couples you met in this chapter, when partners engage in power struggles about punctuality, both tend to resent it. The partner attempting to cajole or corral the other to be on time resents having to take that role, and the partner being cajoled resents being controlled. To escape from the grip of these power struggles, you will need to come to appreciate one another's reasons for relating to punctuality as you do and then find a compromise.

Another way to identify the presence of punctuality power struggles is to look at the difference in your scores about anxiety levels when punctuality is breached. Do you feel more anxious about being late for your partner than your partner seems to feel about being late for you? Or is it your partner who is more anxious about being late for you? That might signal that one of you feels controlled by the other about being prompt and worried about the relational consequences if you are late (criticizing, yelling, ignoring, blaming, or other unpleasant reactions).

Alternatively, you may be engaging in more of a two-way power struggle, with each of you attempting to exert control over the other's standards of punctuality. One may be trying to get the other to relax about being on time and loosen the standards of what defines "late," while the other is repeatedly asserting the need to be on time and has a more restrictive definition of promptness and lateness. Or your struggles may be more activity specific: You may be trying to get your partner to be more on time for social occasions, while your partner is trying to get you to be more on time in handling bills and returning books and videos.

If there are major differences in your perceptions about your and your partner's respective behaviors and beliefs about punctuality, it's important to talk about those differences. And since overall impressions emerge from our subjective summations about what we've seen in specific activities, it will help you to clarify your perceptions of one another and examine how you each rated yourselves on punctuality for specific domains of activity. You can compare your responses using the following questions:

- How similar or different are you in your self-ratings of your own punctuality for each activity?
- How similar or different are you in your self-ratings of the importance of being punctual to each activity?
- How much do you agree with one another's self-ratings?
- Do you think each other's self assessments are accurate?
- Do you think your partner underestimates how late she or he is for particular activities?

For instance, your partner may think he is rarely late for dinner at home, but you may think he is often late. You may think you are rarely late paying bills, but your partner may think you are often late. You might even find you are pleasantly surprised to hear that your partner thinks you *overestimate* how late you are in getting to a particular activity. You might blame yourself for often being late to dates with your partner, for example, and he or she might reassure you that you're not as late as you think!

Compare your scores on reasons for being late. The partner who is generally more punctual will of course have a lower score. Examine the reasons for lateness for which you scored high, a 4 or 5. Answer the following questions for each one:

- How much do you *want* to address this reason for lateness? For instance, you may not want to work on changing your personality, but you might want to work on managing your time better.

WORKSHEET **6.1**   RELATIONSHIP RHYTHMS ANALYSIS: PUNCTUALITY

List your surface conflicts (common areas of conflict) that relate to punctuality:

REVEAL
What did you experience and learn about
  punctuality growing up in your family?
How is your approach to punctuality
  affected by the culture you grew up in?
How does knowing more about the
  meaning of punctuality to your partner
  reduce your upset with them about their
  behavior?

REVALUE
What things do you appreciate about your
  partner's approach to punctuality?
How does the difference in your partner's
  approach to punctuality provide you a
  useful opportunity to grow and become
  more flexible in your approach?
How do your respective approaches
  to punctuality (either similarities or
  differences) still help the relationship?

REVISE
What can you change to make your
  approach to punctuality more compatible,
  less a source of conflict?

REHEARSE
What's your practice plan? Make a
  commitment to specific activities you will
  do on a daily, weekly, monthly, and yearly
  basis to change and/or better align your
  approach to punctuality.

- How much do you believe you *can* reduce the effect of this reason for lateness? For instance, you may believe you can find a quicker route to work, but you may not feel you can do much about the unexpected demands from your boss, at least for the time being.
- For those lateness reasons that you want to work on and think you can change, what might be some ways to do so?

It's great if each of you can help one another think through these questions in a supportive fashion. One of you may have some good ideas for the other on how to address a factor that causes lateness. If you think your partner might be able to set a firmer limit about last minute, unexpected work from a boss, try to phrase your idea like this: "One thing you might do is ask him for a brief morning meeting where you plan the work of the day. That way, he might be less likely to suddenly think of something else you have to do just as you're about to pack up to come home. What do you think?"

Step 3: Start Finding Solutions. Complete the Relationship Rhythms Analysis Worksheet on Punctuality. Try to get beyond your frustration and power struggles regarding punctuality and learn what personality styles, family experiences, and cultural beliefs shape your and your partner's approaches (*reveal*). Then, no matter the extent of your differences, reflect on how your partner's approach to punctuality might provide either a useful counterbalance to your own or an opportunity to become more flexible in your approach to timeliness (*revalue*). Next, think about how you each can change somewhat to create less conflict and greater synchrony in how you handle showing up on time (*revise*). Remember that, in some cases, this will mean the late-inclined one makes greater attempts to be on time, and the punctual one relaxes standards a bit. Finally, set a specific plan to practice the new patterns and to support each other's attempts, even if imperfect (*rehearse*).

Punctuality is the most obvious and overt of the various problems about time that couples struggle with. For such a seemingly uncomplicated, concrete, nonpsychological act as punctuality, the factors that affect it are surprisingly complex and multilayered. Personality styles, family backgrounds, culture, and a wide range of life factors all affect people's beliefs and behaviors about punctuality. So it's not surprising that many couples—coming to their relationships with their unique personalities, family histories, and cultural backgrounds, as well as work pressures and other life challenges—struggle with each other around punctuality. And differences in punctuality can lead partners to attribute all sorts of negative characteristics and motivations to one another. Partners can feel controlled by one another and can feel unloved by one another, all because of failing to meet at a point in time. Marriages can be broken by the failure of partners to negotiate what it means and how important it is to be "on time."

This chapter has equipped you with greater awareness of your own and your partner's behavior and values, and a step-by-step way to work out useful compromises about punctuality.

The Great Juggling Act, Part I: Balancing Work Time and Relationship Time

ON THE EVENING OF their first session with me, Richard, 47, a television producer, showed up first. His wife Clara, 43, a management consultant in the fashion business, was running late. When she wasn't traveling for business meetings, Clara worked part-time, mostly from their home two hours north of New York City, where the couple was raising three young children. "She had to train it in and it was hard to catch a cab," he reported, sympathetically. Richard, a classic tall, dark, and handsome type, still exuded the sparkle of a man who'd had great success selling entertainment, but the sparkle seemed a bit dulled by a thin film of exhaustion that seemed to hang like a veil over his face. As he described his "constantly on the go" work life, filled with multiple daily meetings and frequent business flights, he sank into my couch like it was a water bed, seemingly grateful just to let gravity pull him into a semi-prone position. Ten minutes later, Clara—who'd called last week saying that she and Richard needed "urgent couple therapy"—blew into the office, apologizing profusely for her lateness. Clara radiated pizzazz and glamour but, like Richard, looked exhausted under her well-composed sheen. They'd met at a work function 10 years prior and immediately felt a powerful attraction, which then translated into weeks of spending every available minute, despite their busy jobs, having sex and talking into the wee hours.

But as Richard told the story of the last few years, he seemed aware, and Clara nodded in assent, that now they'd become another statistic in a story that characterizes so many couples today—way overstretched with work, with more electricity connecting them to colleagues and clients via Internet and mobile phone networks than to each other. They spoke of hopelessly watching the life drain out of their once passionate love. Although I shouldn't have been surprised, given that these were two people skilled in the arts of selling story lines and management campaigns, I was struck by the clarity with which they described the factors that had led them to this point of months without sex or intimate talk. Richard said, "As life has gotten more hectic, it was easy to fall into the pattern that most dual career couples with small children have—seeing each other less, doing things with each other less. We realize that we have to spend more time together. But because we're both so busy, and so stressed, we could easily just disappear from each other's lives. We have fun when we spend time together, but with our schedules, it's hard to make that happen."

The event that served as their wake-up call was an e-mail Clara noticed a few days earlier on Richard's open laptop one evening—from a female former colleague confirming a dinner date for the following week. The tone of the e-mail sounded too cozy for Clara's comfort, and she confronted Richard, who vehemently denied any romantic intentions. He reminded Clara that he'd had a long, close working relationship with this colleague, who now was seeking some guidance on next career steps. Nevertheless, given Clara's distress, Richard changed the dinner to a lunch, and now the couple sought my help to get their marriage back on track.

Although couples raising kids face particular challenges preserving time for their relationship, so do couples without kids. Indeed, one reason many working couples put off having children year after year is that they look at their overstuffed lives and can't imagine fitting a baby into the equation.[1]

Dan and Lucy was one such couple. Both were 40 years old, and both worked 70- to 80-hour weeks, Dan as a corporate lawyer, Lucy as a principal in a software start-up company. Having met three years before, they were still getting along great, but worried that their high-paced and fully packed work lives would eventually cause them to drift apart. Already, they could see the signs—each often felt overwhelmed and preoccupied with their work responsibilities. Their days were hectic, filled with meetings, answering hundreds of e-mails all claiming equal urgency. They were constantly interrupted in their attempts to complete crucial time-consuming projects, which often got pushed off into late nights or weekends when everyone else was gone from the office. If they had lunch at all, it was sitting at their desks reviewing documents and making calls. Despite their desire to go out regularly and enjoy the many dining and entertainment offerings of the city, especially before launching into possible parenthood, most evenings they'd get home by 9 or 10 P.M., collapse on the couch with food delivered to their door, and numbly watch TV until bedtime. Dan noted anxiously, "With our lives so out of whack now, I don't know how we'll ever be able to raise kids." Lucy's eyes suddenly welled up as she proclaimed in a tightened voice, "And of course, my biological clock is more like a time bomb already—I'm already afraid I won't be able to have kids."

One thing I did immediately to relieve a bit of Dan and Lucy's discouragement and tension, as well as Richard and Clara's and that of countless others I've helped to create better work-life balance, was to share with them the research findings that show they are not alone.[2]

As demonstrated throughout this book, *revealing* the hidden time structure that causes your couple conflicts—by naming the particular time issue and knowing the research that documents it—is the crucial first step to changing that structure and eliminating the conflicts it creates and supports. And when it comes to work-life balance, there's an abundance of research on every aspect of this pervasive time problem.

In this chapter, I describe the challenges most people face achieving work-life balance and some specific personal strategies you can implement to get the balance back. I say "personal strategies" because, as many work-family scholars have argued, our nation's laws and our companies' policies about work-family balance ultimately must change if each couple is not to be left alone to fend for themselves when it comes to this crucial issue.[3]

But until those laws change, and even when they do, you'll need some strategies for building a better balance between work time and the-rest-of-life time. After all, even if we had laws guaranteeing paid leave for new mothers and fathers (which we don't), you could elect to break the law and go to work one week after giving birth, and you wouldn't get arrested for it! Quite the opposite. As frequently happens now, your company might encourage you to ignore your legal rights and even the company's various provisions about opportunities for flextime, earned vacation, and maternity leave to show your dedication through face time at the company.[4]

It's critical to evaluate what you can personally do to change your own situation and to erect a firmer wall between work time and other time. This will raise the quality of your presence and enjoyment in both domains— work and the rest of life. As high-performance sports and corporate coaches Jim Loehr and Tony Schwartz write in their book *The Power of Full Engagement*: "Full engagement begins with feeling eager to get to work in the morning, equally happy to return home in the evening and capable of setting clear boundaries between the two."[5]

Learning how to manage your stress and time at work is a critical component of an overall couple strategy for attaining work-life balance. Because each of us is like a channel that links the river of the workplace to the river of the home place, tensions from work can gush over into home life, or vice versa. So we need strategies for limiting the negative influence of work stress on our intimate relationships—and vice versa.

I hope that when reading this you'll feel part of a huge international support group of millions (Work-Life Balance Anonymous?), because you'll learn that others experience these same daunting challenges in balancing work and the rest of life. The toughest part is learning not to blame yourself when that balance seems out of reach. When we blame ourselves and our partners entirely for circumstances caused primarily by trends and forces in our larger society and world—in this case, the international culture of work—we become consumed with guilt, shame, hopelessness, and bitterness toward ourselves and our partners. This self- and other-blame reveals our tacit or explicit endorsement of the destructive Myth of Total Control, introduced in chapter 2: the belief that we are the masters of our destinies, no matter what sorts of real time pressures are exerted on us by our workplaces or other circumstances beyond our total control. As a result, if our lives seem out of balance, we feel like failures or see our partners as failures, rather than joining our forces to take charge of our time. We're more able to take responsibility for productive changes in our work lives when we first know what we're up against. Stopping the blame game is the next important step in taking charge of creating a better work-life balance, both as individuals and as a couple.

A World in Work-Life Imbalance

America is the developed world's center of work-family imbalance.[6] Yes, you read that right. The world's beacon of freedom and justice hasn't done so well by its citizens when it comes to work-family balance. The United States is the only country among the 30 industrialized democracies in the Organization for Economic Cooperation and Development (OECD) that has no paid maternity leave laws. If you have a new baby (biological or adopted), you're entitled by law to 12 weeks of *unpaid* leave[7]—but only if you're in the lucky half of companies with 50 or more employees. Otherwise, you're legally entitled to no leave at all.[8]

And you're entitled to this leave only if you are a mother. American fathers have no legal rights to paid or unpaid paternal leave, unlike their counterparts in Germany, where fathers can share in the 14 months of part-time paid parental leave provided mothers or fathers for up to the first three years of the child's life.[9] Likewise, just over our northern border, Canadian mothers can take an average of 17 weeks of leave, and receive 55 percent of their salary; in progressive Quebec, fathers can get up to 5 weeks of leave and receive about 70 percent of their salary. And unlike in the States, in all the other OECD countries, no new parent on leave need fear they'll be replaced while out caring for their newborn child.

In a recent comprehensive analysis, economists Joan Williams and Heather Boushey note that because the United States has fewer laws to protect working families than any other developed country, "it should come as no surprise that Americans report sharply higher levels of work-family conflict than do citizens of other industrialized countries. Fully 90 percent of American mothers and 95 percent of American fathers report work-family conflict."[10]

This last statistic is of major importance, as it shows that work-life balance is not just a "women's issue." Defining it as a women's issue is likely to keep it from being addressed, both at the company level and at the level of federal legislation, in a comprehensive and satisfactory fashion. But research consistently shows that men are as concerned about having more time for parenting as are women. James Levine, former director of the Fatherhood Project® at the Families and Work Institute in New York, notes that in his seminars to top-level executives at American companies, fathers aren't even seen as a unique category of employees, unlike mothers, or persons of different ethnic or racial backgrounds, persons with disabilities, and the elderly. In their classic ground-breaking book *Working Fathers: New Strategies for Balancing Work and Family*, Levine and his coauthor Todd Pittinsky write,

> For many people, *working mother* has come to symbolize conflict. When a woman works outside the home, our society assumes she must feel a constant tug-of-war between her "job self" and her "parent self." But working father is a redundancy, isn't it? Saying that "fathers work" is like saying "fathers father." The prevailing assumption is that men do not feel that tug-of-war between their "job selves" and their "parent selves."[11]

Levine and Pittinsky offer the findings of survey upon survey showing that the percentage of fathers torn by work-family conflict matches if not exceeds the level of conflict experienced by mothers. As often occurs in research, other studies have shown that women's work-family conflict is more tightly connected to their sense of well-being than is men's.[12] But the majority of the facts show that the issue of creating better work-family balance is an issue that now unites, rather than divides, men and women. Mothers and fathers don't want only a few weeks off after the birth of their babies for the critical bonding that occurs during this early phase of attachment.[13] They want regular, uninterrupted breaks from work to restore, renew, and rejuvenate their couple and parent-child relationships. In other words, they want time for leisure and recreation, those dirty words in the postindustrial era in which the measure of a man or woman is constant productivity in the workplace, not their contributions to family, friends, or community.[14] But U.S. laws don't safeguard vacation, and even when companies provide vacation benefits, there may be subtle or blatant messages that those who take vacation risk being overlooked for promotions and bonuses if they keep their jobs, and may be on the short list during periods of downsizing.

The facts. Of the 138 industrialized countries, the United States is the only one that has no laws protecting workers' entitlement to a vacation, and 25 percent of American workers get no paid vacation time at all.[15] Although a national survey by the Families and Work Institute indicates that over three-quarters of employees have access to paid vacation and the average number of days allotted is a little more than two weeks,[16] that's only half of the minimum yearly vacation provided to Europeans. Few employees take their full allotment—37 percent took less than a 7-day vacation including weekend days, 12 percent took 1-3 days, 25 percent took 4-6 days, and 36 percent did not plan to use their vacation at all.[17] Yet people who do take vacations need 3 days on average to relax *into* vacation mode.

So, if you're taking only a week off, you're losing almost half of your vacation time letting go of stress. And if you're taking off just one to three days, you're not getting a psychological break at all. Taking one's maximum vacation leads to more of a sense of relaxation and reenergizing, and shorter vacations lead to a more rapid return of overwhelm. It's not surprising to learn that with many people taking off a week or less, 43 percent report feeling overwhelmed by work when they return. And the 19 percent of employees who use vacation time to attend to family matters or as sick time—often, because their companies don't provide a sufficient number of sick days or personal leave days—certainly don't reap the refreshment benefits of vacation.[18]

Working during vacation—and, depending on the survey, anywhere from 21 percent and 63 percent[19] of people work or are in contact with the office through laptops, pagers, or voicemail while on holiday—keeps the stress up and doesn't seem to help much in staving off the sense of being deluged on full reimmersion at the office. Fully 50 to 60 percent of what I call "vacaworkers" feel overwhelmed upon returning to the job full time—even after taking all their vacation days.[20] This could be because the job is simply unmanageable and no amount of work allows them to keep up or catch up, or it may be that because they don't set firm boundaries on work during vacation, they never really relax. If you don't close the door on work during vacation time, it's probably because you haven't practiced shutting off work during your regular work week either.[21]

Sadly, rising to the top of your profession may make you *more* likely to take work everywhere rather than freeing you from this tendency. The Families and Work Institute survey found "employees with the greatest job responsibilities and demands are those most likely to work during their vacations: managers and professionals, higher earners (and) employees who work the longest hours. . . ."[22]

Ian, a high-powered corporate lawyer, and Samantha, an art book editor, both in their late 30s, came to me because Ian's apparent inability to set a firm boundary between work time and couple-and-family time was resulting in rapid burnout at work and frequent firestorms in their marriage. Ian checked his BlackBerry at any available moment: between sentences of attempts at intimate conversations with Samantha, just before bed, immediately upon waking up, even while sitting on the toilet (he said this was his favorite spot because he knew Samantha wouldn't see him doing it). When she did see him with the device, she criticized him bitterly for "always running away into work." Asked how she felt about the BlackBerry, Samantha fixed her steely gaze on me and said, "I hate the f***ing thing. I'd like to throw it out the window." Ian laughed nervously as he recalled the time one of his sons threw the phone in the pool.

Although Ian was a committed and attentive dad, he was often distracted by work. Ian brought his BlackBerry on all family vacations (and vacations were never longer than a week). Samantha described a moment in Italy when they were window shopping; she went into the store briefly, the two kids in tow, and came out to find he'd disappeared around the corner, where he was pacing back and forth on a call to the New York office. Ian noted, with an ironic grin and an air of jaded resignation, that his company, like many others, issued a memo to all high-level principals indicating vacation spots where they could be reached by BlackBerry and those where they could not. The message was clear: Vacation in a BlackBerry-accessible locale if you want to be in this company.

Negative Spillover from Work

Long work hours, hectic workplaces, fast paces, and little opportunity for the "pause that refreshes," only intensify what social scientists have long known: Whether people are overworked or not, stress from one's work life can spill over into our intimate relationships and family life.[23] One classic study demonstrated that work-family conflict leads to psychological distress, which then results in marital tensions through the negative interchanges between partners.[24] Stress spilling over from work is one of the main causes of sexual difficulties in partners.[25] Because work stressors and economic challenges are two of the most influential aspects of a couple's daily context, it is crucial to acquire adaptive attitudes and effective skills that will protect your relationship from them.[26] Much research by my colleague, prominent marital researcher Guy Bodenmann, and others has documented that it is the everyday hassles of work and family life, rather than more discrete, one-time critical life events, that most degrade the quality of a marriage if partners do not enact specific coping responses.[27]

But the good news is that positive aspects of marital interaction—like effective communication, warmth and support, and avoidance of hostile, critical, and contemptuous exchanges—have been shown to reduce the negative impact of work and other economic stressors on individual partners and on their relationships.[28] Several studies have also shown that time together is an important ingredient in a couple's overall stress protection plan.[29] Bodenmann puts decreased time together as first in a list of four major ways that chronic external problems, like work-related stress, affect couples negatively. Work stress also negatively affects couples by eliciting more negative and less positive couple communication styles; by increasing the likelihood of psychological and physical problems such as sleep disorders, sexual difficulties, and depressed or anxious moods; and by bringing out the worst of our personalities—our insecurities, rigidities, and defensiveness.

Lorenzo and Claudia had been living together for six years. Claudia was eager to marry, but Lorenzo didn't feel ready. Although the couple had decided that the problem was Lorenzo's "commitment issues," exploration of their daily rhythms revealed the time side of their problems. Lorenzo was a physical therapist, working long hours at the hospital. With the new budget cuts to his department, he worried that he might get laid off. Once home, he spent most of the evening unsuccessfully trying to relax and connect with Claudia, but couldn't stop ruminating about the possibility that he might lose his job. As an African American man whose hard-working father had repeatedly been passed over for promotions and was eventually laid off while less-skilled white co-workers kept their jobs and moved up the ranks, he was understandably worried that he might suffer the same fate. Lorenzo's family had fallen on hard times for several years until his father was able to regain employment. Claudia was an administrator at a local college, and though her pay was relatively low, her job was stable. Lorenzo's worries were so extreme that he'd become depressed and developed a sleep disorder, and took medication for both conditions.

When Claudia brought up the topic of marriage and having children, Lorenzo would withdraw further. Although he was generally a friendly and warm person, he was now angry much of the time. This left Claudia unsure whether to stay in the relationship, and occasionally she'd lash out at Lorenzo. She felt he was being rigid; he felt she was pushing him too hard. Their sex life suffered.

My first step with this couple was to put their challenges in larger context by noting how Lorenzo was not alone in being totally preoccupied about losing his job. His was not a commitment issue—instead, he was afraid of not being able to be the kind of husband and father that he wished to be due to realistic larger economic forces that had resulted in massive layoffs in many sectors of the U.S. economy. I also validated his concerns about the history of racism in employment practices, and noted how intent he was to protect Claudia, himself, and the family they might create from the experience of unemployment. This helped both partners appreciate the "honorable explanation" behind Lorenzo's fear of getting married. Lorenzo also came to see that, rather than being pushy, Claudia really loved him and had faith that he was so talented in his occupation that he'd find a way to find a new job even if he lost his current one (which was unlikely, as he was one of only three physical therapists left in the department). I taught the couple the communication skills described in chapter 9 and also the decompression chamber exercise (see chapters 1 and 8), both of which lowered their level of antipathy and helped them reconnect emotionally and sexually. I also taught Lorenzo some relaxation techniques to help him cope better with his work stress. This helped him with his sleep difficulties and reduced his depression considerably. Eventually, he stopped his medications.

I also encouraged him to take a chance and plan the life he and Claudia wanted with each other, knowing that life held no guarantees and that he might get fired and would have to find new work. I pointed out how sad it would be if the two of them broke up because of the larger economic problems facing our country. Two years later, I saw the couple for a follow-up session. They'd married, and he'd been promoted to director of the physical therapy department. A baby was on the way.

We can see in this couple how the links between work life and partner work stress led to a lack of relaxed time together, sleep difficulties in one partner, bickering, hostility, and emergence of the worst of their personality tendencies, which only reinforced their communication difficulties and ended their attempts at sexual intimacy. By identifying the work stress issues underlying their conflicts, Claudia and Lorenzo were able to regain and affirm their dedication to a life together, whatever the economic future might bring.

Overwork: State of the Problem

In terms of hours worked per week and year, the United States has long been considered the champion in the overwork marathon, its citizens working more hours per week and more weeks per year than people in other hard-working countries like Japan,[30] Germany, Great Britain, and Canada.[31] Some recent surveys suggest that other countries appear to be usurping America's first place in this dubious distinction. For instance, a recent International Labor Organization survey found that in developed countries, the British led the way in work weeks in excess of 48 hours, followed by Israelis, Australians, Swiss, and Americans.[32] Worldwide, the Peruvians have the longest work week! But another yearly survey, conducted by the OECD, found South Koreans consistently in the lead over the past decade in average annual hours worked.[33] Just as it's nearly impossible—short of deep-sea diving and climbing Mt. Everest—to find a spot where you can't place a cell phone call and log into your e-mail (you can do it even in Katmandu, that venerable Buddhist destination and mecca for Western hipsters trying to drop out and get off the grid for a little while), it's becoming increasingly difficult to find a place on the planet that hasn't bought into the lifestyle of overwork.

Clearly, with this range of findings on which country wins the title for world's most overworked nation, surveys vary in how they define overwork, when they were conducted, and what kind of work they assessed (did they survey professionals and office workers only or include day laborers and farmers?). So it's difficult to determine definitively which country's workers toil the longest.

Although some studies indicate an increase in work hours across social class and occupation,[34] a more fine-grained analysis indicates that work hours vary by social class, and stress may be caused by overwork for some, while for others stress comes from being unable to *increase* work hours to make more money.[35] Of course, as we have been reminded all too well since the American recession began in the fall of 2008, job loss and unemployment can create psychological stress and relationship distress.[36] The fear of being the next person laid off has, for many, fueled the willingness to work longer hours, to prove their company loyalty and indispensability or simply to do their jobs in the face of reduced staffing.

Just to complicate the picture more, some researchers suggest that work hours per American worker have not increased much, if at all, over the past 50 years![37] Instead, they argue, there has been an increase in *total family work hours*, mostly due to the increase in rates of both partners working—due in turn to the increase in women entering the workforce since the 1970s. Over the past 20 years, the number of couples in which both partners work—so-called dual-earner couples—has risen significantly. In 2003, 78 percent were dual-earner couples, compared to 66 percent in 1977.[38] As eminent researchers Jerry Jacobs and Karen Gerson wrote, "It is not the amount of working time but rather the loss of someone to take care of domestic needs"[39] that is largely at the core of partners' sense of increasing work-family imbalance.

More broadly, as both partners max out on work hours, this inevitably leads to loss of the critical couple resource of time—not just for handling housework and raising children, but for the relationship, for personal time, for participation in community and politics, for recreation, as well as for stillness, silence, and doing absolutely nothing.

Financially, we may still be one of the wealthiest nations in the world, but we are one of the poorest when it comes to time for activities other than work. Study after study has documented that beyond the level of financial resources necessary to attain the fundamental needs of adequate shelter, food, clothes, and health care, greater wealth is not correlated with greater happiness. Rather, the quality of our close relationships is most highly associated with happiness.[40]

Whether or not work hours have increased in general, we do know from a recent (2005) comprehensive survey of U.S. employees, conducted by the Families and Work Institute (FWI),[41] that one third of Americans consider themselves overworked, and that hours worked is one factor in feeling overworked. Yet another study, of 500 families across eight cities conducted between 1999 and 2000 by the University of Chicago's Alfred P. Sloan Center on Parents, Children, and Work found that overworking is pervasive: "approximately 40 percent of the parents report arriving early to work or staying late for three or more hours in a given week; nearly 60 percent reported working at home, with 54 percent indicating that they feel pressured to bring work home in order to keep up…long work hours appear to contribute to higher levels of stress."[42] Yet as we'll see, feeling overworked is not only or even necessarily about the pure number of hours you work per week.

So what leads to this sense of overwork? And what can you do to change it? Some problems that affect us as workers in our particular careers and workplaces have solutions that must be deployed by each partner individually while at work or in the transition time between work and home. Other work-life challenges need to be solved by joint partner action (we'll cover those in chapter 8). Here, let's look at what makes work life often feel so stressful and what you can do to take charge. By decreasing your work-related stress on the job and in the transition between work and home, you'll decrease the negative spillover into your relationship.

Work Stressors and Work-Stress Solutions

You probably have a gut sense of whether you're having difficulty balancing work with the rest of your life. Or if you don't, your partner probably does. Sometimes when we're deep in work mode, it's hard to judge how in or out of balance our lives are, but our partners (and sometimes our kids or friends) will gladly tell us! To get a clearer sense of how much this is a problem for you, rate each of the following five items using this scale:

1 = Not at all   2 = Rarely   3 = Sometimes   4 = Often   5 = Almost always

1. I feel my work pressures are too much to handle.
2. I find myself thinking about work while spending time with friends, partners, or family.
3. If things are busy at work I can't really get into fun, pleasurable, sensual, or sexual activities.
4. The important people in my life get tired of talking with me about my work problems.
5. I feel I can't let go of work stress once I get home.

Now rate the next five items, but note that the items are in the *reverse* order:

1 = Almost always   2 = Often   3 = Sometimes   4 = Rarely   5 = Not at all

6. On weekends I relax so much I forget all about work.
7. I use specific ways to decompress after work and can reconnect with friends, partners, and family.
8. I can switch gears pretty easily once I leave work.
9. I feel really good about how I've been able to balance time for work and my personal life.
10. I feel I have enough time for important relationships and for taking care of myself.

Add up your ratings to find the total. If it's between 40 and 50 (an average score of between 4 and 5), you're likely struggling a fair amount with managing the boundary between work and the rest of life, including your couple relationship. Even if you scored low overall but 4 or 5 on any item, the rest of this chapter will help you develop some better work-life coping techniques. (You can find the entire Work-Life Balance Questionnaire on my Web site: www.syncyourrelationship.com.)

Stressor: Too many simultaneous responsibilities and too little time

One factor that creates a sense of overwork is the degree to which you feel you've got too much on your plate and not enough time to accomplish it all. Research shows that job pressure has increased over the past 25 years,[43] and job pressure leads to a sense of overwork and its associated higher stress levels. In the 2005 FWI survey, 89 percent of respondents said they experienced high levels of job pressure.[44] Over half of employees feel they often have to work on too many tasks at once, and this sense was higher in companies that had been downsizing. Those who've survived the flurry of pink slips dispensed since the economy's near collapse in 2008 are expected to carry the load left behind by laid-off colleagues. Because of the decline in the global economy, I'm betting that as you read these words, the portion of employees who feel overwhelmed due to having too many tasks to focus on is even higher today.

Solutions: Address the source to normalize the load

This is a tough one, because most of us are not great at admitting to ourselves or others that we can't handle the load. Even if we're clear to ourselves that we're beyond our comfortable capacity for tasks, we may be worried about keeping our jobs and so don't want to talk to our boss, clients, students, or whomever we feel accountable to. There may be periods during which it's most prudent to "grit and bear it"[45]—especially when the colleague in the nearby cubicle just got laid off and you're the next likely one to go. But one way to approach the boss about staff cutbacks and workload increases is to point out how certain tasks are interfering with other tasks that she or he really wants you to accomplish. There are several excellent books listed in the endnotes that offer step-by-step approaches to asking for shorter hours and changes in workload.[46] Here's a vignette of a client whom I helped to successfully negotiate with his boss for a change in his overwhelming schedule.

Ed was a 50-year-old automobile executive who'd been laid off two years earlier after 20 years in a company that had gone through a major downsizing. Desperate to get a job to support his family, finding that at his age and level of seniority he was turned away from the lower-ranking positions he applied for, he finally found one in the new U.S. branch of a European automaker, only to discover that his superior was a disorganized, impulsive, impatient workaholic who dumped tasks on him without a clear plan. Not the easiest target for a calm, collaborative planning session to decrease one's workload!

Ed faced a dilemma—risk damaging his marriage and burning out because of working crazy hours, or risk losing his newfound job by initiating a conversation with his seemingly maniacal boss. I counseled Ed to take the chance and ask for a meeting with his boss to discuss the boss's ranked priorities, to suggest a step-by-step plan to get the work done over time rather than all at once, and to delegate the busywork to less senior staff in the company. If approached not in a whiny, helpless, or combative tone but in a "I want what you want" style, at worst his boss might order him back to the salt mines and we'd have to figure out how Ed could plan his time as best he could to avoid going back to the job market, a prospect he loathed. To Ed's surprise, his boss was not only receptive but actually expressed appreciation for Ed's planning skills. From then on, Ed and his boss had a weekly meeting to review priorities, to confirm how Ed should use his time, and which tasks could be delegated to someone else. This normalized Ed's workday, interrupted his escalating anxiety, and enabled him to get home to his wife and kids.

Although a number of studies indicate that having more control and autonomy at work is associated with less work stress,[47] as usual, it's not as simple as that. If you are the person mostly in charge of your workload—because you are the boss, are self-employed, or because your job requires you to make many decisions about how much to take on—you may handle the pressure well, or you may fret a lot about how many clients to serve, how best to grow the company, how much financial risk to take, how many programs or products to offer, how many sales trips to take or conferences to attend, or how many studies to do and papers and books to write.

When one is at the helm of one's own endeavors, it can be difficult to pace one's work goals. In addition, certain personality styles may do better than others in positions of control and decision making. In one study, degree of control over meeting job responsibilities was associated with reduced likelihood of poor health for persons with a high sense of effectiveness and who did not blame themselves for negative work outcomes. But for those with little sense of effectiveness and a heightened tendency to blame themselves for negative work outcomes, control over their work was associated with *increased* likelihood of poor health.[48]

Lauren was a social activist and inspiring speaker who had started a nonprofit program to help immigrant women get technology skills. After the program was featured in a top newspaper and on a television special, the phones didn't stop ringing and she'd been flooded by requests from organizations around the country that wanted to be local sites for the program. Seemingly brimming with self-confidence, Lauren often felt choked and anxious with all these opportunities and unable to keep up. She traveled constantly and neglected her personal life. Edging toward 40, she'd broken up six months before with a man she thought she would marry, and her crazy schedule did not permit her time for dating.

To me it was clear that her problems were not psychological. Lauren needed to take the natural next step to grow her organization to keep up with the demand. Unfortunately, like many in the nonprofit world and others who start a for-profit company without training in business, she did not have a plan for how to take the next step to expand. I've worked with many successful people who get caught up in blaming themselves for not being able to work hard or fast enough to keep up as the work piles on. They wonder if they are smart enough, skilled enough, or dedicated enough, and as they get increasingly frazzled and feel like they are drowning, they focus on their personal deficits rather than whether they are set up organizationally. I always start by evaluating, as best I can from their description of their business, whether they have all the structures (staff, space, funding, technology) necessary to expand without being at the center of every decision and all efforts. Usually they don't. So, I help them stop blaming themselves and instead focus on changing how they've structured their organizations and their time. Until they add resources to take the load off of themselves, they will continue to suffer stress.

Searching for psychological explanations for one's stress when one's workload is simply impossible to manage is counterproductive. Anti-anxiety medication or relaxation training will reduce the stress only temporarily but not eliminate the root causes of it. Stress is defined among psychologists as "an imbalance between demands of a situation and the response capability of a person or a system."[49] If one continues to build success with the same inefficient structure in place, anxiety will increase along with greater demands. When I think a person needs further consultation—from an expert in management, technology, finance, and the like—I make it clear that this will be a crucial step in reducing both the person's stress and the stress on a relationship.

Lauren needed to hire more skilled administrative help and needed to recruit other colleagues who could take her place to train local agencies in setting up the program. She started to take steps in this direction, hiring two new teachers and a new administrative assistant, and immediately felt a burden being lifted.

I've certainly had lots of personal experience feeling overwhelmed with work—all due to my growing success as a psychologist. Like Lauren, I learned the lesson that success brings more opportunities, and if we don't select those that we most value and want to develop, we can feel scattered among too many projects, accountable to too many people and too many deadlines.

A few years ago, I had a huge amount on my plate: In addition to a full teaching load at the university and supervising ten graduate students' dissertation research, there was committee work, directing a research center, my own research, grant and scholarly writing, a busy private practice, posts in professional organizations, national and international presentations, and I was also trying to be somewhat of a present father and husband. I felt like I was being crushed by my work; I was deeply unhappy despite all the markings of a flourishing career and home life.

It seemed ironic that, as I climbed to the pinnacle of my career, achieving everything I'd ever wanted, that I felt so miserable, like it was all too much, and that my real life was passing me by. Around this time, I started having a recurring anxiety dream whose meaning was immediately apparent to me.

In the dream, I am at the Jomo Kenyatta International Airport in Nairobi, Kenya (where my wife and I had actually lived for the first two years of our relationship). I have come to Nairobi for some important meetings and am waiting to board my flight home when it suddenly occurs to me, "I forgot to see the animals!" I had gotten so caught up in work that I didn't even go to the Nairobi National Park to see the wild animals (a regular Sunday activity for me and my wife years earlier). And in the dream, I start weeping uncontrollably, and then it is time to board the plane.

After having this dream a few times and waking up at the age of 45 in a panic, feeling that my life was going to be over unless I cut down on my work, it became clear that I needed to make choices. I needed to cut out some activities, give up certain goals (so that I could achieve others), and learn to say "no," even when I thought I had to say "yes" in order to build my career. It's taken a few years to whittle my work life down to a more manageable size. I've also realized that learning to manage your time is a lifelong process.

Like Lauren, Ed, and yours truly, if you are overworked and overwhelmed, you may need to take one or more of the following actions, depending on your particular line of work:

- Scale back your aspirations—decide what is really most important and necessary for you to achieve, at least at the present time
- Prioritize and organize your goals in terms of a more do-able projected timeline over months or years
- Hire new staff members, especially someone who can handle much of the day-to-day running of the company or organization
- Hire an organizational consultant to help you organize the roles and responsibilities of your staff
- Obtain advice on how technology can be utilized to streamline rather than add to your workload.

Stressor: Multitasking and workus interruptus

Speaking of focus—with all these tasks to do at once, many people find themselves constantly interrupted and desperately trying to multitask to get things done. Problem is, for the most part, multitasking doesn't work. In fact, it can reduce rather than increase productivity. Multitasking, coupled with the increase in fragmented focus, increases stress. The 2005 FWI survey found that 60 percent of people who reported they *very often* had to handle too many tasks at once felt overworked but only 22 percent felt overworked if they *sometimes* had too many tasks; and they were three times as likely to feel overworked if they were *very often* interrupted, as compared to those who said they were only *sometimes* interrupted.[50] Several studies in basic cognitive science have shown that we lose time when we switch between tasks that require more than the most basic mental effort.[51] Far from making us more efficient, multitasking tends to decrease the quality of our work, and increase the sense of fragmentation and anxiety.

Solutions: Three things to combat multitasking

1. *Create an interruption-free creativity zone.* If at all possible, organize your daily work rhythm so that you have at least one hour a day to work on long-term projects that involve creativity, thinking, and writing. Some prefer and can arrange to make this the first hour of the day, some make it the last, and some insert it in the period when, for whatever reason in your particular line of work, requests for interactions with others or responses from you are at a minimum. Alternatively, you might schedule at least half of the slowest day in your work week for this kind of concentrated work. It took me a few years of schedule alterations to do it, but I now work at home on Fridays and spend most of it writing. I limit my phone calls and e-mails to those I *want* to initiate because they're related to my long-term creative projects and avoid those that require a response to some completely routine matter that someone else has cast as "urgent."

2. *Do one thing at a time.* In the rest of your day, pick one task to do at a time. Avoid the habit of skipping from one thing to another. Just like a stone skipping across the water, your mind cannot go deep when you move from one activity to another and then back. If you are working on meeting several deadlines simultaneously, work on one activity for at least 30 minutes, take a one-minute break to breathe, read a magazine, stare out the window. Punctuate the "story" of your day as you are living it with semicolons, colons, and periods. Don't live life like a run-on sentence with a few breathless commas inserted here and there.

3. *Mindful eating at the monitor.* One of the unhealthiest forms of multitasking is eating while working at one's desk. Studies show that workers who eat at their desks tend to order more fast food and eat more than if they take a break for lunch. We gobble our food so fast and are so distracted that our satiation sensors cannot keep pace with the volume of food we're consuming.

In working with Dan and Lucy—the couple introduced earlier who couldn't conceive how they'd ever fit a child into their 80-hour work weeks as a lawyer and software start-up president—I suggested that they start taking a half hour lunch break each day. They stared back at me with a mix of incredulity and embarrassment. These two masters of the corporate universe didn't even feel entitled and powerful enough to take 30 minutes to eat. So I came up with another idea to start with—"mindful eating at the monitor."

Borrowing from the ancient Buddhist tradition of mindful eating,[52] at lunch time they were to eat as usual at their desks but with this important difference: Rather than chowing down quickly and attempting to simultaneously pay attention to the work in front of them, each time they took a bite of sandwich or salad, they were to close their eyes and really taste the food as they chewed slowly and completely. Then they could open their eyes and get back into the work, until the next bite. Likewise, when they took a sip of soup or water or soda or coffee, they were to close their eyes and really taste the liquid, feel it in their mouths and feel the coolness or warmth (depending on the liquid) running down their esophagus. By alternating concentrated eating and drinking with concentrated working, they would be able to enjoy their food, take little calming breaks, and emerge from lunch a bit more refreshed, which would reduce their cumulative stress level at day's end.

To provide them an immediate sense of what it feels like to actually chew food (since neither could remember a time when they had ever eaten this way), I again borrowed an exercise from Buddhist practice. I gave each of them a raisin, asked them to roll it around between their fingers and feel its crinkled creases, then raise it to their nostrils and smell it, and then place it on their tongue, roll it around and feel its texture before biting into it and beginning to chew. There they sat on my consulting room couch, side by side, eyes closed, Lucy in pearls and a snappy gray suit, Dan in his dark Brooks Brothers jacket and slacks with a crisp white shirt and a go-get-'em red patterned tie, moaning softly as the raisin juices ran down their throats. "Wow," said Dan. "Yeah," said Lucy. They opened their eyes and looked at me incredulously again, but this time, not because they couldn't imagine taking the break I had suggested but rather amazed at the flavor of a single raisin. Dan said, "I really don't think I've ever tasted a raisin before, although I've eaten plenty of them." Lucy, still in the pleasurable grip of the raisin juice, could only intone again, "Yeah, wow!" You would have thought I'd slipped them a little LSD, but no, it was just the act of slowly eating a raisin.

The couple implemented mindful eating at the monitor for a week. They loved it, and without my even suggesting a next step, they made a date for lunch, spending a whole 90 minutes away from the office. To make a long story short, they ended up having a baby, and when the financial crisis of 2008 hit, they both lost their jobs. But rather than panicking, they decided to use the time to fully immerse together in being new parents—a step they could never have imagined when they came to me on the corporate treadmill. Having learned to live more frugally over the year and a half that they were out of work, they returned to work life with the goal of preserving couple and family time as their first priority, selecting their work commitments in a way that would not violate that commitment.

Stressor: Constant accessibility through technology

The proliferation of communication technologies has erased the physical boundary between work and nonwork hours.[53] Devices fully stocked with applications, Internet-equipped mobile phones, increasingly portable computers of ever-decreasing size and weight, not to mention multipurpose machines that allow us to fax, scan, copy, and print documents in just a small corner of our living space—all allow constant access to centralized databases, as well as to our clients and customers, bosses, coworkers, and employees. We can stay connected whenever and wherever we are and can carry out just about any work function at home.

As a result, home offices and telecommuting are on the rise[54]—which can be a good thing if you can meet the even greater challenge of creating firm boundaries between work time and home time when you work at home.[55] Telecommuting can allow more flexibility between work and child care, can cut down on transportation time and costs, and is even good for the environment by reducing fuel consumption.

Yet all this connectivity can come at the cost of ongoing stress for the worker and negative spillover into relationships. When a couple is trying to enjoy a relaxing dinner, a day in the park, or even a night of sexual frolic, and one partner checks her or his e-mail, it's like one lighting up a cigarette and the other suffering from the secondhand smoke. As one wife said to her husband in a session, "When we're on vacation, and you're checking e-mail or making calls to the office, it doesn't matter if you're only doing it for a few minutes. It spoils the whole 'we're away' vibe. I can see the tension in your jaw—you tighten up, and then when you're off the call or text you're distracted-looking again—and apart from worrying about you because you never take a break, it has a real effect on me. Now I'm all tense, I don't feel we're together anymore, and we might as well be home with you at work and me with the kids instead of on a fancy vacation in the Alps."

By making more porous the "membrane" separating work from the rest of our lives, technology has made shutting off work during after-work hours ever harder for many. There is also the potential for workers to be exploited by bosses who expect 24/7 availability for no extra wages.[56] The 2005 FWI survey found that one third of employees connect with the workplace after work hours at least once a week, and those with this level of contact rated themselves twice as overworked as those who said they had little or no contact with work after hours.[57]

The hyperspeed of back-and-forth communication enabled by mobile technologies has contributed to our general sense of franticness and of being flooded by information and by requests for rapid replies.[58] When we relied on the postal system to correspond with one another, we could expect to have a lag time in giving or receiving a response. Now we're expected to provide a deeply considered, thoughtful pronouncement on a complex question in a minute or less.

Solution: Create "no-tech" zones

Simple to say, simple to do—just push the off button! But I certainly empathize with how much anxiety can accompany that simple movement of a finger....

Okay, empathy time's over, now do it. I can see you have at least one of your devices on even as you are reading this book! Come on now, push the off button. You did it! Good job!

Seriously—when doing work that needs to be uninterrupted, or during the rhythms of relationship you set up with your partner, your family, and with yourself for alone time, turn off the BlackBerry, the laptop, and don't answer the phone. For instance, after a long day at work, if you're tempted to make just a few more phone calls or respond to a few more e-mails to wrap up a few more things, you might instead hear a little voice inside your head saying, "I'd really like to get home and see my partner and my kids, and they need to see me, too. This work can wait."

In one couple I counseled, he was a successful real estate broker who feared that if he switched his cell phone off even just for the two hours per night he had available to dine with, hang out with, and bathe his young kids, he'd risk missing a client call that would make or break him. So for two weeks, I had him keep track of all the calls he received from 6:30 P.M. when he arrived home until 8:30 P.M. when the kids went to bed. Turned out there wasn't even one urgent call, just routine stuff that he could have easily addressed in the morning. Turning off the phone made a huge difference for him, his kids, and his equally hard-working wife who, despite her share of end-of-the-day loose ends, felt obligated (as more mothers do than fathers)[59] to set aside the work day when she came home and tend to the kids' needs. Now they could share in the routine hassles as well as the pleasures of time with the kids at the day's end.

When I strongly suggested the idea of no-tech zones to Ian, that hardcore BlackBerry user you met earlier, he agreed to "give it a go." He realized he could turn off the phone from Friday evening until Sunday evening, when he needed to check the progress of the Asian stock markets, and he and Samantha decided to schedule their yearly family vacation for August, when he would not be required to do his monthly newsletter and interview. That allowed him to keep the BlackBerry off for the entire vacation, with dramatic results in his and his family's ability to truly relax together.

Stressor: Releasing work preoccupations

Our difficulty managing work stress can become a stressor in and of itself. We become frustrated when we can't turn it off and immediately relax; when we find ourselves distracted during dinner, a movie, or play with our kids; or when we're going over to-do lists in our heads while making love to our partners. We expect our brains to work like a light switch: Turn on work mode; turn off work mode. We want the same level of robotic control over our sleep—we work up to the very last moment, stretching the work day (which, after sunset, should more accurately be called the "work night") into the wee hours, phone or laptop in bed with bored or already sleeping partner by our side (if they haven't kicked us out yet), plugging away until the diminishing number of hours left before wake-up time promise a next day of exhaustion. Then its lights out, we shut the lids of our laptops to put them in sleep mode, and we shut our eyes expecting our brains to go into sleep mode just as quickly. Sometimes it works, often it doesn't.

A fair amount of the epidemic of addictive behaviors—whether to drugs, alcohol, cigarettes, or pornography—can be explained as a means for people to medicate themselves to blot out work stress and to transform anxious hyperarousal either into temporary excitement or numbness. In addition, there's a huge growth in prescriptions for sleep medications, a proliferation of sleep-inducing natural substances like melatonin, and even sleep-inducing bottled water.

Difficulty releasing work tensions can also invade and spoil weekends off and vacations. Research shows that those who ruminate a lot about work problems during time off do not reap the refreshment benefits of a vacation.[60] You may be in Boca Raton for a sunny vacation, but if you are mulling over how frantic your work life is, you and those whom you are with won't enjoy the down time.

Solutions: Pay attention to yourself

We need to approach our work day with more self care, remembering we are human beings and not machines. We often travel through our workday with a solid, straight, unflagging path of activity. As the afternoon wanes and evening's poking its head around the corner—a time when we should be starting to wind down and prepare to reunite, dine, and relax with loved ones, friends, or just by ourselves—many of us start a whole new frantic push to gear up, trying to get our second (or third, or fourth) wind to finish up some critical piece of work that "just can't wait" until tomorrow.

Unfortunately, that deadline may not be a fiction of our own obsessive, self-blaming, workaholic brain. Because so much of the work world now operates in this high-urgency fashion, it may be a real deadline that we feel compelled and responsible to meet. We push on another hour or two, or three, until it's done or we're done—that is, unable to function further. In the 24/7 global economy, it seems there are only three honorable options for ceasing and desisting one's work day: (1) we finish the job; (2) we are so wiped out we collapse; (3) our partners threaten divorce if we stay one more late night at work. Actually, many companies, even some with a so-called family-friendly culture, seem not to care too much about the third consequence—after all, we might be more available to work longer hours if we were divorced.

But numerous studies in chronobiology (discussed in chapter 4), clearly demonstrate that our bodies, including our brains, require a break every 90 to 100 minutes.[61] When we ignore the need for a break, we push our bodies to continue releasing corticosteroids, which stimulate our sympathetic nervous system and keep us in a state of strained arousal. We jack ourselves up with stimulants or anxiety and try to carry on, but all the while we're depleting our energy reserves and creating a state of long-term burnout.

As I discussed in chapter 1, burnout is a psychophysiological state that can resemble depression or anxiety. Researchers define burnout as a state of emotional, mental, and physical exhaustion caused by excessive and prolonged stress.[62] Signs of burnout include:

- Disengagement: Loss of interest/motivation for a role that one originally sought
- Reduced energy

- Feelings of helplessness, hopelessness, cynicism, resentment
- Lowered self-worth and self-efficacy
- Lowered productivity

It is hard to bounce back from burnout, so it's better to prevent it by ensuring better work-life balance from the start.

Sports performance coaches Loehr and Schwartz recommend regular, ritualized breaks between spurts of energy output. Their extensive experience with top-flight athletes and high-performance "corporate athletes" shows that those who have regular rituals of decompressing and "chilling out" between periods of high exertion are more successful than those who see a game (or a sale, or a project) as one long arc of consistent activity. You need to oscillate like a wave between work and rest. Adhering to the wave keeps you healthy and promotes well-being. Ignore your inborn rhythms at your peril!

In other words, *take regular breaks!* Refresh! Renew! Shift your attention for a few minutes away from work and onto pleasurable stimuli to activate other parts of your brain and to give your parasympathetic, calming, soothing side of the autonomic nervous system a chance to counterbalance the fight or flight mode of the sympathetic nervous system. Do some puzzles, listen to some music, eat a really great piece of chocolate, look at photos of your loved ones...the possibilities are endless.

Three days a week, I climb the long staircase from the commuter train at Marble Hill in the Bronx to the elevated subway platform on my way to teach at City College. And every time, for the past 10 years, I've seen the same slack-haired, simply dressed, nerdy-looking woman with little glasses on the platform. She's always got a laptop hanging from her shoulder. Though we live in the same town, I don't know her. (Who has time to meet their neighbors?) While I check my e-mails on my BlackBerry, she usually completes a Sudoku puzzle. I finally decided to talk to her; I was curious about what she does for a living. She's a statistician in a laboratory at Columbia University Medical School, and she is extremely shy. Her whole life is about math, numbers. She loves her work but to "warm up" for it and "cool out" from it, she told me, she does puzzles. I admired her for her consistent work-balance strategy! As a result, I started one of my own: listening to jazz on the platform. It gets me ready to deal each day with the challenges of the academic world.

Decompress before you get home. Overstressed working family members either tend to be moving at a pace way faster than their partners or kids—still hyped up on work time—or are in a numbed-out state of entropy, barely able to keep up with the flow of life in front of them. Decompressing before you get home is important to prepare you to sync your life pace with your partner's and your kids'.

So I advise that you use at least the last part of your commute home to soothe yourself, calm down, chill out, change your mood, and prepare to connect.[63] Everyone's got ways to do it—although by now you may have lost track of what works best for you.

For me, music is a dependable source of soothing and reenergizing. The last leg of my commute is a seven-minute car ride from the train station home. I've equipped my rusting but dependable 1993 Honda Civic with great speakers so that I can jack up the sound and rock or jazz out for a few minutes before I get to my driveway. Or, depending on your transportation mode, you can read a book, the newspaper, or a magazine, or listen to an audio book, MP3, or the news. Even bad news can be very therapeutic—it allows you to take all your outrage and anxiety about your boss, colleague, client, or underling and transfer it to oil spills, mismanaged governments, or disappointing sports and entertainment heroes. Catch up on sports scores, talk with a friend, help out a stranger. Do puzzles.

Recently, taking the long flight of stairs down from that same subway platform where I sighted the Sudoku-solving statistician, and after a long day in a very long week, I spotted a woman carrying three heavy bags of groceries. I offered to help her carry them. She initially declined, and I then pointed out that carrying heavy loads was one of the few ways most men can be reliably useful. She smiled quizzically at me and replied, "You said it, I didn't," as she handed over two of the bags. We had a nice chat for a minute about women, men, and chores, our shared frustration that there was no elevator from the train to the street. She got help, and I felt useful. I found myself smiling rather than continuing my stress-laden frown on the platform as I awaited another train.

Practice mindful breathing and walking. While waiting during your commute, try mindful breathing exercises and add mindful walking. Again, I'm borrowing from thousands of years of Buddhist practice. Breathe in as you take one step, breathe out as you take the next step.[64] Really feel your foot roll from heel to toe as you step. Feel yourself connecting with the earth, then try two steps per breath, and then four, until you are walking at a "normal" pace but mindfully breathing. Then repeat. If you are on a train platform, don't walk off the edge—please keep your eyes open, I don't want to be sued.

Add hobbies to your life. Many of us have little imaginings, little passing fantasies of things we'd like to try or do before we die. We often daydream about these when we are most stressed at work. That's a signal from your brain—it is telling you, "You need to do some nonwork activities to feed me a varied diet." These activities, which have no consequences if you achieve them or not and which are totally off the grid of work, family, or any real responsibility, can be great things for decompressing after work. Because they mean nothing except the interest you bring to them, they can become deeply meaningful, private, and personal. And most importantly, they can be great for feeling that you have a life besides work and family responsibilities. Doing something that you didn't go to school to learn, that nobody expects you to do for any reason whatsoever, an activity that is totally *for you*, can be wonderful. You may decide to tell your loved ones or not.

I recently ordered a Shakuhachi bamboo flute. Although I'm a professionally trained drummer, I always wanted to learn to play that mournful, soulful, traditional Japanese bamboo flute. And now I have one, and I play it on the subway platform, way above 225th Street, on my way to work. Everyone looks at me with either interest or like I'm a weirdo, and both are cool. My Sudoku-playing neighbor smiles shyly at me—now she knows we are both nerds, doing our own nerdy things to get ready for the day!

Get organized. In this book I haven't discussed much about time management because there are so many wonderful books on the topic, I have nothing else to add. For sure, we all need to get organized—but as I've hopefully demonstrated, time management is not the sole or sufficient path to a more satisfying balance between work and nonwork life.

In this chapter, you learned that if you are stressed out about your relationship to work, and if you struggle with balancing work time and relationship time, you are far from alone. You are part of a worldwide pandemic, although if you are a denizen of the United States, you're likely struggling much more to preserve time for life than many peers around the globe. You learned a wide range of practical tools that you can use to decrease work stress and establish better boundaries between work and home. In the next chapter, we'll look at what you and your partner can do to further reduce the impact of work stress on your marriage and preserve high quality and quantity time together.

The Great Juggling Act, Part II: Couple Strategies for Balancing Work Time and Relationship Time

THE INDIVIDUAL WORK-STRESS COPING skills in the previous chapter are a critical component of an overall work-life balance plan for couples. But to fully succeed in achieving work-life integration, you also need to directly address the couple side of work-life conflict—the ideas and behaviors on work-life balance that get you into difficulty in your relationships. Marital conflict often results from lack of time together due to long work hours, exhaustion (including reduced sleep), negative energy spilling over from the work day and partners' mismatched work schedules. A vicious cycle develops. Too much and too stressful work leads to relationship problems and individual distress, including depressive symptoms, which leads to distraction and inefficiency at work, which leads to putting in more hours, which leads to greater exhaustion, which leads to less time and quality energy for our relationships and for managing household and child-care responsibilities, which leads to relationship conflict, which may lead to choosing to stay even later at the job because we feel unappreciated at home, which leads.... It becomes a steady downward spiral that reduces our pleasure and presentness both at work and at home.

Rosalind Barnett, Kathleen Gerson, Ellen Galinsky, and other pioneering researchers in the study of work-life balance have demonstrated through numerous studies that when partners work together as a team, sharing the burdens and pleasures of domestic life, and when both partners work or engage in other fulfilling, productive activities, then partners, children, and workplace all benefit. And it can be done.

In this chapter, you'll see how synchronizing with your partner's pace, punctuality, time perspective, and rhythm—those time sides of our relationships discussed in previous chapters—are central to correcting work-life imbalance. And you'll see how by applying my four Rs to changing couple time patterns—Reveal, Revalue, Revise, and Rehearse—you can create your optimal work-life balance.

Revealing Our Unreasonable Expectations about Work-Life Balance

Factors that can greatly affect how satisfied we are with our work-life balance are our expectations and images about what a healthy and happy work-life balance looks like. If our expectations are unrealistically high, we're bound to be disappointed. If our expectations differ greatly from those of our partner's, we're likely to experience conflict.

I find that partners struggling to achieve work-life balance often hold one or both of these problematic ideas:

- Work hard and efficiently and you'll find free time
- Work-life balance is a state of perfect equanimity

Let's examine the problems with these ideas about work-life balance.

Misconception #1: Work hard and efficiently and you'll find free time

Many of us approach our work lives (including, of course, managing the lives of our adorable progeny and pets and the many upkeep demands of our living spaces, finances, and so on) armed with detailed to-do lists and prioritized planning systems. We hold out the hope, despite daily and weekly evidence to the contrary, that once we get through those lists and finish those tasks, time for our relationships will remain—time to relax with our partner, catch up on the day, and chill. And, we cling to the notion that such time is only worthwhile *if* it occurs spontaneously, without effort to make it happen. Although everything else in our life seems to require planning and effort, somehow relaxation and relationship time will just naturally occur. We continue to hold this belief even as we watch each day pass with little or no time or energy left over for our mate. The days turn into weeks, the weeks into months and years, and suddenly you and your partner realize you've rarely had enjoyable evenings together, haven't had a weekend off in months, and haven't had a vacation in years.

Partners may differ on whether or not they endorse this belief about work-life balance, and their differences often emerge from different basic time perspectives. The more future-oriented partner is likely to endorse this notion of take care of work first then turn to the rest of life; the more present- or past-oriented partner is likely to prioritize time for relationship, for pleasure in the day. As Joe Robinson put it in his classic book, "Do you live to work? Or work to live?"[1] Many couple conflicts center on this theme of what should be the basic approach to achieving work-life balance.

In a recent survey of executives, Ellen Galinsky and her team at the Families and Work Institute in New York found that when it came to prioritizing work versus family or personal life, 61 percent were work-centric, but a strong 32 percent claimed to put equal emphasis on both. Galinsky calls this second group "dual-centric" and found they were much more likely to feel successful at work than folks who prioritized either work or family and personal time.[2]

Of course, without conducting what social scientists call a prospective or longitudinal study[3] it could be that those who've achieved a certain level of success feel freer and more financially able to devote a larger portion of their time to family and personal life. But even if attaining some measure of success contributes to the decision to be dual-centric, it's notable that Galinsky's survey found that a solid one third of executives today want a better balance between work and personal time.

This basic difference in their approach to work-life balance underlay the conflict between Ron and Denise. They approached me after my workshop at their church on couple communication, asking if I could work with them privately to learn the communication skills I'd described (see chapter 9). Together for four years and married for two, they had an 18-month-old son, Mark. Ron owned a company that provided lighting and sound for outdoor events and festivals. Denise was a singer and dancer on Broadway, who had elected to cut back on her career for the next few years to raise their son and limit her work to singing commercial jingles. Overtly cheerful, upbeat, and still very much in love, they were nevertheless getting into some stressful snafus when they talked about housework and Ron's long and unpredictable work hours.

In particular, Ron's current contract, his biggest ever, had taken a serious toll on their marriage: 14-hour days with unpredictable arrival times back home, occasional Saturdays spent in the office, constant calls and e-mails from his clients and employees throughout the day and sometimes well into the evening, and unexpected crises in one aspect of the project threatening to shut down whole aspects of the show. Ron came home a self-proclaimed basket case, feeling unable to connect with Denise and Mark. "It's like all the energy that got me home and through the door drains out of my body and I'm just done, I've got nothing to give." After numerous attempted forays into Ron's world—asking him about his day, wanting to be included and trying to be supportive—Denise's understandable reaction now was to shut down as soon as she saw Ron come through the door. When Ron tried to reach out to cuddle on the couch or in bed, Denise withdrew. With tears in her eyes, Denise said, "I feel like, don't touch me, don't bother me...because to try to connect is just a reminder of how little I've seen him all day."

Lately, Ron had suggested that Denise not cook but instead order in, so that he wouldn't have to clean up the kitchen afterward. Turning to Ron, she said, "That really hurt my feelings, because it's one of the only ways I know to take care of you, especially since you won't talk with me about your day." Ron sighed sadly but appreciatively said, "And she *is* a great cook. It's just that I'm trying to cut down on the stuff I need to do at home during this high pressure time." With a bitter smile and notable irritation, Denise countered, "Yeah, I tried to get us on a schedule for doing chores, because otherwise, he won't do them, and then who gets to do them? Me!" Ron sighed again and said, "I know, it's not fair, but it's like I've been on a schedule all day, so I just can't come home to another schedule." Within just a few minutes of describing their time-pressed life, this upbeat couple looked totally deflated.

In our first session, Ron revealed his belief in the mistaken idea that working harder and more efficiently would restore time for him and his family. He declared in a tone of strained hopefulness, "I just need to get more organized, get things done faster, and work harder. I'm trying to get my staff to handle more of the crises without calling me each time. And once I get through this big job, I'll be home regularly for dinner, we'll have time again, real quality time, we'll have weekends again, we can go away...."

Denise interjected, "Yeah, but there's always another project, and one contract comes right after the other, and there's never a break." Feeling hurt and unappreciated, Ron shrugged his shoulders and said to me, "She thinks because I own the company that I can dictate the schedule and the workload. But my clients do." Denise despondently sunk into my office couch, saying, "Well, if you don't make some time for me and for Mark, or at least let us know when you're coming home in the evening, I guess we *all* just have to center our lives around your clients."

Aside from the little amount of time they shared together as a couple and that Ron spent with Mark, Denise complained that she never knew when Ron would arrive home. She'd learned to suspend belief when Ron called saying he'd be home in an hour. One hour would spin into two or three hours before Ron would drag in, exhausted. Denise lived with the daily tension of never knowing whether or not to cook dinner, or what to tell Mark about whether he'd get to spend a little time with his dad that evening.

As a couple therapist, I always try to show partners how each one has a point. But sometimes you have to say, "Both of you have a valid point, but in this case, one of you is more right than the other." In this case, Denise was most right. Yes, Ron's work life depended on serving his clients. But unless he took charge of the boundary between his work time and family life, there would be an endless string of jobs that would build his business but disassemble his marriage. Being more efficient and working even harder was not the solution.

Richard and Clara from chapter 7—the television producer and management consultant, with three kids, overstuffed work lives, frequent business travel, and barely overlapping schedules—were both true believers in the just-get-organized approach to establishing more couple and family time. Both were forever tinkering with their schedules, trying every time-management course and book they could find. And still they'd find themselves overwhelmed, exhausted, and late coming home. Richard cried, "I just can't find a way to fit it all in, and prioritizing only goes so far. I've got so many top priorities, I can't even get half of them done!" Clara shrugged her shoulders despondently: "I know what you mean—I'm suffering from the same malady."

The same was true for Ian, the corporate lawyer married to Samantha, the art book editor. His obsession with his BlackBerry was only partly a strategy to avoid intimate conversations with her. Mostly, he felt he had to stay on top of the hundreds of e-mails he received each day. "If you miss a few days, you've quickly got thousands to wade through, and you feel completely out of control."

All of these folks kept hoping that, somehow, some way, they'd get on top of their workload and find time for one another. In hoping for this, they unwittingly operated under the sway of the Myth of Spontaneity. Come on, face it, if you're beyond the first few all-consuming months (or if you're lucky, year or two) of your love affair, how often, deep in the mosh-pit of your busy work week, do you happen upon your equally stressed partner and simultaneously get overwhelmed with desire, *and* have the time to act on it? I'm going to guess, not often. Please recall:

The Myth of Spontaneity

Love time, fun time, pleasure time with our partners is only genuine and enjoyable if it occurs in the spur of the moment, inspired by overwhelming desire and passion.

Solution: Arrange, protect, and preserve time for each other

The appeal of the Myth of Spontaneity is so great, it's no wonder my clients are initially reluctant, or at least a little disappointed, to have to embrace the key antidote I offer them. Because the key antidote is, simply, that we must *create* time, *carve out* time, *set up* time, and then *protect and preserve* time for each other.

It's understandable that most couples balk at this initially because after putting so much effort and organization into their work lives, they wish that time together for relationship pleasure would be something they wouldn't have to make an effort to attain. Wouldn't it be nice just to get that time, served up on a silver platter, as the just reward for all our hard work? But in truth, most of us simply can't just "find time" to be together. Time for life and love is not lying around like a barely exposed flower peeping out of a concrete sidewalk, waiting to be discovered. Our calendars are already full. We need to take the radical step of creating rhythms of relationship, setting in motion regular times during the day, week, month, and year when we can spend some quality and quantity time with one another.

Richard and Clara operated under the influence of the Myth of Spontaneity. After all, if spontaneity worked for them in the early months of their romance, why not now? They were busy with work then, too. Indeed, their mutual attraction was based in part on admiring each other's work success. But in those early hazy days of love, their brains, like those of most lovers, were flooded with the neurotransmitters of romance (dopamine, norepinephrine, endorphins), and their veins filled with testosterone, the primary hormone of lusty sex. And as their hot romance transformed into the warm glow of their growing bond, their brains were further immersed in a bath of oxytocin and vasopressin, the hormones associated with attachment—what Helen Fisher calls the "cuddle chemicals."[4] Along with all this activity at the brain level, each felt they'd met their soul mate. With all these circulating love chemicals and great expectations, Richard and Clara prioritized time for each other. They just did it, were driven to it rather than planning it. But now, with these inner love drugs reduced, years into a life with the customary accumulation of constraints and responsibilities that come with kids, expanding careers with frequent business travel, owning and worrying about property, investments, and other stuff, the decrease in passion that accompanies domesticity and familiarity, plus the wear and tear left from unresolved conflicts, they'd stopped making time for each other.[5]

So even though, or rather precisely *because*, they were incredibly busy, and even though they'd lost some of the initial burning passion that drew them to each other, I suggested they create regular rhythms of relationship—times for fun and intimacy. With all Clara's business travel and Richard's late nights at the office and business dinners it took a few weeks before they even were in the same place long enough to start their rhythm rolling. But they did it, and soon it became the "organizing time frame" (as they called it) that led them to reevaluate the busyness of their work lives. Clara cut back on travel; Richard got others to attend some of the TV network events he'd previously covered.

This has been my experience repeatedly—once a couple gets the taste for more time together and sees they can make it happen, their priorities start to shift around so that love life starts to balance out work life.

Misconception #2: Successful work-life balance is a state of perfect equanimity

Many people believe they've attained a balance between work life and the rest of life only when they feel at peace with the exact amount of energy and time they allocate to all the different aspects of their lives. They seek the holy grail of the perfect distribution of time into the domains of work, couple relationship, children and family time, extended family, friends, community, household management, and self. And that's only a generic list covering the most common categories. There are many other ways people can divide the time pie in terms of where they wish to, or must, invest their energy and attention.

Underlying this mistaken idea about work-life balance are two of the other broad myths about time: the Myth of Perfection and the Myth of Total Control.

The Myth of Perfection

It is possible to do everything we want and everything asked of us, if we only organize our work life and coordinate it with our partner's work life in a seamless, well-ordered sequence using time-management principles.

The Myth of Total Control

No matter how many forces are affecting how we spend our time, ultimately we must blame ourselves if we're not managing our lives well. And if our partners are not managing well, we blame them too.

Although as an abstract notion the goal of perfect balance is appealing and often depicted on the covers of lifestyle magazines, it creates false hope. Striving for a standard of work-life balance signaled by a state of blissful equanimity leads to chronic dissatisfaction, because few, if any, of us can attain a perfect allocation of time among all these involvements for any length of time. There are just too many variables. The reality is that the work-life rhythm is complicated, with many elements and "moving parts" that may shift from day to day, week to week, month to month, or year to year. Just consider a short list of the factors that can require us, temporarily or for longer periods, to increase the amount of time we spend in work versus home life:

- A new assignment or project that needs an initial burst of time and attention
- A colleague is out sick, on vacation, or traveling, and you've got to pick up the slack temporarily
- A colleague has been fired; you've got her job—in addition to yours—until another person is hired
- You've got to take an important business trip; you'll be away for a week
- It's that time of year again—most jobs have their predictable busy periods (tax season for CPAs, hot, dry summers with brushfires for firemen, end of grading periods for teachers, June weddings for ministers and rabbis)—and yours just arrived
- Your commuter rail just cut the train you've been taking; you'll need to take an earlier train because the later one won't get you there on time

Now consider a few of the many factors that can temporarily or for an undefined period increase the amount of time we need to devote to our home life:

- You're getting married and going on your honeymoon: someone else will have to cover

- You haven't taken much of your vacation time and it's about to disappear unless you do
- You're moving
- A child is sick: one of you must stay home
- You are sick—and you make the wise decision to stay home, spare your company your germs and your impaired performance, unlike the increasing number of people who come to work ill due to the often-unspoken workplace rule of presenteeism[6]
- You've lost the child-care person for your infant; you'll need to stay home for a few days until you find another, then catch up on work once you do
- A parent is dying; you want to spend more time with her and need to help her settle her affairs
- Your marriage is on the rocks because one or both of you have been working so hard, and now it's either devote more time to the relationship or call it quits

Solution: A new metaphor for work-life balance

Instead of a perfectly balanced set of scales with work as one set of weights and the rest of life as the other, imagine a seesaw in a children's playground. The current state of affairs for many people in the relationship between work and the rest of their lives looks like one extremely big, heavy kid (representing work) holding the seesaw on the ground, with his arms defiantly folded and a smug grin on his face, while the smaller, lighter kid (representing the rest of life) remains suspended in the air, flailing around, crying "Let me down!" There's no mutual influence, no flow of energy back and forth, and while the big kid (work) might get temporary satisfaction out of outweighing the smaller kid (life), in the end, neither can have much fun or get much exercise with this imbalanced arrangement.

When the work aspect of our life weighs so much more than other aspects, our life gets stagnant, one dimensional, boring, and stressful. Our relationships with our partners, kids, parents, friends, communities, and selves get shortchanged. And although I've focused mostly on the effects of negative spillover from work onto relationships, research shows that the quality of our personal relationships and leisure time affects the quality and quantity of our work.[7] Marital conflict spills over into work, resulting in reduced energy, distractedness, and missed days on the job.[8]

Research supports the idea of creating a healthy, rhythmic seesaw motion and flow between work and relationship time. Pioneering work-life expert Rosalind Barnett and her colleagues provide much evidence that multiple roles for both partners (parent, partner, and worker) rather than singular roles (in the past, men as workers, women as mothers and home-makers) result in positive health and relational outcomes by buffering the impact of negative events in one or the other role. Other positive outcomes of multiple roles include increased family income and shared responsibility for earning; increased social support and opportunities to experience suc-cess; an enlarged number of perspectives on one's life; an increased number of possible shared experiences for partners to talk about; and a challenge to partners to confront and take apart constraining gender roles and increase equality and fairness.[9]

James Levine and Todd Pittinsky provide ample support that fathers long for more time in their partner and parent roles, and, in contrast to the stereotype that men's self-concept is wholly centered on their career suc-cess, men judge themselves and their happiness as much or more by how they function in personal domains.

Even the kids are happy when both parents work. Ellen Galinsky's land-mark survey of kids' perspectives on their parents' work found that kids are proud to have both fathers and mothers working. Their main wish is that when the parents are home, that they be less stressed and more emotionally available to them.[10] And we now know, from all the data shared here and in the field of work-life studies, a large percentage of what we call work stress is actually work-life *balance* stress. It's a vicious cycle: Less satisfaction with work-life balance leads to greater stress for parents returning from work, which leads to more conflict with partners and less satisfactory contact with (or even, withdrawal from) kids,[11] which reinforces the assessment that work and life are not in good balance, which leads to more despair. Yet, the data all suggest that it works well overall for *everyone in a family* when both parents work *and* both parents spend time with their kids.[12]

This doesn't mean one can't be happy as a stay-at-home parent. Rather, these studies simply show that if you have children and want to work, you needn't feel guilty or worried that this will cause psychological difficulties for your children. As long as young children have good quality child care, research shows that there are no differences in the intellectual develop-ment, attachment, or psychological well-being of children whose mothers worked during the children's first year of life versus those whose mothers were with them full time.[13] Child development is much more affected by the preexisting warmth and sensitivity of parents toward the child, parenting stress and attitudes, separation anxieties, and work stress.[14] So, reducing parent work stress is one of the most important things you can do to ensure healthy, happy kids.

And for women, one source of work stress is when their husbands don't approve of them having jobs.[15] Men can alleviate some of their female partners' stress and the stress that might be transmitted to children simply by showing support for their wives' working.

Given that both partners work in most couples and that many factors can affect each partner's work-life routine, I recommend not setting the goal of attaining perfect, unchanging balance. Instead, aspire to a flexible, resourceful balance that recognizes an ongoing tension between time spent at work and time spent in personal life.

Back to the seesaw image. Just as it'd be difficult on a playground to find two kids of the exact same weight to balance on the seesaw (and not much fun for them to just remain in perfect, unmoving balance), the seesaw of work-life balance requires constant motion, adjustment, and energy transfer from both sides. Imagine that instead of two different kids on that seesaw, it's you on both sides—your work side and your personal-life side. And *you* need to balance things out with *you*, as well as with the people and tasks needing you on either side of the seesaw. Expect some degree of tension between your commitments to work and the rest of your life. Allow the sense that you are spending too much time in one area to signal to you that it'd be good to devote more attention to the other. Learn to prepare for and enjoy the flow from home to work to home life and back again to work, rather than bemoaning each shift of focus and energy.

This approach of expecting and harnessing the tension of work-life balance functions on a day-to-day basis as well as in the greater arc and plan of your life. For instance, if you feel a bit swamped with kids' activities, or after a long day of togetherness with your partner you'd really like to spend a little time apart and dig into some work, do it. Of course, make these shifts responsibly, so others aren't left holding the bag or feeling hurt at being abandoned. Talk to your kids and your partner and tell them you need a little time to get some work done. With young kids who need supervision, make sure your partner can and will take over. Or work out a schedule for a weekend day in which you and your partner split the day, each getting a few hours for work or private time while the other tends to the kids.

These tips can help establish the day-to-day balance of work and life. For the longer-term planning of your joint lives, it's important to notice and take seriously when you or your partner generally feels out of balance in the overall focus on work versus personal life. Syncing your respective personal timelines, and your visions of the future (a topic discussed in chapter 5) has much to do with figuring out the optimal balance between time and energy devoted to work and time and energy devoted to your partner, children, and other personal life relationships.

Solution: Clarifying your couple time priorities

One of the most important correctives to the Myth of Perfection is to make peace with the reality that you cannot do everything you want to do, for as long and as frequently as you might wish to do it, at every phase of your life. You have to make choices as a couple. This is where your differences in *time perspective* can lead to conflicts. If one of you is more focused on the present and wants to savor the life phase you are in right now (whether that's dating, early years of marriage, being a student, starting a career, having children, or growing old), while the other is more focused on making future dreams come true, you may have quite different ideas about how you want to allocate your time and energy. Likewise, if one of you is present oriented and wants to spend more time with your new baby, while the other of you is more past oriented and wants to keep up your old friendships and nightlife activities, this can lead to conflict in how you want to spend your nonwork time.

To get a sense of how you each actually spend your time, how you each would prefer to spend your time, and how in sync you are as a couple, complete my Time Allocation Questionnaire, available at www.syncyourrelationship.com. Or just list your typical activities during the work week and write down the estimated time (or percentage of time) you spend doing each of them. Then write how much time you'd *prefer* to spend in those activities, and add any activities missing from the list. How closely matched are your own actual and preferred time allocations? Which activities are different? Would you prefer more time with your partner? More or less time working? And so on.

Now, compare your time allocations with those of your partner. Do you concur with each other's self estimates about how much time you spend in various activities? Or does one of you, for instance, think the other underestimates the amount of time actually spent in work and overestimates the amount of time spent together or with the kids? Think about the impact on your relationship of the differences in how you actually allocate time, as well as how you'd each prefer to spend time. For instance, do each of you have different preferences for the amount of time you prefer to spend working (at home, out of the home)? Do each of you have different preferences for the amount of time you prefer to spend alone with each other, versus time with each other and friends, with friends without each other, with your extended families? If you have kids, what are your respective preferences for the amount of time spent with each other and your kids (e.g., together as a family) versus individual time with your kids? How about time by yourself? Time on the Internet? And so on.

If you're like most couples, you and your partner probably have some different preferences for how to spend time. Talk about your preferences and see if you can resolve some of those differences using the communication and problem-solving skills in chapter 9.

Now do the same set of comparisons for how you spend your *weekend* time. Talk about the differences that are revealed. Try to find a happy medium!

More Solutions for Creating Work-Relationship Balance

The first thing you can do as a couple to create better work-life balance is the most important: *revising* and *rehearsing* the rhythms of your relationship.

Create a regular rhythm of sexual and emotional intimacy

Put into motion a regular weekly or even biweekly time for physical intimacy. Set aside at least two hours so you've got time to get into it and not feel like you're rushing into yet another appointment. Don't fall prey to the Myth of Quality Time, thinking that irregular little bits of time with your partner will do as long as you're focused. Too much pressure!

The Myth of Quality Time

As long as you are focused and attentive, it doesn't matter how small the segments of time you have for one another.

Create time when you will have no distractions: when the kids are in bed or watching cartoons in the morning, or off to friends for a sleepover or with their grandparents—whatever you can to arrange for a little privacy.[16] Turn technology off and get it out of the bedroom. No last-minute BlackBerry checking. Arrange your love chamber in a way that's sensual and enjoyable—smells and sounds you both like, sheets that feel good to the touch. Put aside work worries and concerns about home maintenance and kids as best you can, and let your bodies speak to one another.

Remember—just as when we try to settle down to meditate or exercise, enjoy a quiet walk in the woods, immerse ourselves in a great concert or an engaging action film—we can't switch off the images and worries from the day's travails the way we flick off the bedroom light. Expecting simply to "wrap up all your cares and woes" and swing effortlessly into sex is an example of the Myth of Perfection, and it will raise your anxiety and interfere with pleasure and arousal. The more you notice how difficult it is to concentrate and be present, the more anxious you'll become and the less you'll be able to get aroused. That's because, as you learned in chapter 3, anxiety is the experience-feeling side of the fight-or-flight response that readies us to cope with danger. When we're arming for battle, our minds and bodies are not exactly in the mood for snuggling or sex. The parasympathetic, calming side of the autonomic nervous system is largely reduced when we deal with conflict, but it's precisely that part of the nervous system that must be activated for sexual arousal to occur. Instead of worrying that you are still worrying, expect and allow yourself a transition from those worries into fuller presence with one another.

Even if you still have some issues to resolve as a couple, and even if it's been a long time since you touched, and even if you're not sure you can get turned on, give your bodies a chance.

Of course, don't force it. If, for whatever reason, you are not yet comfortable trying to resuscitate your sex life with each other, try sensate focus in which you take turns giving each other a nonsexual but sensual massage, and in which the receiver gives verbal or nonverbal feedback about what feels good and what doesn't. If you find this exercise too structured, share a shower or bath, wash or brush each other's hair.

Or if even these activities feel too physical for where you're at as a couple, spend the time doing something else that will bring you joint sensual pleasure, but without physical contact. Literally take time to smell some roses—or other flowers. Feed each other little treats (chocolates, spoonfuls of caviar, berries, or sushi), or share a slice of pizza or a hot dog. Take a slow walk.

You may feel so deluged by work and home responsibilities that only the smallest changes seem realistic at first. If the idea of creating even a weekly "date night" (you knew that was coming again) causes you to cackle or hoot bitterly as that seems impossible for now, then start with less—but make it a *regular* time so that you can count on it happening in your life. Make a *once a month* date for sexual intimacy or for a night out. Or once every *two* months. My clinical observation in working with hundreds of couples is that the regularity, or what I sometimes call the count-on-ability, of the time together is more important than the absolute frequency. Regular but infrequent sex that is consensually initiated and planned in advance is more important than sex that occurs irregularly and only after one partner bitterly complains that he or she is not getting enough and feels neglected.

And don't think that just because you planned a night of intimacy this means the sex can't be spontaneous. Within the time you plan, be as spontaneous and adventurous as you want! Research suggests that variety is indeed the spice of life when it comes to sexual motivation and excitement. Adding some novelty gets the love hormones and neurotransmitters flowing again.

Once you set a relationship rhythm in motion—that is, once you engage the fourth step in my method, *rehearsing* your new rhythm by keeping it running for a few weeks—it will start to run almost automatically. You won't need as much effort to create time with your partner and won't need to be motivated to create time by all the conflict that comes from the frustrating *absence* of relationship rhythms. Marital conflict that comes from the absence of pleasurable relationship rhythms is like the couple version of a defibrillator—it may get the "heart" of your marriage going again, but it's a pretty stressful and ultimately damaging way to jump start making time for each other.

Make small moments of connection happen

Small, frequent, and regular moments of pleasure and connection, or larger, less frequent but regular times for one another, can get your pleasure motors running again. Once you see that you can disentangle yourself from the vise-like stranglehold of work and other responsibilities, once you learn that when you set limits on work, nothing terrible happens (you don't get demoted or fired, you don't miss crucial calls or deals), and once you witness the decreased burnout and resentment and feel the renewed enthusiasm you bring to work by reclaiming your relationship time, you'll feel more like you are running your life rather than your work life is running you.

Here are a few ways to use small amounts of time to connect despite busy days.

Implement 60-second pleasure points

If it feels too hard to set aside even as little as two hours once every two weeks, or even once a month, for fun and frolic, try instituting 4-to-6 60-second pleasure points across the day. Do two in the morning before you separate for work, two while you are apart, and two when you reconvene at day's end. Sixty-second pleasure points are fun, pleasurable, or sensual things you can do with your partner in which the activity lasts a minute or less.[17]

When I suggested this to Ron and Denise, they took it and ran with it. When physically together, they hugged and kissed, did a three-way family hug with Mark, and did something they called the Bear Family, in which they pretended to be bears sniffing each other behind the ears. As devout Christians, they also reinstituted family prayer. Ron started giving Denise 60-second back massages, sometimes extending into several minutes. "He used to give me massages all the time!" said Denise. "They were these big elaborate affairs, with candles and oils. My envious girlfriends used to say, 'He does *what??*'" When apart, Ron started calling to say "I love you"; Denise snuck Post-its all around his office with loving messages for him to discover, and Denise started faxing Mark's drawings to Ron, who'd then fax back a note on the drawing—"Great, Mark!"

Create a daily decompression chamber

Time diary research has established that most couple fights occur at the end of the day, when partners come back together.[18] Makes sense: This is the period of the day when both partners have long passed the physiological biorhythmic "break point" that occurs in mid-afternoon (around 3 P.M. in a day that starts at 7 A.M.), so they are already running on borrowed energy. If the couple has kids, they're now back from school, and whichever partner is in charge of administering snacks, mediating fights, and supervising homework is hard at work. The other partner, especially if she or he hasn't taken my advice about taking little stress-relief breaks during the workday, is basically fried from all the meetings, e-mails, phone calls, and business-related interactions. Each partner is longing for some relief, a relaxing end to the day. But each may believe the prospect of fulfilling such a fantasy is slim: There are still chores to do, kids to feed, wash, and bed down, the last bushel of e-mails to respond to, and, if the end of the day has become a flashpoint for the couple, anxious anticipation of a rough reunification. On top of it all, each partner may be moving at quite different *paces* and feel out of sync. For all these reasons, I spend a lot of time with couples working to create and refine their end-of-the-day decompression routines.[19]

Here's how to do it. Talk together about what each of you needs in order to decompress at the end of the day. Map out a sequence in which each of you gets the personal, private time you need as well as time together. Build into the sequence the necessary (and hopefully, largely pleasurable) time you need to spend with your children, caring for your pets, your plants…and think about including daily chores and other life-sustaining activities.

Connect while doing daily chores

"Wait, what? Chores? I thought this was supposed to be my time to decompress?" you cry plaintively.

Remember the fifth great myth about couple time?

The Housework-Fun Incompatibility Myth

Chores cannot be used for quality couple or family time.

Cooking, cleaning up after cooking, folding laundry, raking leaves, mopping floors, shaking out rugs, cleaning the guinea pig cages (a Saturday morning ritual in my home for me and my two kids, which allows my wife some time to herself); sorting bills into folders, compiling the monthly expenses for taxes or general financial review; and doing the weekly drop-off, pickup circuit (dry cleaning, shopping, post office, video store)—all are relatively mindless activities, allowing plenty of time to reconnect, catch up, regroup, and sync your paces. The beauty of using chores as reconnection and decompression time is that they all have to happen on a regular basis—that is, they have their own natural rhythms into which you can just slide in time for chilling out and reconnecting with your partner (and kids).

Unchain your partner from your unpredictable workday

A large part of the tension between Ron and Denise was because his unpredictable daily work rhythm also made her daily routine unpredictable—and unlike him, she had no control over his schedule. An emerging body of research finds that it is not the length of partners' hours per se that causes work-relationship conflict, but the degree to which their work schedules are in sync. When partners' work schedules are out of sync, this can result in conflict.[20] As we saw in chapter 4, when one has more power than the other to determine daily and weekly rhythms, anger and resentment usually follow. Remember, the biologically instinctive tendency for human partners, like other creatures and like the subsystems of our bodies, is to sync their daily rhythms. In the not-so-olden days, when the workday began and ended with the rising and the setting of the sun, couple partners could achieve this readily. Lights out, bedtime.[21] Rise and shine when the sun returns. But ever since the invention of the electric lightbulb and the industrial implementation of artificial light, there's no larger natural force that guides the diurnal rhythms of humans.[22] We work as long as we or someone in charge of us wants us to work.

When one partner feels powerless to control the schedule and is frustrated constantly waiting for their partner to come home, the other partner feels guilty, anxious, and resentful of the pressure of one more deadline to meet. So until the schedule can be tamed and brought into a regular rhythm, it's better to arrange more flexible ETDs (estimated times of departure, for those with changeable morning schedules) and ETAs (estimated times of arrival, for those with fluctuating ends of the day). This will unchain the partners from the vagaries and vacillations of their work schedules.

With this idea in mind, each night, Ron gave Denise a two-hour window of when he'd be home. And with a few weeks of practice, he stuck to it. That allowed her to go on with the evening and either make dinner for them as a family or just for herself and Mark. Although his work schedule still dominated their lives during the week, she was no longer so completely tethered to it. She felt less resentful and more in control; he felt less anxious and guilty.

Be punctual in getting home

As the example of Ron and Denise demonstrates, nowhere is being on time more important than when you arrive home (or to another after-work rendezvous spot) after the workday. If you promise to be home at a certain time, or on time to the theater or restaurant for your date night, for goodness sake, BE ON TIME! Reread chapter 6 if you've forgotten just how deep punctuality goes for many people. All the good intentions to rectify work-relationship imbalance will be undone in your partner's eyes if you are constantly late coming home from work.

Take short breaks and long vacations

After completing a job, Ron would schedule a five-day break, taking off from Friday until Wednesday. These minivacations ensured that the family would have some quantity time together.

Revalue: Honor Each Other's Work and Contribution

Those of you who've become attached (as I hope you have) to my four-step approach to solving time problems—Reveal, Revalue, Revise, and Rehearse—may have noticed that I haven't talked yet in this chapter about the second step—*revalue*—as it pertains to achieving better work-relationship balance. Well, that's because I wanted to end with a bang—by discussing an issue that often requires a process of revaluing—the ever-inflammatory couple issue of chores and child care.

I want to share some practical tips about how to talk about these activities successfully and how to create greater fairness in how child care and housework are distributed. Successfully negotiating a fair distribution of the overall work must first include an opportunity for each partner to *revalue* what the other partner does to contribute to the overall welfare of the couple and family. In working with couples on this issue, I've found that before we can make adjustments in who does the dishes and who throws out the garbage, who does the shopping and who arranges the kids' play dates, it's useful to step back and discuss each partner's feelings about how they each spend the day.

Whether or not a couple has conflicts about the amount of chores and child care each does, all couples can profit from a conversation about how they feel about each other's work life. Not counting sleep, most of us spend more hours apart than together, and we spend them apart largely because we're working, either at home or out of the home. So it's important to have a conversation in which you and your partner answer these questions:

1. How do you each define "work?" Do you agree with each other's definitions?
2. Do you value each other's work? Do you view each other as making equally valuable, useful contributions to your life together?

When couples conflict about work-life balance, almost always one or both partners communicate, sometimes subtly and sometimes explicitly, that they don't value the other's work efforts, are not sympathetic about his or her work stress, or feel that work stress bleeds over into their relationship too often. Their comments suggest that they don't think the partner is doing a good job of balancing work and life, or that they don't think the other makes enough money to warrant all the time spent on work. Or that the partner doesn't work hard enough or is not ambitious enough; or works *too* hard and is *too* driven and only cares about work; or that the other doesn't manage time, staff, bosses, or clients well, and it's the partner's fault that they feel so overwhelmed.

The following are two topics (in addition to child care and housework, which we'll get to shortly) that often come up for couples when discussing how they feel about one another's work life.

When one partner works but doesn't make (much) money

As a therapist working in New York City, a world center for the arts, I have the opportunity to work with many couples in which one or both strive for a while to achieve fame and fortune with their art. An artist or writer toiling away at making paintings or writing books may not yet be earning money but is still working. Whether their chosen work is *possible* given the couple's economic needs is another question. The artist may need to get a paying job and do their art after hours until such time as the art makes money, or may have to face economic realities and forego their dreams of being self-supporting through their art.

The seriousness and worth of our endeavors should not be measured solely by whether we make money and are able to support ourselves and our families by doing the work. Consider this short list of great artists who, at least for an extended period of time, did not make enough money doing their art to support themselves and had to hold part- or full-time day gigs: writers Dostoyevsky, Kafka, and Chinese poet Tu Fu were civil servants; composer Steven Reich drove a cab; and the great jazz guitarist Tal Farlow designed signs for a living.

Rob and Jill fought intensely about their different definitions of work, how they spent the workday, and how much each contributed to their financial well-being. Jill was an associate director of a nonprofit arts organization; Rob was a professional musician and independent producer. Jill brought in most of the income. Rob had periods when he played regularly with bands but then had long periods without steady work. The music projects he'd produced had so far made no money. Together six years, married for two, she had originally agreed to this arrangement, as Rob was playing more regularly then and had just launched his production facility. In fact, their problem at that time was since Rob was often on the road or playing at night, they had little predictable time together. But for several years, his work and income had been irregular, and she thought it was time for him to get a day job to contribute more income. Rob felt "betrayed" by Jill's request, saying he'd been clear with her about the ups and downs of the music business, and that she was going back on their agreement to endure the down periods. Jill felt frustrated and silenced by Rob's response.

Luckily, Rob's playing schedule became more regular shortly after our discussion, and he decided to return to college (which he hadn't completed) as a step toward preparing himself for another career should the music business again take a downturn. But more importantly, the couple had finally talked in a more open and mutually understanding way about a topic that had up until then been explosive.

Problems when a partner works for a family business

When one partner works for a family business, all sorts of complicated power, loyalty, and jealousy issues can arise in the couple's relationship and between them and the extended family members in the business. For instance, when Saul (whom you met in chapter 4) took over the family business after his father died, he felt hugely responsible to honor his father's legacy by continuing to expand. Through the mourning process and then through taking his father's place at the helm of the company, he became even closer to his mother and sister, who also worked in the company. Jessica felt pushed to the side. So, part of establishing a better balance between work and relationship time meant Saul needed to set some limits on his availability to his mom and sister, and to remember to prioritize time with Jessica.

Revaluing Domestic Labor: Everything Including the Kitchen Sink

Conflict often occurs when one partner is working and earning income while the other—typically the female in a heterosexual couple—is temporarily or permanently in the role of stay-at-home parent and homemaker. The partner doing work that draws an income may show lack of appreciation by implying, or outright declaring, that child-rearing and home-making work can't compare to the stress level of his "real job." This is often accompanied with a further statement that she should "stop complaining" about his work schedule or her responsibilities. And sometimes this attitude comes with such positions as he should not contribute much time to upkeep of the home or that his interactions with children should be limited to play or other mutually pleasurable activities, and remarks about the relative value of remunerated work versus unremunerated house and child work.

In contrast to the model of the 1950s and early 1960s of the male breadwinner and the female homemaker, for today's preponderance of dual-earner couples, it's the challenge of caring for children and carrying out chores while holding down full-time jobs—and doing so in a way that feels fair and respectful to both partners—that's largely responsible for couples' endemic sense of time crunch.[23] When one or both partners feel the arrangement is unfair, anger, resentment, and bitterness can flourish like a virulent mold in the unkempt corners of a kitchen countertop.

In heterosexual couples, child-rearing and housework are still overwhelmingly handled by women. Although a number of studies document an increase in the number of men doing more parenting and recognizing the benefits to themselves, their children, and their marriages,[24] most men have been relatively slow to take on a more equal share of housework—efforts hardly commensurate with the rapid rate of increase in women joining the workforce over the past 40 years. Even when men do contribute, it's women who are more likely to perform the most time-intensive and routine (daily) household tasks—meal preparation; cleaning; shopping for groceries and household goods; washing dishes and cleaning up after meals; washing, ironing and mending clothes; dropping off and picking up dry cleaning and shoes for repair; ordering stuff for the home online.[25] Women, more than men, often include within their work commutes complex sequences of children's appointments and chores, a phenomenon known as "trip chaining."[26] Women also manage the schedules and payment of child-care workers and housekeepers when a couple is fortunate enough to be able to afford that help.[27]

In contrast, men gravitate to the less regular and less time-intensive activities of fixing things around the house, yard work, and bills. The time dedicated to routine tasks is approximately three hours for every one hour of the nonroutine.[28]

All too often, when men do chores, it's described as "pitching in" or "helping out." And some good-intentioned (or repeatedly solicited) guys help out quite a bit, without delay, and with great competence. But the phrase "helping out" suggests that the main responsibility remains with the female partner. With virtually all of the couples for whom division of domestic chores has been an issue, I've found that what women long for is that their male partners will completely take charge of one or more task domains: not just "help out" scouring the kitchen when reminded, but initiate it and complete it to mutually agreed-upon standards. Only taking it over 100 percent gets it off the woman's to-do list, reduces her stress, and creates a more fair task distribution.

In some couples, conflicts about the tasks men are willing to do or not do, or that women are willing to turn over to men, are based on traditional beliefs about gender roles. For some men, their definition of masculinity limits their willingness to participate in housekeeping, childrearing, and other tasks they view as "feminine."[29] For some women, a reluctance to forfeit control over the home and childrearing—referred to as "maternal gatekeeping"—may reduce participation by men and contribute to women's disproportionately greater responsibility for housekeeping and childcare.[30] If your arguments about who does what involve stereotypic gender roles, it might be time to become more flexible in how you think about being a man (or woman) in order to achieve more equal participation and fairness in taking care of the home front.

Some guys I've worked with have insisted that if they are going to take over a particular role such as to feed, bathe, and put the kids to bed on a particular weekday evening, they want to do it "my way"—that is, according to their self-defined standards. In response, I will sometimes jokingly sing the chorus of Frank Sinatra's classic song of the same name and note that, by most historic accounts, Old Blue Eyes (a.k.a. "The Chairman") didn't do much housework or child care. He wasn't thinking about those activities when he sang that song. (You typically don't find the chairman of anything with a mop in hand scrubbing floors or rubber-gloved doing dishes.) And let's face it, Frank did divorce three times.

Instead of taking the "my way" stance, I suggest that the couple needs to come to consensus about their standards and ways of doing things. Sometimes husbands actually can contribute useful refinements to the ways and means of doing household chores and parenting! But if the wife has already perfected a routine with the kids, a best method for stacking the dishes, an efficient way to clean and fold the laundry, or a clever way to assemble the weekly shopping list, husbands coming in to take over a particular task should not reinvent the wheel, but rather learn the method and add refinements if necessary.[31]

Although the issue of women's overburden with domestic life is often particularly acute in dual-earner couples, these conflicts may captivate your couplehood even if one of you, likely the female, has chosen to handle the bulk of the child-rearing. Most readers are in relationships formed years after the second wave feminism of the late 1960s and early 1970s, when the gender imbalance in educational opportunity began to be corrected. Even if you elected to stay at home full- or part-time for a few years to raise children, you are more likely still to identify yourself with your career and education and may still do some part-time work at home. You are likely to view yourself not as a housewife or homemaker but as a professional woman, with equal right to be in the workforce and often with an extensive work history, who has for the time being elected to be a full-time mother for any number of reasons. You and your partner are committed to having one of you be the person spending most of the time with your children in their early years, [32] or perhaps your particular job or profession doesn't allow you to work part-time (or worthwhile part-time positions are not presently available), or possibly the money you would make working full-time would not sufficiently offset the high cost of full-time child care plus commuting. Furthermore, in addition to the continued bias against men taking off from their work to be full-time parents and homemakers, men's salaries on average still outstrip women's for the same work. [33]

Rather than simply fulfilling an outdated, strictly gendered, culturally prescribed role while your male partner is out there in a fulfilling career, you likely view yourself as intellectually equal to your partner, have made the choice to be a full-time parent, and expect something approximating more equal contribution from him when it comes to the work of caring for kids and maintaining the home front. And if you are a new parent, you are likely to know (or discover soon) that child-rearing and home management are indeed hard work, that these jobs are rarely directly compensated, and that they are not often appreciated by those who receive the benefits of your hard work—or certainly, not in the regular, structured ways one receives recognition and reward for a job well done in the workplace. [34]

A number of studies document the strong relationship between the degree to which women perceive housework as fairly divided with their partner and rates of depression among women—and the related effects on marital quality. [35] In contrast, given the few hours most men devote to housework, it is not surprising that men's perceptions of the fairness of housework distribution are unrelated to either their own or their wives' degree of unhappiness or marital distress. [36]

In addition, women carry more of the load of the connections between the couple and extended family. Women are significantly more likely than men to attend to the needs of the older generation, potentially fueling women's sense of resentment and resulting in conflict between partners. [37]

We might expect that with dual-earner couples being the norm and with the cultural impact of feminism there would by now be a widespread shift in attitudes away from the traditional divisions of responsibility for the home and care of children and elders. There are strong trends in this direction, but as Kathleen Gerson notes, it is an "unfinished revolution." [38] Although many younger couples may ascribe to and practice a peer marriage prior to having a child, [39] the vast majority settle into a neo-traditional arrangement after the birth of the first child, at least for the child's early years, with men typically working longer hours and women taking or shifting to employment that allows them to fulfill home and child-rearing responsibilities.[40] Women who refuse to travel, relocate, or work overtime typically sacrifice long-term career advancement. They get transferred to the so-called mommy track, where they can expect to languish in posts not commensurate with their skills and can forget about possible promotions.[41]

I've never met a couple in which the partners determined the exact financial value of all this labor and paid the home-based partner at the rate deserved. Keep in mind that the average salaries paid to professional nannies, child-care workers, and housekeepers are abysmally low. The salaries are accepted because the women providing these services are often financially poor women of color or first-generation immigrants, and often undocumented. Paying one's equally educated partner the going rate for these services just won't do.

When the working partner—usually a guy who seems to have somehow missed any exposure to the feminist movement or the idea of fairness—continues to hold the idea that homemaking and child care aren't really work, I sometimes suggest, with a challenging smile, that he think about what he'd do if, God forbid, his wife died tomorrow. Assuming no relative would be able to move right into those roles, how would he manage all these daily tasks? How much would he have to pay? And would it be the same as having his wife raise his child? Usually, this gets the guy at least talking about, and often reconsidering, his somewhat sexist perspective on the value of the domestic work done by his wife.

If pointing out the actual financial value doesn't affect his view, I find it useful to note the distinction between the experienced value and rewards of paid work versus housework and child care, as a prelude to suggesting that in the interest of fairness to their female partners (and improving wives' marital satisfaction), men may need to do more around the house. If more persuasion is needed, I quote Scott Coltrane, a (male) expert on the role of housework in marital relationships: "The single most important predictor of a wife's fairness evaluation is what portion of the housework her husband contributes." Coltrane further states that "marital satisfaction—including women's desire to have sex—increases in relation to the amount of routine housework that is shared by spouses."[42] (By the way, if you're a guy and you want to wriggle away from this important fact by thinking, "Oh, that Coltrane guy is probably a nerdy professor," I've met Scott—he's a tall, athletic, manly man!).

Likewise, in rigorous prospective studies, famous couple researcher John Gottman found that male partners' doing of housework was significantly related to high future marital satisfaction and a decreased likelihood of divorce.[43]

All couples, whether heterosexual, gay, or lesbian, need to negotiate a fair balance about housework, childcare, and time devoted to career. Same sex couples generally share childcare and housework more equitably than do heterosexual couples.[44] Nancy and Jelena, both talented scientists relatively early in their demanding academic careers, had an eight-month-old son. Nancy had been the one to carry the pregnancy, but now wanted to share parenting responsibilities "50-50." Jelena agreed, but Nancy often felt hurt and angry when Jelena did not take the lead. Jelena countered that Nancy's level of future planning and organization was too detailed and unnecessary. I was able to help them reveal that their different underlying time perspectives (Nancy highly future focused, Jelena more present focused) resulted in these conflicts. They came to revalue their differences—Nancy seeing how Jelena's present focus could help her worry less, Jelena seeing how Nancy's extraordinary gifts in planning could help her avoid the occasional unanticipated snafu. They agreed to a weekly planning meeting in which they would distribute child and home chores, and decided that "50-50" was better as a general guide than as a strict standard.

Let's go back to the initial dialogue between Ron and Denise about their respective work days to see how some of these attitudes had deepened the hurt feelings that were contributing to the growing emotional gorge between them. In that early session, Ron sighed as he recalled his parents' relationship when he was growing up: "I always had the sense, even though they did different things—Dad worked at the company and Mom ran the home and took care of us—they were together in purpose. Dad would come home every night at 5 P.M., and Mom would get us ready a half hour before, saying, 'Remember, your father's coming home soon, tidy up.' And then he'd listen for an hour to a classical music program while Mom made dinner, and we had dinner together every night. I know our lives are not like that, and [turning to Denise], I don't mean this as a criticism, but I kind of wish we could approximate what they had. I guess I don't understand why there's always so much stuff all over the floor—Mark's toys all over the place, coats on the couch, and shoes scattered all over the living room instead of lined up in the entry hall...I mean, you've got just one kid to take care of, a relatively small apartment, and all day to do it."

Tears in her eyes, Denise countered, "I try to keep up the place, but with an eighteen-month-old boy running around dropping his stuff everywhere, and also my handling our bills, shopping, taking him to classes and play dates, to the doctor for checkups, and cooking, not to mention talking to my mom about her troubles every other day, you'd be surprised at how the day flies by. Plus, as you know, I still do a few hours a week of singing on jingles…." Ron smiled tightly and nodding in a pseudo-understanding way, said, "No, I know, you've got a lot on your plate, too. But what's hard for me is when you get so irritated that I can't reliably predict everyday when I'll be home. You're already home. And it's hard that you seem so irritated about my work hours when I'm the one supporting this family." Denise, clearly sensing that Ron did not value her role as real work, shrugged in resignation and sank deeper into my couch.

The conversation then turned to Denise's feeling that Ron excludes her from the events of his day and doesn't turn to her for comfort or soothing. "Honestly, Ron, I'd like to be supportive of you and connect to you that way. But when you come home and I ask you about your day, you just mumble 'it sucked,' and that's the extent of our conversation. So I withdraw, because I feel like you've just said 'don't bother me, don't touch me.'"

Ron's expression shifted to one of sincerity, as he said softly, "I know, you're right, I need to do better about that, I'm not good at talking, but I've lived it all day, now to come home and talk about it, it's like, ugh, I just want to forget about it. But I guess I don't do anything to let you in." Denise looked at me with an expression of "I can't believe he's actually realizing this!"

This softer moment was my opening to start them on a new conversation—one in which they could come to *revalue* each other's roles, and then *revise* some of the problematic time patterns underlying their ineffective ways of balancing work time and relationship.

Our conversation concluded with Ron acknowledging that his expectations about Denise's willingness to be the same kind of fully committed housewife and mother that his mom had been was unreasonable, given that Denise too had a flourishing career and saw her stay-at-home status as temporary. When Mark started kindergarten, she would return more full-time to her career as an in-demand Broadway singer-dancer. We also discussed how times had changed, and that many men of their generation were doing more domestic chores than their fathers did. Ron agreed, albeit initially with some reluctance, to my suggestion that, when he returned home from work, by which time Denise and Mark were often already asleep, *he* wash Mark's baby bottles and collect and put away Mark's toys, and while doing so, think about Mark's playful journeys around the apartment. That would take a bit of the load off Denise and help her feel there was a fairer arrangement between them. In turn, Denise agreed to Ron's request that coats and shoes be put away by day's end.

In the following session, Ron reported proudly that "the house looks great" and reflected that he felt good about contributing more to the daily upkeep of the home. In line with what research would predict, since he started taking some of the load off Denise by sharing more of the clean-up, she was feeling more amorous toward Ron. He also noted that doing the chores helped him decompress: "After a day of what I do, dealing with all sorts of crises and complaints, washing baby bottles in our quiet apartment is such a relief!"

In this chapter, we went beyond individual work-stress coping skills and took the next step in achieving work-life balance: looking at how you think and what you do as a couple to create and preserve that balance. We challenged two major misconceptions about how to attain work-relationship balance—the "work harder and get better organized" theory and the "search for perfect equanimity" theory. We identified how four of the five major myths about couple time—the Myths of Spontaneity, of Perfection, of Total Control, and of Quality Time—drive those two problematic theories of work-life balance. You were introduced to an alternative: the seesaw theory of flexible, dynamic work-life balance, which is supported by the latest research. You learned specific strategies for attaining this realistic balance and for preserving not only quality but quantity time for your relationship. You saw that by challenging the fifth major myth about couple time—the Housework-Fun Incompatibility Myth—you could not only locate ready-made rhythms for connection in the chores you must do anyway, but also create a greater sense of fairness between you and your partner. This could increase the likelihood of igniting or restoring sexual passion in the female partner, especially if the male partner takes up more of the home-management and child-care tasks.

You learned how some of the other time issues covered in this book—pace differences, time perspective, punctuality, and rhythm—figure centrally in the challenges couples face in achieving work-relationship balance, and how to use your awareness of your differences to help build a better balance. And through the stories of other couples I've helped and the techniques I've shared with you, you've learned how to apply the Four Rs of changing couple time patterns—reveal, revalue, revise, and rehearse—to create your optimal work-life balance.

So you have the right ideas and you've got the tools. Now it's up to you to use them!

Syncing and Flowing as a Couple

I WANT TO RETURN to this book's original theme. It started with me and my relationship to time. I was a professional drummer and then became a psychologist and couple therapist. As I trained for my new career, I instinctively applied what I'd studied about making music to understanding couples. It won't be a surprise to hear that most therapists assimilate or integrate the new theories and techniques they learn into the theories with which they're already familiar and comfortable.[1] For instance, if a therapist was first trained to think psychodynamically—to think about how the unconscious meanings and feelings from early childhood motivate behavior—when she adds some behavior techniques (such as relaxation training) to her helping repertoire, she's likely still to think about how the client's unconscious feelings will be affected by learning these relaxation techniques.

Similarly, I assimilated the theory and practice of couple therapy into a theory from outside psychology altogether—music theory, especially rhythm. Doing so has allowed me to make some new discoveries about relationships that I wouldn't have noticed staying only within the theories of psychology. I brought my experience of creating great relationships through playing the drums to what I was learning about creating great couple relationships.

Being a drummer in a band is similar to being a partner in a couple. The art, craft, and science of making great music with others are quite similar to making great music with an intimate partner. Both allow us to play. And relationships that feel like play, instead of hard work, are what we desire. As the psychoanalyst Donald Winnicott wrote, "It is in playing and only in playing that the individual child or adult is able to be creative and to use the whole personality, and it is only in being creative that the individual discovers the self."[2] And it is in play that partners discover and truly enjoy one another.[3]

Let me explain.

The role of a drummer in any ensemble—whether it's jazz, soul, funk, rhythm and blues, country, or even classical music—is to impose temporal order on the music. Our job is to "keep time." We are charged with establishing and keeping "the groove," the "time feel," the beat, so that others can relax and feel energized to play the melodies and harmonies that make up the rest of the music. So, we drummers must exert our musical opinion on the rest of the group—we have to be leaders. As the great drummer Mike Clark, who while playing with the famed jazz pianist Herbie Hancock revolutionized jazz and funk drumming—and whose beats are frequently sampled by such diverse artists as Janet Jackson, Prince, Grandmaster Flash, Britney Spears, and Christina Aguilera—says, "As a drummer, you have to have a point of view."[4] If we drummers impose our rhythmic point of view on the ensemble without listening, we dominate and alienate the other musicians. And they will ignore us—or worse, we'll get fired! So we must be forceful yet listen all the time. We must be responsive to their rhythmic needs yet keep our own groove going.

I think that fits pretty well with what happens in relationships when partners aspire to have equal power and influence on their joint lives. Each partner has a point of view, each expects respect for that point of view, and each needs to respect the other's point of view. You have to understand your partner is another human being—an independent human with his or her own pace, approach to punctuality, time perspective, and rhythms—not to mention particular problems balancing work and life.

If you want to approach being in an intimate partnership in the same way that a drummer approaches being in a band, what are the key things you need to know to make your relationship great and keep it great over time?

Big Ears: Cultivating Deep Listening and Clear Communication

One of the highest compliments a drummer (or any musician, for that matter) can receive is to be told, "You've got big ears." This is not a comment on the anatomical size of one's ears; it means you're a sensitive listener—"you hear me and respond supportively." If instead a drummer is rockin' (or swingin') away, eyes closed in blissful self-absorption, immersed in his own beat without regard for what the other musicians are playing, he or she is likely not to keep that gig too long. In order to play with others, you have to listen.

You also have to speak clearly. Drummers who play beats that are too complicated and that keep changing don't establish the dual feeling of comfort and excitement that is the hallmark of a great beat. One of my greatest drum teachers, Fred Buda of the Boston Pops Orchestra, put it this way: "The job of the drummer is to create a rhythmic carpet for everyone else to walk on." When it's hard to understand what the drummer is "saying," the guitarist or bassist will turn around quizzically—they can't get a clear read on what he or she is playing, so they can't do their thing. Fired.

As a couple, you may communicate quite well. If so, keep doing it! But if you find communication difficult, especially about problems, I highly recommend a set of research-tested techniques from a program called PREP® (Prevention and Relationship Enhancement Program) developed at the University of Denver's Center for Marital Studies.[5]

Step 1: Avoid Hostile Communication Patterns: The "Time Out" Rule

The first step in the PREP® approach is to identify quickly when you are falling into destructive communication patterns, and to stop. In chapter I I introduced the four major problematic communication patterns identified in research with thousands of couples: Escalation, Withdrawal, Invalidation, and Negative Interpretations. Here are some specific forms of escalation to note and to avoid.[6]

- Summarizing self syndrome: arguments in which each of you reiterates the same point over and over, often with increasingly critical or contemptuous affect (as in "You don't know what the hell you're talking about," followed by "Oh, I see, you are the expert. Huh, some expert!")

- Yes, but: prefacing statements with a "yes, but," which gives the patina of listening and seeing the other's point of view, even though what follows shows you still insist on your opinion and your way.

- Cross-complaining: responding defensively to your partner's complaint about one area of your life together ("You didn't clean up the kitchen like you said you would") with a complaint in another, sometimes wholly different domain ("Well, you never initiate sex…so we're even").

- Kitchen-sinking: piling on every complaint you have about the other, rather than focusing on what's making you mad now. Example: "We need to talk. I am just so fed up with you. You are constantly late, you never call to check in with me or the kids, I have do to all the housework, you're nasty to my parents when they come to visit, you're

gaining weight, and you look terrible, you seem to have no trouble
spending money on yourself, but when it comes to me, you're a total
cheapskate, and, and, and…you leave your dishes in the kitchen sink,
as if I'm supposed to clean up after you." This leaves the partner feeling bad, defensive, and unsure where to begin to respond.

- Character assassination: rather than sticking to the specific action
  that upset you ("I am so angry that you picked Jimmy up late from
  soccer!"), making global statements about your partner's personality ("You are the most irresponsible parent I've ever known.").
  Sometimes character assassination takes the form of downright
  name-calling ("You're such an idiot." "Face it: You're just a cold,
  cruel, shell of a man." "And you're just a jerk." "Pathetic loser.").
- Catastrophic interpretations: also known as "always-never" statements. Global statements about the frequency of your partner's
  behavior that take the form of "You're always late, you're never on
  time," "You're always rushing around and making me nervous,"
  "You never clean up after yourself, I always have to do it." Even
  when statistically true, framing one's complaints in this global way
  usually (not always!) generates defensiveness. It's better to stick to
  a particular event, even if the problem has happened frequently.
- Blaming: laying total responsibility for the problematic situation
  at your partner's doorstep. ("The reason we have no time together
  is that you can't seem to manage your work." "The reason we don't
  get invited to parties anymore is that you always want to leave just
  as the fun is starting." "We'll never be able to move on to the future
  unless you stop constantly talking about what we did wrong in the
  past.") You might ask what to do when it's factually true: It may be
  that the reason a couple has no money is that one partner gambled
  away a small fortune, or the reason they rarely see one another
  is that one partner is frequently away on business. But like with
  always-never statements and character assassinations, it's best to
  avoid phrasing things in a blaming fashion. Instead, stick to telling
  your partner how you feel when he or she behaves in certain ways
  in particular situations. Be specific! That will help you and your
  partner know exactly what needs to change.

Make a pact with one another that if you start into an argument and
find yourselves escalating in any of these ways, or withdrawing, invalidating, or making negative interpretations and mind-reading statements, you

will stop! Call "Time Out" or "Stop Action," or raise at this moment your own personalized verbal flag that says, "Let's cease and desist," and schedule a time to talk about this issue within 48 hours using the skills I will teach you next. ("Too Hot," "ER," and "Red Balloon" are some of the unique phrases invented by couples I've worked with to call a time out.) Believe me and the research—continuing to argue using any of these destructive patterns leads to naught. A couple that fights dirty won't recall the substance of their argument, but the hurt will stay with them. You'll remember that the person who is supposed to love you criticized and blamed you and, on top of that, invalidated your feelings when you tried to express your point of view. Break out of this mode of communication; take a little time to breathe and calm down. (Don't spend the "time out" ruminating about how bad your partner is—distract yourself, listen to music, do anything but build up steam to become even more upset!) Then reapproach the issue using the following skills.

Step 2: The Speaker-Listener Technique

In the Speaker-Listener Technique, one partner is the Speaker and the other the Listener. First decide on the topic. Money? Kids? Sex? Time together? Work-family balance? Housework? The Speaker then takes the "floor," and PREP® even has some nifty cards called The Floor that look like a floor tile and have the rules of the Speaker-Listener Technique printed on them.[7] Use this, or some physical object to remind you both of who has the floor. When you're the Speaker, speak for 10 to 15 seconds, keeping it really brief—a sentence or two, at most—and talk about your thoughts, feelings, opinions, and points of view on the topic. Avoid suggesting specific solutions at this time—prematurely offering ideas for solutions can cut short the important process of sharing your feelings and thoughts. A second part of the PREP® communication problem-solving method will help you come up with creative, collaborative solutions. Right now, just take some time to explore and express how you see the problem and how you feel. As one couple to whom I taught this technique said, "It's good, because we're always in such a rush to solve things, we never really talk."

The Speaker speaks, and then the Listener paraphrases—basically, as the Listener, just repeat what you heard your partner say. Don't try to get too creative or poetic in summarizing what he or she said. And certainly don't interpret it—as in, "What you're really saying is that you have unresolved rage about your father that you are now imposing unjustly on me." (All psychotherapists reading this book, take note—leave your finely honed psychological interpretive skills at the office, and talk to your partner as an equal.) Instead, repeat back what you heard, and don't forget to include any feelings your partner mentioned, using your partner's own words—upset, frightened, anxious, sad, lonely, and so on. Don't turn up the volume on feelings—if your partner said, "I feel a little upset when you come home late," don't paraphrase that as, "You get furious with me when I am late." Stay with the language and feeling-intensity level your partner uses. Roll the words around on your tongue; hear the words in your inner "aural chamber." And don't just be a parrot—try to imagine what it feels like for your partner to see the problem as he sees it and to feel what she feels. This way of speaking opens a door into empathy and mutual understanding, and it helps you move from a you-versus-me-based relationship to a we-based relationship.

It helps if the Speaker states her or his issue in the form of an XYZ statement: a kind of communication algebra in which X stands for the partner's behavior, Y stands the situation, and Z stands for the feelings. "When you come home late (X) and we've planned to have dinner together for a change (Y), I feel frustrated and hurt (Z)." You can switch the order of the elements around: "I feel angry (Z) when you insist that we must spend all holidays with your family (X) when we rarely see mine and my mother is not doing well (Y)." After stating the main issue in the XYZ format, the Listener will know the territory, and the Speaker can leave the XYZ format aside and just riff on why this is upsetting—give examples, trace history, stuff like that.

If the Listener doesn't quite accurately repeat back what the Speaker said, the Speaker should just repeat the part that the Listener didn't quite get right (without any commentary like, "Ah, you see, you don't care, you don't listen to me"). Just repeat it—there are all sorts of reasons the Listener might not accurately repeat your words. Don't assume the worst!

After the Speaker has taken four or five turns—each one about 10 or 15 seconds long, and each time with the Listener accurately paraphrasing—switch roles. If you were the Speaker, you now become the Listener, and if you were the Listener, you are now the Speaker. As the new Speaker, you should stay on the same topic to avoid cross-complaining, in which one partner addresses one issue and the other takes up another issue, leading to no resolution of either. The Speaker makes four or five statements on this topic, each accurately paraphrased by the Listener, and the floor goes back to the Listener, who becomes the Speaker once again.

When you return to the Speaker role again, I suggest that you devote your first turn to summarizing anything you heard from your partner that was new, or that you heard differently or more clearly. This avoids the pattern in which each partner uses the Speaker-Listener Technique to politely reiterate his or her point of view—a kind of civil version of "summarizing self syndrome." The whole point of using this admittedly hokey, structured technique is to reduce the emotional intensity around talking about problems so that you can each really hear one another's points of view.[8] When the other partner gets the floor back, you should do the same—use the first turn as the Speaker again to summarize anything new or more clearly heard. This process of reflecting deeply on your partner's point of view starts to build better bridges of mutual understanding.

Any one conversation about problems shouldn't go on for more than 90 minutes (remember what you learned in chapter 4 about the biological rhythms of interaction—after 90 minutes, the body and mind need a break). To make certain that you get back to discussing unresolved problems, create a "problem-discussion time" during your week. Any successful business or other organization has regular staff meeting times. As a long-term couple, you are an organization of two, with plans, responsibilities, and expected and unexpected challenges. Setting aside an hour to an hour and a half once a week to discuss and solve problems ensures that you will stay on top of the issues you're facing and that you will practice good communication skills.

Creating this regular relationship management time also helps you partition problem discussions from the rest of your time together. You can then more fully enjoy the time you set aside for couple pleasure, work, or family time, because one or both of you is not constantly itching to bring up some problem that hasn't been fully discussed. Building in time to talk about problems helps you to recognize what research has documented repeatedly: that all couples have problems, and it's better to make space for them than to try to resolve them all at once or to become discouraged that you have problems at all.[9]

When you've each said everything you have to say about this issue—whether this occurs in one sitting or over multiple conversations—you're ready to move to the next step, problem solving.

Step 3: Problem Solving

By the end of a good Speaker-Listener conversation, you will arrive at one of three places:

1. You have clarified how each of you feels and realize all that is called for is apologies (one-way or mutual). This category might include scenarios where the husband learns that his wife gets upset

when he attacks her mother's political views and decides not to do that anymore. Or the wife who learns that her husband feels hurt when she doesn't smile when he comes home after work tries to smile more. No need for problem solving: It's clear what to do.

2. You started with different points of view, and by the end of the Speaker-Listener you've arrived at the same point of view. But you still need to figure out a plan for what to do next. Problem solving will help.

3. You started with different points of view, and by the end of the Speaker-Listener you've heard and appreciated each other's perspective, but you still hold to your ideas. Now you need to bridge these to create harmony. Problem solving will help.

There are four steps to problem solving, summarized by the acronym ABC+F.

A: *Agenda setting.* Pick the problem you will work on. If you've been talking about house chores, you may need to narrow it down to who's going to handle scouring the kitchen counters or who's going to take out the garbage on which days. Life is filled with such mundane issues—don't avoid them; embrace them!

B: *Brainstorming.* Come up with every idea you can to solve the problem, without censoring any ideas. Get into what hypnotherapists call a "Yes Set"—anything is possible, and you never know how one wacky idea might lead to another that solves the problem. In other words, no No's allowed. Even if you think a spontaneous suggestion from your partner or yourself makes no sense, write it down (one of you should be taking notes).

C: *Combine, Compromise, and Contract.*[10]

Combine: Look at each of your top suggestions. How can you use the natural complement of your different points of view to your advantage? Which of your respective most treasured suggested solutions can you combine into a usefully complex plan? For instance, if one of you wants weekends to be lazy time, and the other likes to explore and do lots of stuff, can you devote one weekend day to laziness and one to activity? Or alternate weekends? If one of you is future-oriented about money and savings, and the other wants to spend on pleasures and needs of the here and now, can you find a way to put aside a certain percentage for the future and guarantee a certain percentage for now?

Compromise. Combining is much easier than compromise. Compromise always means giving up something. But research shows that compromise is a necessary act for long-term relationships to survive and thrive.[11] The social psychology "law of reciprocity"—which governs everything from doing something nice for your partner after they've done something nice for you to buying something from a salesperson who first gives you a gift or "free offer"[12]—suggests that, over time, when one partner compromises, the other will return the favor. Of course, there are certain big compromises that are hard to reciprocate. For one couple I worked with, he agreed to adopt the wife's niece, even though this would potentially change his career path. It's not yet clear how she can reciprocate. In another couple, she agreed to move to a town she didn't know and away from the city she loved, because that's where he found the best job. In yet another, he acceded to his wife's passionate wish to have one more child, even though he worried about money and had always said he only wanted one child. At some point, the compromising partner will likely feel compensated—maybe not around a single decision of the same magnitude but in smaller ways that add up. And if the other partner cannot fully reciprocate the act of compromise, he or she can at least appreciate it and show that appreciation in many ways.

Why should you make compromises? Because you want to be together, and your partner needs or wants something so badly that, if you can't agree to it, the relationship might break apart. Plus, we love our partners and want them to be happy. It may not be fair or balanced, but it's real life. Welcome to the realities of long-term love! I'm not here to clean it up for you with simplistic self-help formulas. I'm here to prepare you to cope with reality. Add that to my 4 R's of change: Reveal, Revalue, Revise, Rehearse, plus *Reality*.

One of the most important compromises that you will both inevitably make in a life together (if you haven't already) involves discovering that there are differences between you that cannot change—or that can change a little but not completely. Instead, you will need to *accept* these differences and find ways to work with or around them.[13] Throughout this book, you've learned how all relationships contain fundamental differences in partners' time orientations, in life pace, in feelings and behaviors around punctuality, in time perspective, in rhythms, in ideas about establishing work-life balance, and in preferences for how to allocate time. In completing each chapter's self-assessments and comparing your answers to your partner's, you've probably discovered a lot of differences that affect your relationship. You may have discovered how some of these differences have spun out into full-fledged polarizing patterns, in which you feel like timing opposites, with each of you trying to rein in the other's pace, or punctuality, or work schedule, or other time styles. And you've learned a whole toolbox of strategies for *revaluing* those differences, *revising* them enough to escape polarizing conflicts, and *rehearsing* the new patterns so that they become easy-flowing, automatic rhythms in your life.

Time dissonance is often based on differences in how we experience emotion, and in beliefs and habits established in our families and cultures of origin. Rather than expecting yourself or your partner to change these ways of being in time, I've encouraged you to learn to *reveal* how they show up in conflicts about communication, chores, children, sex, and other specific difficulties. Then, combine and bridge those basic time differences as a way to solve the specific difficulties. Acceptance is one of the most important attitudes and skills to cultivate in your marriage.

Contract. Once you and your partner have come up with a plan to solve the problem, write it into your to-do list, your phone, your datebook, or your organizer. Specify Who will do What by When and How. Unless you make a contract with one another, and agree to a time frame to carry out the concrete steps in your solution, it's not likely to happen. Not for lack of motivation; just because you are already busy, and it's hard to remember new plans.

F. *Follow-up.* Set a date and time to review how the problem-solving plan went. Having a deadline to review progress helps focus our energies and makes us accountable to one another. If there were unanticipated snags and snafus that interfered with achieving the plan, discuss how to overcome those, or go back to your brainstorming list and see if other ideas might help solve the problem.

Step 4: Identifying Hidden Issues

Getting stuck at any stage of the problem-solving sequence—unable to set an agenda, critiquing each other's brainstorming ideas, finding little chance of combining or compromise—suggests there's more to discuss. You need to return to the Speaker-Listener Technique and talk more about your respective feelings and positions on the issue. In particular, getting stuck suggests that the issue you're talking about—whether it's work-life balance, planning for the near or distant future, frustrations about one another's pace, or anger about chronic lateness or monitored timeliness—represents even deeper "hidden issues." Hidden issues include:

- Closeness and caring: You might feel that you're just not loved or cared about. You might feel the expectations for expression of caring and affection are too great.
- Power and control: You might get the sense that your partner is trying to take charge against your will, controls the situation, and always gets his or her way. Or you might have the feeling

that you are left with too much responsibility and control—as in the "overfunctioning-underfunctioning" polarity described in chapter 1.

- Respect and recognition: You might feel that your partner does not respect you—about specific things like what you do for a living, how much money you earn, your opinions or knowledge on a certain topic, or in general as a person. Or that your partner does not recognize the efforts you make to contribute to your shared life.

- Trust: You might sense that you cannot really trust your partner or that your partner doesn't trust you—with money, with tasks, with the children, to behave well in public or family situations, to be sexually monogamous (if that is your arrangement), to honor commitments not to gamble or abuse substances (if this has been a problem), to tell the truth, or to honor long-term commitments to the marriage.

- Integrity: You might feel that your partner behaves or asks you to behave in ways that violate your basic values, the law, or your physical and emotional integrity.

Acceptance. As discussed above, acceptance is essential to a satisfying and long-term marriage. It becomes a problem when you sense that your partner doesn't accept you for who you are, what you do, and what you believe. If your partner does damaging, hurtful things or consistently evokes in you one or more of the other hidden issues (or if you do this to your partner), even when you've asked him or her to talk about these behaviors and stop, you need not accept this mistreatment. The line in the sand—when to stay or when to go—is different for every person, so there are no clear guidelines for when enough is enough. Relationships, our partners, and we ourselves are not perfect and can't become so, and we must learn to accept our partners with their strengths and faults. Acceptance, however, is not unconditional. You need to decide when your partner's lack of caring, attempts to assert too much control over you, disrespectfulness, untrustworthiness, and lack of integrity (or attempts to violate your integrity, including through abuse) are too much to endure. If you've given it your best shot and used (or tried to use) the techniques described to discuss your hidden issues, and nevertheless your partner refuses to change, you may decide you cannot accept your partner enough to remain together.

Assuming things are not that bad yet, let's look at how to address hidden issues. First, identify the hidden issue or issues that underlie the problem for each of you. Then talk about them using the Speaker-Listener

Technique. I've devised a variation of the XYZ that I call the XYHZ, which simply inserts hidden issue language in your statement of what concerns you. Let's use the XYZ examples I presented earlier:

"When you come home late (X) and we've planned to have dinner together for a change (Y), I feel unloved and uncared about (H), and I feel frustrated and hurt (Z)." "I feel angry (Z) and like you have all the control over our time with extended family (H) when you insist that we must spend all holidays with your family (X) when we rarely see mine and my mother is not doing well (Y)."

Because hidden issues usually underlie more than one specific problem, it's useful to talk about all the different ways in which you feel uncared about, or controlled, or disrespected, and so on. The potential danger of doing this is that you may slide into "kitchen-sinking," and your partner will feel overwhelmed. To avoid this, make it clear that you are having a hidden issues conversation, rather than just launching into a list of complaints.

After you have identified the hidden issue (or issues—as I said, there can be more than one operating underneath any single problem) and where it pops up in your relationship, turn the floor over to your partner, who should identify the hidden issue or issues he or she experiences attached to the initial problem. For instance, if you raised the issue about your partner being late to the long-awaited dinner together, and you've then catalogued other situations when you feel unloved (partner doesn't ask you about your day, partner rarely offers to call your parents to see how they are doing, partner doesn't express affection in public), your partner might then say, "I understand that I hurt your feelings when I'm sometimes late to our dinners. I feel hurt that you don't seem to recognize how hard it is for me to leave work on time—even though I've told you how overwhelming and impossible this job can be." She may then go on to list the ways in which she feels unrecognized for the efforts she makes and the many ways she does show love and care.

Once you've both had a chance to explore and express your respective hidden issues, you can then go back to the original problem (for instance, making those special dinners happen) and try to rework the solution, or you might decide to take on and solve some of the other issues you've identified through this process.

Communication Skills and Deep Understanding

The communication techniques I've described here will ensure that you and your partner discuss problems clearly and productively rather than destructively. They will help you meet the inevitable challenges of a life together as teammates rather than as opponents. They will help you to either resolve your differences or recognize the differences between you that you need to live with and accept. And they will guide you in exploring and resolving deeper, more extensive issues that surface in specific problems and conflicts, including those about time differences.

Practiced over time, these communication techniques and the attitude of mutual respect they embody will help you attain deeper understanding of your partner and of yourself. And deep mutual understanding is a central component of emotional intimacy. In order for there to be a strong and realistic sense of "we"—to move beyond a relationship in which there is only a "you" and a "me"—you need this deep appreciation and understanding of one another. And these ways of being in a relationship are not developed in a strict temporal sequence, in which first you get to know yourself, then get to know each other extremely well over time and, in lots of discussions, identify your differences and resolve them, and only then are ready to become a "we."

One of the greatest misconceptions of pop psychology is the notion that before you can love and truly know someone else, you need first to love and know yourself thoroughly. If this were the case, and if we followed this rule exactly, there would be few intimate relationships, and the human race would be extinct. Knowing and loving oneself is a lifelong process that occurs through relating to others. And the process of relating to others is rife with conflict, rifts, ruptures, tears (as in rips), and tears (as in crying). It's those hard, confusing, conflicting moments with a person we love in which we realize we're not as much a "we" as we thought we were. We need to stand back, see how we're each feeling, learn how the other is feeling, talk about it, and then try to resolve, repair, and reconnect.

This process of rupture and repair builds a better sense of self, greater understanding of our lover, and a more realistic, accurate sense of who "we" are as a couple. Conflict is inevitable in relationships. The key is to manage it well so that it becomes the energy that propels an upward spiral of growth in your relationship rather than a downward spiral of destructiveness and dissolution.

And by the way, this process of relational rupture and repair not only characterizes intimate couple relationships but is critical to the healthy attachment between parents and infants (and later, children) as well as close friendships.[14] Struggle, moments of failure, difficulties—all are critical to growth, inventiveness, and creativity in both human relationships and our relationship to our work. Relationship conflicts can be transformative for both partners and the relationship.[15]

In my work with couples, I notice that some clients are genuinely surprised that friction stole its way into their relationship. They are upset about not being a seamless "we," and this hampers them more than the actual problems and differences. On the other hand, when one or both partners refuse to address problems, these typically fester and become more intense. Problems that we don't face now will lead to discontent later on. Use the tools I've provided you to discuss and reconcile the problems you encounter in your relationship, and you will also glean the gift of deeper understanding.

Offer Frequent Thanks and Compliments

Two of the most important and yet neglected relationship maintenance acts in long-term marriages are the compliment and the thank you. When we're falling in love, it seems we're overflowing with them—complimenting our partner on how they look, how they smell, their brilliant ideas, their tastes, and how they treat us. And we also thank them a lot—for treating us to dinner, for cleaning up the house, for how nicely they spoke to our overbearing mothers or uptight fathers at the first nerve-wracking visit with the in-laws. Yet as we build a life together and the years pass along, we start to take our partners for granted. How many times can you thank someone for cooking dinner, cleaning up the kitchen, taking care of the kids, working hard to bring in a good salary—stuff we do every day? Answer: frequently. More frequently than you probably do it now. And is it really necessary to tell your partner, who should *know by now,* that you love him or her and find him or her attractive? Answer: most definitely. You'll be surprised at the way these simple acts, complimenting and thanking, grease the wheels of the relationship and create a bank account of good feeling and mutual appreciation that will help you endure the inevitable minor frustrations and hassles of shared living. You are simply less likely to bicker, fight, and find fault with someone whom you know appreciates you, and whom you appreciate. Laying the groundwork of mutual goodwill also makes it easier to address difficult conflicts. Research bears me out: John Gottman and his team found that couples who expressed their admiration and appreciation for each other were happier in their relationship, and their marriage lasted longer and proved more stable.[16]

Compliments and thanks are a great warmer-upper when you do want to ask your partner to change his or her behavior in some way. If you wish he'd put his dishes in the dishwasher, a good way to bring this up is to start by thanking him for what he already does for the relationship. "Honey, I really appreciate how hard you work, and that you rarely complain even though your hours are so long and you often don't get to eat dinner till late. But I'd really appreciate it, when you're done eating, if you could rinse your dishes and stick them in the washer. Would that be OK?" Or if you wish she'd clear her mail off the dining room table, you might say: "You know, I really appreciate that you are so busy with work and then taking care of the kids when you get home. I don't mean to add more to your load, but I'd so appreciate it if you could put your mail away after you've opened it. It's just getting a little cluttered on the table, and I'm worried one day I'll spill a little spaghetti sauce on a catalog or a bill or something. Would that be OK?"

While I'm on the topic of asking your partner to change, one of the most useful principles discovered by behavioral psychologists in studies of learning in all creatures, from slugs to humans, is the principle of shaping. Shaping is defined as "reinforcing approximations to the goal." That means when someone is trying to learn to do something, it is encouraging if they are rewarded for their attempts in the right direction. Author Amy Sutherland writes about how she got her husband to put his dirty shirts in the hamper. When he did it, she expressed thanks or gave him affection; when he didn't, she ignored it, a technique called the least reinforcing syndrome, which is based on the idea that any response to the problem behavior is likely to reinforce it. By positively reinforcing our partners' attempts to do something we've asked of them, rather than criticizing those attempts as imperfect, and by ignoring the times when they do forget to do it entirely (as long as they are generally trying), we reinforce the positive behavior and, to use the technical term, extinguish the problem behavior. Sutherland learned these techniques while doing research for a book on training exotic animals.[17] They work for kids, pets, employees and employers, and annoying parents and in-laws, too. Let's face it, we're all exotic animals. Or maybe even exotic animals are just as boring and predictable as we are!

And these behavioral principles work with band members. Nothing damages the trust and flow in relationships among members of a musical ensemble more than harsh criticism of a fellow player's performance. Because playing music is a "full body" experience, uniting thought, feeling, and action, one can feel quite vulnerable in the act of performing. To play well, a musician must put heart and soul into it. So if one musician comes down hard on another after a performance, or during rehearsals or recording, it can be quite hurtful and cause the criticized one to pull back, making it difficult to reenter the state of creativity and connection. And it affects the other members as well. The criticism breaks everyone out of the group trance that develops in playing music, leading everyone to become self-protective and disconnected going forward.

Likewise, harsh criticism by one partner of another's efforts and contributions can cut deep, leading to a mixture of hurt, anger, shame, resentment, and withdrawal. Emphasizing what you liked about what your partner did (whether it's in the bedroom, in the kitchen, or wherever else activities occur), gently asking for changes, and encouraging approximations maintains a sense of "we," and it avoids sending the partner into withdrawal or angry counterattack.

Getting in Sync and Sustaining Deep Connection: Flow

Throughout this book, you've learned how, by getting in sync through the many facets of time, you can achieve a healthy and happy intimate relationship. Now I want to take you a step further. I will teach you how, by getting in sync as partners in time and rhythm, you can attain a level of connection and intimacy with your partner in which you feel great pleasure, completely relaxed, not self-conscious, undistracted, and totally focused on each other. In this state, we become fully immersed in the moment, in the now, not worried about the past, and not worried about the future. This is the state of flow, a state Mihály Csíkszentmihályi and his colleagues extensively researched and found common to all creative, productive, enjoyable activities and relationships.[18] It's kind of a peak experience, which many athletes, performers, and others have trained for years to achieve. But to date, there's been no concrete advice about how to attain the experience of flow with an intimate partner.[19]

I'll draw upon all the time themes of this book—temporal orientation (time feel), pace, rhythm, punctuality, time perspective, projected time lines, work-life balance, and time allocation—and show how to weave them together to create a great and enduring "we." Because there is much to be learned from examining the direct parallels between how a musical ensemble gets in sync and attains flow and how a couple gets in sync and attains flow, I'll start by describing how it works in a musical ensemble and then show how it works similarly in couples. I think this comparison will help you remember the main messages of this book. As long as you remember to think of you and your partner as a band, everything else I've taught you about the role of rhythm in couplehood will come "flowing" back to you! I know because I've pretested that idea with hundreds of now happy couples.

To create the moments of connection and shared creativity that characterize great musical performances, any ensemble must first get in sync on their goals for a particular tune. After picking the tune, what time feel will they play it in? George Gershwin's American classic "Summertime" has been recorded in many different time feels—originally a ballad, it has been played as a faster-tempo swing tune, a Brazilian bossa nova, a blues-type shuffle, and even a slow funk tune. A band has to decide what time feel they will play the tune in.

I once unwittingly contributed to a moment of conflict between two of the jazz greats, trumpeter Dizzy Gillespie and singer Betty Carter. I was an 18-year-old freshman at the New England Conservatory in Boston and was invited to spend a week as part of the backup rhythm section for Dizzy and Betty for a week-long master class they were conducting at Harvard. A few days into it, one of the singer students asked to play "Summertime." We started to discuss what time feel to use. Having recently heard a recording of Dizzy with his band play it as a slow funk tune, I brightly suggested it. He loved the idea, but Betty didn't, and in a sharp-tongued tone she was famous for, she lashed out: "Dizzy, we're here to teach these students *jazz*, not rock and roll!" Dizzy, characteristically friendly, mellow, and unflappable, dropped his grin and clearly looked embarrassed: "OK, Betty, OK." I just hid behind my cymbals, hoping to avoid a similar tongue lashing. Thankfully, we got on with the tune—needless to say, played as a slow, jazz ballad! But that's the kind of conflict musicians can experience when it comes to deciding on the time feel of a tune.

For a band that hopes to create a career together, there is often long-term planning about what styles of music they will strive to create over time. What are their musical goals? What do they want to be known for? How can they respond to new developments in the world of music, the larger world of art and politics, and to the technological developments of recording music? The Beatles are a splendid example of a band that had a vision of themselves evolving over time, always responsive to the whirlwind of cultural styles and political events that characterized the 1960s and early 1970s, yet somehow retaining a core musical identity.

Likewise, for couples to achieve flow, they must share goals (research shows that having shared goals is the fundamental condition for mutual flow between people),[20] both in the short term—for instance, deciding what to do on a Saturday (parallel to the decisions a band makes about a particular performance)—and in the long term (parallel to the decisions a band makes about its career), about the lifestyle they seek to build, whether or not to have children, how to balance work time and relationship time, where to live, how much to emphasize making money (and how much money), where and how much to travel or pursue other leisure activities, and other life goals.

For instance, as a couple, you may decide your weekends have been too hectic lately—too dominated by chronos—and you want to create a more off-the-clock, relaxed time feel this weekend, more of a sense of time-suspended aeon. Now you've got to figure out what you will do to achieve this—what particular activities, at what pace, how much time to allocate to each activity, in what sequence, when to start and stop each activity, and whether and when to take breaks. One version of such a weekend might include getting up late, making love, taking a shower together, going out for brunch or making a leisurely lunch at home, wandering around the city, strolling in the woods, or taking a walk wherever you live for a couple of hours; then separating for an hour or two to exercise, surf the net (not for work, just for fun), or just stare at a wall (relationship break time); and getting back together in bed for another love-making session or just to cuddle a bit and nap, followed by cooking a relaxed dinner or dining out at a favorite low-key restaurant, then maybe a movie and bed. Alternatively, you might get up early to watch the sun rise or listen to the rain together, have breakfast, read the paper, and lounge around on the couch all day, moving in and out of conversation and having food delivered. There are as many possibilities as there are couples and tastes for particular activities.

Back to the band: After deciding on the basic time feel, the group needs to refine the particular rhythms they'll play on the tune. For instance, funk is a time feel, but within funk there are infinite variations of specific rhythms that can produce that feel. The same goes for all the musical time feel styles mentioned above. Often, it's the drummer who suggests a rhythm, and the rest of the band then makes suggestions for refining it. Sometimes, though, another instrumentalist or the singer has an idea for the rhythm.

In addition to figuring out the rhythm of a tune, the band must establish whether or where the tune will have "breaks"—short or long periods of silence, usually punctuated by accents and particular rhythmic figures that the band plays in unison. The band also needs to decide whether or when to take breaks between tunes. A two-hour concert in which the band moves immediately from one tune to another can be extraordinarily exciting but may leave the audience (and the performers) exhausted. A two-hour concert with an inter-mission and pauses between tunes for a bit of stage patter and stories from the lead singer can create a sense of intimacy and moments for recovery. But breaks that go on too long can result in loss of momentum and boredom.

Similarly, as a couple, once you create a pattern of a weekend day that you enjoy and that achieves the desired goal of chilling out and connect-ing, you may decide to repeat it—each weekend or less frequently (either by choice, or because your relationships to work, children, extended family, or other persons and activities don't allow it). When you repeat it, you're engaging in a rhythm—in this case, a rhythm of relaxing.

In creating your relaxing weekend rhythm, you've designed a regular sequence of activities that includes periods of activity and inactivity—that is, time together and time apart, the relationship equivalent of musical breaks—in which each activity starts and ends at particular times, either specific clock times or broader times designated by phrases like late morning, early afternoon, and evening. Each activity within the rhythm lasts a certain length of time and occurs at approximately the same pace each time you enact the rhythm.

Of course, I've given just one example of a time feel for a weekend rhythm. If your weekends have been boring and seem to drag on forever—an overdose of aeon?—you may also want to create rhythms that capitalize on chronos, that provide more activities and that adhere more closely to the clock, as a way of generating a sense of forward movement and excitement. Or you may search out experiences that provide the time feel provided by kairos, seeking opportunities for serendipity and adventure and generating the heightened experience that comes from the unexpected, the new. All three of those time feels are available to you as a couple, and you can create rhythms that reliably generate those time feels through patterns of activities.

Back to the band. Along with the basic feel and rhythm, the group needs to decide the tempo, or pace. All rhythms can be played at an infinite range of tempos. For instance, a jazz ballad can be played extremely slowly, with a more spritely gait, or anywhere between. In addition, across the course of a tune, each soloist may want to change the tempo or time feel: Sometimes a ballad shifts into a double-time swing, or a bossa nova, or a funky groove. The transition into a new time feel and tempo brings a sense of novelty and enhanced immersion in the tune. It's almost like starting afresh, and the contrast between the original tempo and feel and the new one can bring delight to the performers and the listeners. Returning at the end of the tune to a restatement of the melody and the original time feel and tempo can give the listener a sense of coming full circle, coming home after an interesting journey and interaction of energy, emotions, and ideas among the performers and with the audience.

Likewise, couples need to find a way to mine their pace differences so that they can enjoy and make use of the wide range of activities available to them. Couples need to create slow times, fast times, and a balance of these paces over time. This makes life more interesting and makes couples more adaptable to the circumstances around them, which sometimes call for quick action and rapid movement and other times for patience and slowness.

The band then needs to work on starting the tune and ending the tune at the same time. This is the punctuality aspect of music: showing up on time—not just for the gig (which is a huge issue in the music business and can make or break a band), but in the musical moment. This is more difficult than it may seem, because those first and last notes always occur in a split second. When a band fails to start and stop together, it sounds sloppy. This is why some bands forgo attempting to achieve this level of unity by deliberately having temporally loose beginnings and splashy, loose endings to tunes, with the drummer doing lots of cymbal crashes and rolls (sustained notes). On recordings, another trick is to have the tune fade out gradually rather than end precisely. Lots of jam bands, in the tradition of the Grateful Dead, use this loose approach to beginning and ending many of their songs. In contrast, when the musicians achieve perfect synchrony on starts and stops (including the starts and stops of breaks within the tune), we say the band is tight. James Brown's band was the ultimate example of tight; but to achieve it, he rehearsed his band for hours, until they played completely in unison.

As we've seen, punctuality—showing up on time—can be a highly inflammatory issue for couples. As can the process of negotiating and coordinating rhythms. When couples cannot agree on the time feel they want for the weekend, the amount of time they want to allocate to various activities (including amount of time together versus apart during the day), or the sequence of the activities that should make up the rhythm; or when partners differ radically in their paces of doing an activity; or when one partner doesn't show up on time for one or more activities in the rhythm—all these disruptions in the joint rhythm of the day may prevent the couple from fully immersing in a sense of flow and connection. Without the order provided by rhythms, deep intimacy and effortless connection is impossible.

Back to the band. Throughout the performance, all the musicians are listening closely to one another and communicating (often through nonverbal signals, but sometimes with a quick word or two). They are united by a basic framework of melody, harmony, and rhythm but free to contribute their own inspirations within the unifying frame. There is togetherness and separate-ness among the performers—a me, a you, and a we. It flows—in the language of music, it's in the groove and, in the language of drums, in the pocket.

Just like in couples. You need to listen to each other and communi-cate clearly. Interestingly, even the parallel between bands and couples and use of technology is pertinent. The Beatles were pioneers in the use of the rapidly evolving recording technologies, using them creatively to enhance their sound. Yet they retained their identity. Other groups let the temp-tations of the new technologies take over their sound, and they lost their musical identity.

When you lose control of the technology—by constantly texting other people while sitting at dinner together, answering e-mails in bed when your partner is waiting to make love (I've lately heard about a new practice among the techno-savvy—texting each other *during* lovemaking: No com-ment!), taking business calls while sitting on the couch chilling with your partner, or accessing pornography instead of your loved one—this disrupts the rhythms of relationship and opens the important gate between the world outside and the intimacy of time together. And that time together is essential to reaffirming your couple identity. On the other hand, you can use technology to connect with each other in pleasurable ways when apart, or to collect information about novel and enjoyable activities to add to your rhythms, or if your tastes so incline, even to watch erotica together.[21]

Because all relationships can sink into entropy unless they engage new stimulation and challenges, couples seeking to sustain flow need to vary their diet of leisure and other activities. For instance, you can move the compo-nent parts of the rhythm around and still keep the time feel that the rhythm provides. Just as in a band, you may tweak the rhythm based on your joint preferences—having breakfast first and then retiring to bed for lovemaking, or taking an early morning walk, then going to brunch, and then making love. Rigidly followed sequences can start to feel stifling and uninteresting. Flexibility is important for keeping your rhythms lively, so that they create the temporal structure for the deep engagement of couple flow.

In addition to creating novelty by reordering the sequence of the activi-ties that make up your rhythms, try varying *when* you do them—"performing" your rhythms at different locations on the clock and calendar. Just as a band mixes up its set list—the tunes they will play at a particular performance—changing the time in the day, week, month, or year you do various life activities can bring novelty and fresh experiences, as well as new chal-lenges that can bring you and your partner together in invigorating ways.

It's the balance between those comforting routines and rhythms and the novel experiences, finding the balance between change and stability, that characterizes healthy social groups of all sorts—from countries, to companies, to communities, to intimate couples.[22]

Everyone in the Band Gets to Solo: Balancing Individuality and Togetherness

Csíkszentmihályi points out that for flow to occur in intimate relationships, there needs to be *differentiation*, with each member seen and valued as an individual, able to pursue his or her individual goals, as well as *integration*, the linking of energies in joint activities and purposes.[23] Attainment of relationship flow also requires partners to devote attention to and interest in each other's goals.[24] As partners, you need to support each other's endeavors and dreams, just as your friends would, without focusing immediately on how they would affect you. Much couple research emphasizes the importance of "mutual admiration" and friendship in long-term marriage.[25] If your partner tells you he plans to quit his high-paying job and start a surf shop (especially if you live in Oklahoma or another state without ocean access), before you jump in with your understandable worries about the implications for you and the kids, you might ask, "Ah, that sounds great, honey. Tell me more about that dream!" In a long life together, along with a base of joint goals, there will inevitably be times when one partner's passions take precedence over the other's hopes and dreams, but also times when individual dreams must be deferred because they would interrupt attainment of important joint goals.

The key to preserving a sense of fairness is balance. In musical terms, if there are two drummers and one takes a solo and the other keeps the beat, at some point the principle of reciprocity dictates that they switch roles.[26] In couple terms, keeping the beat may involve taking the lead on running the day-to-day exigencies of the home or earning the bulk of the income, while the other experiments with new career directions.

This of course sounds easier than it is. Life holds few guarantees, and it's possible that once a partner embarks on a new professional direction in life, the dynamic between you two will change. If two members of a band decide they want to play music in a more rock 'n' roll style while the others retain their dedication to playing jazz, that band will likely not survive long term. If you found large differences in how you responded to your personal timelines questions in chapter 5 and your time allocation questions in chapter 8, you need to talk seriously about what these differences portend for the future of your relationship. Using the Speaker-Listener Technique and problem-solving steps, figure out if you can combine and compromise on these critical life-course issues.

When partners treasure radically different goals and visions of life, it may not bode well for their future together. Compromise is difficult but doable. You might agree to shift your own career plans for a determined period of time while your partner pursues graduate school in another city. Then it's reasonable to expect your partner to make your goals a priority, or find a situation in which both of your goals reign. The best balance is achieved when you share a rhythm of life on a daily and weekly basis and a long-term life trajectory of shared goals. These form a base for experimenting with new activities and directions. For instance, it's one thing to give up the big job and try to open a surf shop while raising a family. It's quite another for one or both partners to take up the hobby of surfing to try something new, which one New York City couple did, to great improvement of their marriage.

On the other hand, to sustain a long-term marriage, a couple must expect that at some point, life may hand them a major change that represents a significant challenge to sustaining their rhythms and their joint plans for the future. Some of these changes are unbidden—losing a job and remaining unemployed for a significant period of time, an acute or chronic physical or mental illness, the death of a significant person in the family or extended family, and simply the normal effects of aging, which may affect partners differently. For instance, if one of you becomes physically disabled, that may make certain activities in your accustomed leisure routine impossible or, at least, may change the pace of these activities markedly. When your last remaining elderly parent dies, and she had regularly taken your kids for a Saturday visit with grandma, you may need to change your weekend relaxation rhythm. If your income drops precipitously because one of you lost your job, you may need to forgo certain leisure activities, or the time available for pleasure may decrease because one of you has to work more on weekends. If one of you develops a terminal illness, you may need to radically reconfigure your long-term plans. You may decide to retire now, or greatly cut back on work and living expenses now instead of 10 years from now, in order to enjoy the few years left together.

While some changes and challenges requiring rhythmic and life-course adjustments are unbidden and beyond our control, others may be unanticipated changes in desires and personal goals experienced by one or the other partner. For instance, one of you may feel completely burned out on your job or career and need to go back to school or receive extensive training to prepare for another. Or, if one of you has been a full-time parent, you may want to go back to work once the kids enter school. Or it may be that one of you, who in the early years of your relationship was happy to move to the other's country and believed she would never want to return to her home country, now feels desperately homesick and wants to return. Or one of you decides to become more, or less, religious and wants to allocate much more, or less, time to religious or spiritual activities.

In most parts of the postindustrial world, if we are fortunate to have a certain level of financial and material security and health, many of us can expect to live twice as long as the majority of persons in our same social class even just a century ago. When the vow "'Til death do us part" was created as a standard part of Western wedding ceremonies, the majority of marriages ended by the time at least one partner reached his or her mid-40s![27] Now, instead of 20 years together, couples that wed in their early 20s can reasonably expect to have each other around for 50 to 60 years. That creates an entirely different set of challenges for staying the course of a marriage and set of joint goals. Adaptation and compromise are inevitable attitudes and skills for long-term marriage.

So is accepting disappointment. Some of the goals you planned together may not come to fruition, or at least not in quite the way you envisioned them. Your partner may not be entirely the same person at age 55 that he or she was at 26 when you decided to construct a life together. And neither, by the way, will you be. But you each may be able to adapt and accept the changes and stay together.

In order to stay together and adapt your rhythms and life pathway to a somewhat different course, you will need to use the communication and problem-solving skills I've presented—to talk and explore these new challenges and changes in depth, to develop a new understanding of each other, and to determine whether your goals are still in sync enough to remain a couple.

Finding a New Tune: Moving Beyond a Painful Past

In contrast to the difficulties of adapting to unanticipated changes in external circumstances and personal desires, another extremely challenging issue faced by couples over time is how to recover from past hurts and painful experiences. A miscarriage, a death, an affair, one partner's period of excessive gambling, substance abuse, incidents of physical or emotional

violence in the couple, or use of online pornography when the other partner does not approve—in each of these situations, one partner may be more
upset than another or has been victimized by the other. These events can
freeze a relationship in time if one partner feels unable to move beyond the
event. Time moves on but does not heal, and the present and future become
an uninterrupted extension of the past. Flow is difficult if not impossible
in such conditions: Just as a river that is frozen solid cannot flow, neither
can a relationship frozen by a painful past event. Time stands still, at least
for one partner, and so time stands still for both.

Much as we may desperately want to move on and put the past in its place,
the traumatic event keeps ringing in our heads. When negative events occur
that are outside our expectations of fairness and safety, and over which we
have little or no control, we may experience symptoms of trauma.[28]

What are the symptoms of trauma? Trauma is an overused, vague, yet
powerful word. Persons who have experienced serious traumatic events—
rape, incest, domestic violence, torture, homelessness, natural disasters,
war—on the one hand may have intrusions, such as repeated, unbidden
thoughts, memories, and nightmares. Things (people, objects, events)
in the present suddenly flood them with images and associated feelings
about the event. At other moments, they may experience a sense of emotional numbness, of almost forgetting what happened, a kind of temporary
amnesia, associated with the protective psychological defense of denial.
That state of denial can then be just as quickly disrupted when something
reminds them of the events, and they're back in intrusion land. This pen-
dulum between intrusions and denial is a normal, albeit painful, response
to trauma.[29]

Traumatic events perpetrated by our partners or any close person are
different from car accidents or even violence perpetrated by a stranger.
Our marriage or long-term bond is generally based on a deep level of trust,
as well as the belief that our partners care about us, are not trying to exert
undue control over us, would not violate our integrity or the integrity of the
relationship, and are committed to us and our well-being.[30] Additionally,
though in many cases we may never again encounter the stranger who perpetrated violence on us, and a war or natural disaster may end, or we may
be able to leave the place that reminds us of the traumatic events, when it's
our partner who did something that resulted in a trauma, they remain in
our lives, a constant reminder of those painful, upsetting events. Because
of that, it is difficult to move readily beyond the past, because the person
who caused it is in our present lives.

Overcoming these difficult, significant issues takes work, and in some cases, one partner's sense of physical, emotional, or spiritual integrity and safety may be sufficiently violated that she or he cannot continue in the relationship.

Without diving into any one of these complex issues in detail, I can tell you that if a couple is to move beyond them, certain universal steps need to occur.[31]

Step 1: Talk About the Painful Past

The partner who committed an act that caused the other partner anguish—whether intentionally or unintentionally—typically wants to move on and does not want to talk about it. After all, this event occurred in the past, it is not occurring in the present, and he or she may have apologized already. Why belabor it? The partner in pain wants and needs to talk about it. The partner who wants to move on feels the other is punishing him or her by refusing to move on and by insisting on talking about it. The partner in pain feels the other is punishing her or him by refusing to acknowledge the seriousness of the event or to talk about it.

The bottom line is that if one of you feels stuck and in pain about a past event, then the two of you need to talk more about it. This is based on my lowest common denominator theory of what must be dealt with and talked about by couples. If one partner feels there's a problem, there's a problem for both until both feel they can move on. Quite likely, if you're in this stuck place, you did not engage the communication and problem-solving skills and the approach to identifying hidden issues that I've described here. You need to use these skills, because it's highly likely that one of you (probably the one who did the painful "it," but possibly both of you) at some point withdraws or invalidates the other, or wants to rush to solutions before all the feelings and meanings have been fully expressed and understood.

This detailed, patient, slowed-down approach to communication and building understanding may result in an effective plan. Or one or both of you may conclude that the integrity of the relationship has been so strongly violated that you must separate. If the conclusion is that separation is necessary, it is useful to seek the guidance of a professional therapist or mediator to help make the separation as amicable and as nondestructive as possible—especially if you have children.

Before you decide to divorce each other, it might be useful to try joining together to divorce the problem patterns that cause you pain. Try making one last committed effort to not reenact the problematic patterns that got you into conflict in the first place. Try to step outside of the ice sculpture your relationship has become, which holds you in postures of mutual antagonism. See if you can start to make small changes that please each other. And certainly, if you are going to move beyond a painful past, at least one of you has some apologizing to do.

Step 2: Create Apology Rituals

Simply talking and developing insight about the painful past rarely puts it aside. You need to enact symbolic rituals of apology and of moving on that provide a useful wedge between the past and the present and future. These rituals can be one-time events or can be repeated daily or weekly until they are no longer necessary. One-time rituals may include each partner making a list of old hurts and then stuffing these lists into a bottle and sending them out to sea, setting them aflame, or burying them in the yard and planting a tree over them—with each partner stating commitments to let go of the painful past once and for all and embrace the present. Repeated rituals may involve one-way or mutual apologies for hurtful actions, followed by a statement of dedication to treating each other lovingly and respectfully.

I recommend a general script. It should be repeated in the morning before the partners are apart for the day (assuming at least one leaves the home for work or other activities) and again in the evening upon reconvening. "I want you to know that I know that sometime during the day, you will probably think about what I did and how upset you are about it. Something will probably remind you. And I am sorry for that, really sorry. I am not doing it any longer, and I hope that you don't have to suffer any longer." In the evening, the words are changed to the past tense: "I want you to know that I know that sometime during the day, you probably thought about what I did…"

Important: The partner who has been hurt has no responsibility to forgive the other partner, now or forever. Some behaviors cannot be forgiven. So the goal is not to forgive but to put the painful experience in its proper place, a kind of relationship cul-de-sac, and move on.

This intervention is highly effective, because in addition to including a repeated apology and indication that the person who did the "it" takes responsibility for incurring the partner's hurt, the responsibility is on the person who did the "it" to initiate remembering the effects that the action likely had on the partner. In a way, it disrupts the polarizing pattern of overfunctioning and underfunctioning: Instead of the hurt person being stuck with the task of raising the old hurt, the person who did the hurtful thing takes responsibility. My experience is that after a number of repetitions of this ritual, if delivered sincerely—not in a monotone, parrotlike, disengaged voice of someone who's gone to see a couple therapist and resents having to do this—the person who has been hurt gets bored with it and with the past issue as well.

Step 3: Start Doing Pleasurable
Things Before You Feel Ready

Once you have both committed to the ritual of apology, it's useful to start reestablishing and growing your relationship rhythms of pleasure. Yes, as crazy as this may seem, once you have a commitment to and a plan to address the past hurts, it is critical that you not be overly captivated by the past pain. And that you affirm that you are taking steps to move beyond it. I call this the importance of Defeating the Emotional Logic of the Problem (DELP). Distressed couples, who've been living with conflict for years, cannot imagine trying new patterns that might bring relief and improvement, because the seeming "logic" of their distress is to continue being distressed or even to go their separate ways. Research amply demonstrates that these couples have been all too stable and predictable, rigid, and stuck in unproductive interactions and beliefs about each other—even though they often experience the relationship as volatile and on the precipice of dissolution.[32]

If this describes your relationship, what you need to do is embrace the illogicality of standing up to the relentless pain and alienation that accompanies a history of conflict. It may not seem to make sense to go out on a date again, to talk nicely again, or to touch each other again. But that is precisely what you need to do at the same time that you are apologizing for past hurts and avoiding negative interactions. Remember—your initial attraction to your partner was probably not based on a sense that he or she would be great at talking about and solving problems. You were attracted by each other's minds, bodies, and spirits and the fun and intimacy you had together. So in order to decide to stay in a marriage that has gotten stuck on a sandy shoal on the river of life, you need to push off and take the risk of trying to have pleasure again. If it feels too soon for a full-fledged date or too soon to become physically intimate, use the 60-second pleasure points you learned about in chapter 8—60 seconds or less of pleasure, fun, and intimacy.

The possibility of increasing pleasure and positive connection, not simply resolving problems and avoiding pain, provides the major motivation for the work you'll need to do to secure one another's trust and confidence again. DELP!

Play Regularly

When a band has a long hiatus from playing together, it often takes quite a bit of work to get the groove back—to reestablish the sense of easy "we" and mutual flow that characterize musical ensembles at their best. In these moments, it's hard to learn new material or play at your creative best. You need to stick to the familiar tunes and just try to make those sound good. As Al Cattabiani, resident wise man and guitarist in my rock 'n' roll and R&B band Daddy O, says when we're rehearsing after a spell and someone wants to add new tunes to the repertoire, "We can't really try out any new stuff until we get the rust off."

In the same way, when couples go for long stretches without leisure time, they lose the spark, the glue, the juice—pick your metaphor, but it's all about losing the sense of "we" and flow. Certainly, we may be connected through the daily routines of home care, chores, child care, and reporting on the day's work. However, as discussed in chapters 7 and 8, the daily routines often have a way of reducing, more than increasing, the deep sense of intimacy. To maintain and refresh this sense of intimacy, there's no substitute for play.

Research supports this point. For instance, one longitudinal study found that an increase from an average 1.7 hours per week to 4.9 hours per week of shared leisure time resulted in a 50 percent reduction of the probability of marriages ending.[33] This sort of result has been repeatedly affirmed, and the amount of leisure time a couple spends together has long been found to be one of the most important predictors of relationship satisfaction and lower levels of marital conflict.[34]

Part of what's so appealing about the strong connection between relationship satisfaction and leisure time is that it's intuitive and reciprocal. Common leisure interests play a huge role in determining compatibility and providing a context for self-disclosure during the courtship phase, so it follows naturally that a happier couple wants to spend time together doing the things that they love. At the same time, spending free time together fosters closeness, communication, and shared experience. Partners spend time together because they are happier with one another, and spending time together makes them happier. The converse also appears to be true: The more partners pursue individual, independent activities, the less satisfied they are in their marriages, and unhappy couples are more likely to pursue leisure activities separately.[35] In fact, the amount of leisure time spent together is a characteristic that distinguishes satisfied from distressed couples.[36]

So while happy couples still find time to spend together and reap the rewards of that time together, more dissatisfied couples may be drifting apart as they spend less and less time together.[37]

On the surface, the leisure time–relationship satisfaction correlation may seem like a simple formula for a successful partnership. But putting it into practice is considerably more difficult. We have little available free time in our hectic lives. In the shuffle of competing demands, leisure time is increasingly seen as a luxury rather than a necessity. Domestic labor and social and family obligations are the "new leisure." One partner might like it; the other might not.[38] Learning to use chores as leisure is the key to defeating the fifth myth of couple time: the mistaken notion that housework and chores shall never be associated with fun, pleasure, or connection.

Full-time dual-earner couples tend to give up their time with the nuclear family and with close friends rather than time with institutional social networks (like clubs or social groups) or solitary time. When time is scarce, being with family and friends (including children, spouses, and significant others) is seen as the most flexible and easier to change or decrease. Herein lies a paradox: Though friends and family time is most highly valued, pragmatically, it's the easiest to sacrifice because of easier access to those people.[39] But the result is that we feel less valuable to one another as partners.

It's important to talk about your expectations and desires for how to spend your leisure time. Without open conversation about each other's time allocation, you may watch how your partner dedicates time and assume the worst—that he or she prefers to spend time doing anything other than spending time with you.[40]

People have different ways of thinking about their time, and they use those frameworks both to make their own decisions and to evaluate others' decisions. For couples, successful negotiation about leisure time involves getting onto the same page as well as understanding and respecting each other's needs and desires. Ultimately, the challenge of spending time with our loved ones is about making choices that will honor both partners' respective obligations outside the couple and family, their desires and expectations, and finding a fairly balanced compromise.

It's also important that you and your partner share responsibility for organizing leisure time. Too often, as with domestic chores and child care, it is women that end up managing the social calendar and arranging fun and exciting activities, even if they work just as many hours as men. Given the strong connection between leisure time and couple closeness, it's not surprising that numerous studies have found that women also bear more of the burden of maintaining the emotional needs of the relationship than men do.[41]

The obligation to maintain relationship quality through arranging leisure time can also come at the expense of women's own enjoyment. Women are much more willing than men to spend time pursuing their partners' leisure activities than have them do the activity without them.[42] This is especially common at the beginning of relationships and can set a pattern for a dangerous trend of self-sacrifice on women's part. Women are also more likely than are men to spend time with their male partners' friends and family, even if they don't enjoy their company.[43] Given the increasing demands on one's time by work, children, friends, and relatives, women who spend time doing activities they don't enjoy or with people they don't like may become resentful yet unable to express those concerns.[44]

If you're involved with such a woman or if you are such a woman, it's important to realize that this happens at the expense of women's own interests.[45] It's important that men take part in maintaining the emotional needs of the relationship both by telling their wives what they need and by changing their behavior in response to their wives' needs. Husbands should also share equally the planning and coordination of leisure time with the family and for the couple. Both of these acts have the potential to help wives feel that they have a true partner in day-to-day planning and in tending to the health of the relationship.[46] One study found that when men pursued leisure activities that they enjoyed and that their wives didn't, both parties reported marital dissatisfaction 10 years later. Also, husbands were less happy if participating in mutually liked leisure activities alone, and wives were less happy when men pursued activities they liked alone. This finding suggests that both men and women want to spend time with each other.[47]

Some couples are able to successfully navigate the tricky balance of time together versus alone time. Independent leisure activities are not harmful to a marriage and actually can enhance the relationship when the active partner feels supported and affirmed by the other partner. How much satisfaction one partner gets from a leisure activity and how that affects a couple depends largely on how the other partner feels about the activity. Doing an activity that doesn't involve your partner can be good for you and good for the relationship.[48] But if your partner feels that this independent activity takes away time from the relationship or family too often or too much, it can backfire.[49]

The adjustment to parenthood can take a very big toll on a marriage or long-term relationship. A drop in time for leisure activities, marital interaction, and happiness occurs immediately after a couple's first child is born.[50] After having children, the structure of a couple's leisure life changes dramatically.[51] Leisure becomes less spontaneous, less autonomous, and more home-based.[52]

Differences in how men and women respond to and think about parenthood in relation to leisure also emerge. Because they are more involved in the day-to-day care-giving responsibilities, women consider time with children more like work than leisure. The care giving and domestic work is so overwhelming that leisure time becomes a very low priority. In contrast, for new fathers, parenthood and leisure are much more linked. Men tend to be less involved in the care-giving responsibilities and instead engage in a leisure-based parenting by pursuing their interests with their children.[53] Conflict may arise because mothers may crave time away from the family while fathers may want to spend their free time as a family.

On top of those differences, mothers tend to be the planners of couple time, but fathers are the ones who more frequently come up with the idea to have couple time (presumably because they are less preoccupied with care-giving duties). But while fathers prefer spontaneous couple time, mothers end up planning the kind of leisure time that they want: away from the home and without the children. Even when a couple does manage to get away from the children, challenges persist. For example, if the scheduled activity is not enjoyable to both partners or if one or both of the partners is not in the right mood, an expectation for the time to be extra special can make the reality of a mediocre time a huge disappointment.[54]

It's important to establish strong leisure rhythms before you have a child. Doing so paves the way for an easier time once a child is born.[55]

Not all leisure activities are created equal. Researchers have distinguished between core and balance activities, which serve different purposes in a relationship. Leisure activities provide contexts for couples and families to fulfill the needs for reliability and familiarity as well as novelty and excitement.[56] Core activities are those that are home- or neighborhood-based and require little planning and few resources. They are often spontaneous and informal and include everyday activities, such as eating dinner, playing board games, taking walks, and even adding playfulness to mundane housework. Most everyday activities for couples involve a combination of interactions and usually entail conversation, including catching up, planning, and small talk.[57] These activities supply a safe and positive environment in which the couple can explore boundaries and clarify family and couple roles. These activities can also promote understanding of each other, a context for expressing affection, and a sense of consistency and structure.

In addition to structure and stability, relationships also need opportunities to promote change. Balance activities are those that are less common, less frequent, out of the ordinary, and novel, and include vacations, outdoor recreation (like camping), and going to the theater.[58] These activities are much more common at the beginning of relationships and are necessary for couples to form a romantic attachment.[59] As a relationship progresses through life cycle changes, couples often decrease the frequency of trying new things.[60] Yet exciting and novel activities allow a couple to adapt to new situations and challenges together, sharing experiences of learning and change. Just as a band needs a core set of tunes that define their identity and are easy to play (their greatest hits), they need to add new tunes to the repertoire, or the experience of making music goes flat. A healthy relationship needs both balance and core activities to maintain a level of stability while avoiding the stagnancy of boredom by engaging in novel experiences that foster growth.

The challenges that accompany novel activities improve relationships by promoting each partner's self-expansion.[61] At the beginning of a romantic relationship, self-expansion is in overdrive as partners are spending lots of time together, getting to know each other through conversation, enjoying their favorite activities together, and incorporating aspects of their new partner and their shared experiences into their concepts of self. Those shared experiences are also flooded with positive feelings, making the new partner and the relationship a worthy goal. Over time, novel activities decrease, and the level of challenge drops off. Boredom can set in, making both partners dissatisfied with the relationship. Maintaining a high level of stimulation can foster more satisfaction and passionate love in a partnership.[62] Self-expansion is closely related to flow in that both are fostered by novel, challenging, and energizing activities. And after a flow experience, individuals incorporate their newly acquired information, skills, and experience into their senses of selves.[63]

If these activities are shared with a partner, the relationship is imbued with positive feelings and is seen as a source of growth and exploration.[64] Participation in activities that activate flow and self-expansion lead to increases in relationship satisfaction and positive feelings about the relationship. And again, satisfaction and flow influence each other—partners experience more flow activation when they are more satisfied in their relationships.

Like many couples, you may feel overwhelmed with the practical challenges of creating opportunities for play, growth, and flow, especially when time and money are scarce. But if any time together can be considered leisure time with the potential for flow, you can create new opportunities to cultivate growth and closeness without always having to go all out.

I sincerely hope that this is the beginning of a journey toward creating and sustaining a deeply satisfying life together by putting the power of time and rhythm to work for your relationship. To quote William Shakespeare's *Twelfth Night*, "If music be the food of love, play on." And I would add, of all the aspects of music that parallel intimate relationships, getting in sync in your rhythms is the key to happiness. Put into play the practices you learned in this chapter—using strong communication and problem-solving skills, cultivating deep understanding of one another, thanking and complimenting, being gentle in your requests for change, balancing support for each other's individuality with strengthening the "we," overcoming the painful times that may lock you in an everlasting past, and preserving time for play and leisure—and you will do fine.

Approach your relationship ever mindful of the importance of *revealing* the time side of your conflicts; *revaluing* your differences in time orientation, pace, rhythm, punctuality, time perspective, and time allocation; *revising* the rhythms that don't work for you, and reaffirming those that do; and *rehearsing* the new rhythms until they are automatic. You will meet the inevitable challenges of life and stay in the groove. If you can remember to try these things (don't try to be perfect!), you'll be fine. From one drummer to another (that's you and your partner), I say, "Play on!" And remember—it's about Time!

Acknowledgments

WHEN A BOOK BRINGS together the major passions and endeavors of one's life, and when the ideas have been developed over decades, inevitably there are many people to thank. This book brings together my lifelong love for listening to and performing music, my lifelong fascination with relationships and what makes them work (or not), and my dedication to discovering new ways of thinking about the everyday aspects of daily life.

So I start at the beginning, my family of origin. Thanks to my mother, Meriam Belkin, who taught me to question every assumed idea—my own and others'—to create something new and better, and whose love of the written word she transmitted from my grandfather, Benjamin Bialostotsky, my grandmother, Paula Kahane, and their community of progressive, Yiddish-speaking, Jewish intellectuals living in the Bronx. My grandfather was a well-known Yiddish poet, speaker, and journalist for the progressive New York Yiddish newspaper the *Daily Forward*, and his father (my great-grandfather) was apparently a famous speaker known as the Posvoler Maggid of Lithuania. My grandmother was a critic for the *Forward*. My paternal grandfather, Henry Fraenkel, was a printer, as were two of my uncles, and my paternal grandmother, Stella, was a listener. So I guess with all the writing, speaking, listening, and printing in my genetic and cultural heritage, something stuck. Thanks to my father, Dr. William A. Fraenkel, for teaching me, by his own example in the mental health field, to stand up for principles and to persevere to make the lives of less advantaged people better. Thanks also, Dad, for coming down to the basement while I was practicing drums as a teenager and asking me to stop rehearsing my exercises and play a solo. He'd say, "Just do your own thing." Thanks to both my parents for showing me firsthand what a loving couple relationship looks like and, later, sadly, what happens when things go wrong. And thanks to them for having one jazz album in their record collection that, when I heard it at age eight, hit me like a thunderbolt and inspired my career as a jazz musician.

Thanks to my wonderful sisters, Nina and Amy, who laughed at my jokes, shared my talent and love for music, and sang three-part harmonies with me in the backseat of the car on vacations, driving our parents crazy. Thanks to my talented nieces Tay, Karly, and Ally for keeping me musically current.

I have so many teachers to thank, the list could fill this book. As a high school student, I was fortunate to study with three great drum teachers at the Berklee School of Music: Dave Vose, Fred Buda, and Alan Dawson. Dave straightened out my hand technique and grounded me in the rhythmic basics. Fred taught me to be eclectic, to play any style of music from jazz to classical, and impressed on me the main role of the drummer: "to create a carpet for the other musicians to walk on." He and his wife, Meriam, also fed me a few times when, as a conservatory student with little money, my fridge was empty. Fred, you are like a second father to me, and I'm so glad you are in my life. Alan further refined my technique and my musicianship, teaching me the principles of how to create an infinite variety of rhythms and how to make my solos musical. Alan, you were like another father to me, and I miss you. All three of these teachers had relentlessly high standards for precision, which taught me to think carefully about rhythm and which rubbed off on everything else I did, including my writing. I've also been fortunate over the years to "cop" (jazz language for receive) a few lessons from other masters of the drums: Gary Chaffee, Mike Clark, Johnny Vidacovich, and the great Turkish dumbek player Bulent from Istanbul. And, of course, there are many other drummers and other musicians from whom I learned through watching performances and listening to recordings over and over—teachers from afar—to whom I am indebted. You all live inside me, and I try to do you proud each time I play. You all helped me learn the wide variety of time feels and rhythmic textures, and how to construct simple and complex rhythms—your wisdom has everything to do with this book.

Thanks to the people who taught me how to write: the great writing teacher tag-team of Ray Karras and Robert Kirk at Lexington High School in Massachusetts; Jim Nageotte and Kitty Moore, who edited a book I wrote on an entirely different subject; and Rich Simon, editor of the *Psychotherapy Networker*, who guided me to a less turgidly academic, more engaging and personal style of prose, providing much support during this process, and who also gave me the opportunity to work out these ideas over the years in articles in the *Networker* and at many Networker Symposium workshops.

Thanks to my many teachers and clinical supervisors in clinical psychology, but particularly Norman Zinberg, M.D., at Cambridge Hospital, and Irving Alexander, Ph.D., at Duke University, who taught me how to think in depth about the complex, hidden motivations of people; and Phil Costanzo, Ph.D., my doctoral advisor, who always encouraged me to add one more perspective and one more idea. And special thanks to my teachers of couple and family therapy. To Linda Carter, Ph.D., who turned me on to couple and family therapy and taught me the fundamentals during my internship at Bellevue Hospital/NYU Medical Center, and who created a postdoctoral position and then a staff position to coordinate the Family Studies Program and direct the PREP couples program there—Linda, my career and this book would never have happened without your mentorship and faith in me. To my gifted, creative supervisors Jonathan Lampert,

M.D., Gil Tunnell, Ph.D., Sam Tsemberis, Ph.D., and Ema Genijovich, Lic. And most of all, to my mentor Salvador Minuchin, M.D.—it was a privilege to train with one of the founders of the field. Thanks, Sal, for teaching me to see the deep structure of couple problem patterns underlying their manifold surface conflicts.

Thanks to my colleagues at the American Family Therapy Academy, especially Drs. Gonzalo Bacigalupe, Jay Lappin, Kaethe Weingarten, Elaine Pinderhughes, Thorana Nelson, and Don-David Lusterman, for their support when my perseverance was flagging, and to my colleagues at the Multicultural Family Therapy Institute of New Jersey for providing an environment in which we challenge ourselves to think about the impact of culture, race, class, gender, sexual orientation, and other aspects of difference that provide some families with more privilege and others with less. Thanks to Peggy Papp, M.S.W., and Evan Imber-Black, Ph.D., for helping me refine my thinking about time and rhythm in couples, and to Froma Walsh for inviting me to write a chapter on work and family for two editions of her classic book on families. To my dear friend and office mate, Esther Perel, LMFT, for unflagging encouragement and all the talks about working with couples. To Howard Markman for mentorship and friendship over many years. To Bill Pinsof, Jay Lebow, Paul Wachtel, Virginia Goldner, and Marcia Sheinberg, my fellow theoretical integrationists, who inspired me to create an approach to working with couples that brings together diverse theories to create a more comprehensive and effective approach. Thanks to Peter Steinglass, M.D., who as editor of the academic journal *Family Process* in the early 1990s had faith that I was onto something about time and couples and allowed me to go through three peer reviews to shape up my first article on the topic and finally publish it. And a special thanks to my faculty colleagues at the Ackerman Institute for the Family and at the City College of New York for providing a community of support for high standards of scholarship and teaching.

Thanks to John de Graaf and all my colleagues in the Take Back Your Time organization. It has been an inspiration and great support to have a diverse group of colleagues dedicated to finding a better balance between work and life.

To my many master's and doctoral students at CCNY, some of whom directly assisted me in compiling and digesting the varied and vast literatures that support the ideas of this book: Skye Wilson, Jane Caflish, Carrie Capstick, Stephen Anen, and Natalie Hung.

To Tenzin Dolkar and her daughters Tsering Yangkyi and Kunsang Chodon for showing me what it means to walk in peace and be a strong and happy family despite hardship.

To my filmmaker friends John Walsh and Mary Harron for friendship and encouragement in taking a risk and putting your passions out there and into art.

242

ACKNOWLEDGMENTS

To Anh-Huong, Thu Nguyen, Thich Nhat Hanh, Sister Annabelle, and David Flint for the many lessons in mindfulness.

To Sensei Bob Chillemi, my karate teacher at New York Goju Karate, for other lessons in mindfulness in action and for lessons in focus and flexibility under high speed and pressure. Ööss!

To my bandmates in two bands: Fred Moyer and Pete Tillotson of the Jazz Arts Trio; and Al Cattabiani, Jace Alexander, Bob Caputo, David Stewart, Janice Moore, and Shavonne Conroy of Daddy O—thanks for giving me the ongoing pleasure of being a drummer.

Thanks also to Pete Scattaretico, fellow drummer and owner of The Muzic Store, Inc. in my village of Dobbs Ferry, New York—that's for reading drafts of chapters and giving me another "drummer's perspective"—and thanks for the discounts on equipment!

Thanks to my agent, Jim Levine, who immediately "got" the book and is an endless source of wisdom and perspective on the writing process. Thanks to my editor at Palgrave Macmillan, Luba Ostashevsky, for believing in the project, for brilliant and persistent editing, for teaching me to drop prefaces, and for making this an interesting and engaging intellectual experience. And thanks to production editor Alan Bradshaw for infinite patience in guiding me through the final stages.

Deep thanks to all the couples I've worked with over many years, from whom I've learned and tried out these ideas and practices about time. If I've described part of your story, I've changed your names and other identifying details to preserve your anonymity and privacy.

It's customary at the end of an acknowledgments section to thank one's family for all the support and for allowing one to disappear for hours on the weekend to write. I thank my family for that, but in the spirit of this book, I also thank them for creating the work-family tension that "kept it real" and kept me motivated to finish by their impatience ("When's the book going to be DONE??"), and for still expecting me to be a husband and dad, to make dinner on the weekends, play soccer and make origami with them, help with homework once in awhile, and do my chores. So, thanks to my son, Noah, for all the fun, drumming, and soccer; to my daughter, Lena, for being such a sensitive soul and for drawing the first version of the book cover; and to my wife, Heike, for years of love, friendship, facing challenges, and the chance to learn together what it means to be in a successful longterm marriage. Heike, in the words of one of our favorite dance songs, "I Love You More Today than Yesterday."

Notes

1   Time and Rhythm

1. All names, occupations, and other identifying details have been changed for all persons described in this book to preserve anonymity.
2. See *Why We Love: The Nature and Chemistry of Romantic Love,* by H. Fisher, 2004, New York: Henry Holt.
3. "Introduction to Attachment: A Therapist's Guide to Primary Relationships and Their Renewal," by S. M. Johnson, in *Attachment Processes in Couple and Family Therapy* (pp. 3–17), ed. S. M. Johnson and V. E. Whiffen, 2003, New York: Guilford Press.
4. "Wait Time until Professional Treatment in Marital Therapy," by C. Notarius and J. Buongiorno, unpublished paper, Catholic University of America, Washington, DC.
5. "Gender and Social Structure in the Demand/Withdraw Pattern of Marital Interaction," by A. Christensen and C. L. Heavey, 1990, *Journal of Personality and Social Psychology, 59,* 73–81.
6. "The Psychology of Men and Masculinity," by R. F. Levant and C. M. Williams, in *Wiley-Blackwell Handbook of Family Psychology* (pp. 588–599), ed. J. H. Bray and M. Stanton, 2009, New York: Wiley-Blackwell.
7. *The Courage to Raise Good Men,* by O. Silverstein and B. Rashbaum, 1995, New York: Penguin Books.
8. *Women Don't Ask: The High Cost of Avoiding Negotiation—and Positive Strategies for Change,* by L. Babcock and S. Laschever, 2003, New York: Bantam-Dell.
9. "Marital Processes Predictive of Later Dissolution," by J. M. Gottman and R. W. Levenson, 1992, *Journal of Personality and Social Psychology, 63,* 221–233.
10. The one exception is a trait called neuroticism, which is basically the tendency to view the self and others critically—and no wonder, since frequent criticism tends to tear down a partner's sense of value and acceptance. See "Research on the Nature and Determinants of Marital Satisfaction: A Decade in Review," by T. N. Bradbury, F. D. Fincham, and S. R. H. Beach, 2000, *Journal of Marriage and the Family, 62,* 964–980.
11. *Fighting for Your Marriage,* by H. J. Markman, S. M. Stanley, and S. L. Blumberg, 2010 (3rd ed.), San Francisco: Jossey-Bass.
12. "The Prevention Approach to Relationship Problems," by P. Fraenkel, H. Markman, and S. Stanley, 1997, *Sexual and Marital Therapy, 12,* 249–258.
13. *Peer Marriage: How Love between Equals Really Works,* by P. Schwartz, 1994, New York: Free Press.
14. "Research on Household Labor: Modeling and Measuring the Social Embeddedness of Routine Family Work," by S. Coltrane, 2000, *Journal of Marriage and the Family, 62,* 1208–1233.
15. See *Fighting for Your Marriage,* by Markman, Stanley, and Blumberg, 2010.
16. "The Impact of Vacation and Job Stress on Burnout and Absenteeism," by M. Westman and D. Etzion, 2001, *Psychology and Health, 16,* 595–606.

2   Time in Mind

1. I'll use these three terms—time conceptions, time orientations, and time types—interchangeably to refer to these broad ideas about time. Although time *perspective*

might seem another good linguistic candidate to describe these broad ideas, that term has been used by researchers to describe whether one is primarily oriented toward the past, the present, or the future. More about time perspective in chapter 5.

2. Although overall we experience time as flowing at about the same pace day after day, a number of factors influence our perception of how quickly or slowly time passes in the moment or from one period of our lives to another. The influencing factors include our general level of arousal (the more aroused we are, especially if negatively, the faster time seems to move, and vice versa), whether we are in a state of flow (when we are deeply immersed in experience and activity, we may feel that time is not moving at all), and our age (children judge the passage of time as slower than do adults, and older adults judge time passage as more rapid than do young adults). See review in *Temporal Matters in Social Psychology: Examining the Role of Time in the Lives of Groups and Individuals* (pp. 33–38), by J. E. McGrath and F. Tschan, 2004, Washington, DC: American Psychological Association.

3. There are several excellent educational videos by the great jazz and rock drummer Steve Smith (leader of the jazz group Vital Information and longtime drummer in the pop rock band Journey) that cover the history of time-keeping in drums and that compare the different time feels of some of the greatest drummers. You don't have to be a drummer to enjoy them! *Drum Legacy: Standing on the Shoulders of Giants*, by S. Smith, 2008, New York: Hudson Music, www.hudsonmusic.com. If you're interested in seeing a demonstration by great drum masters on the subtle differences in the art of playing jazz brushes (those sticks with a set of fine wires at the end that make a swish sound), check out the video *The Art of Playing with Brushes*, by S. Smith and A. Nussbaum, 2006, New York: Hudson Music.

4. *The Times of Time: A New Perspective in Systemic Therapy and Consultation*, by L. Boscolo and P. Betrando, 1993, New York: W. W. Norton.

5. My history is not nearly as detailed or erudite as that written by the great physicist Stephen Hawking, and is quite different. It focuses on the sociology and psychology of time and how certain socioeconomic and religious forces have sponsored and privileged one conception of time over another. In Hawking's *A Brief History of Time: From the Big Bang to Black Holes* (1988, New York: Bantam Books), he focuses on the development of chronological time and the ways that physicists like Einstein have questioned the assumed lockstep progression of time into the future.

6. "Understanding Taylorism," by C. Littler, 1978, *British Journal of Sociology*, 29, 185–202.

7. More on issues around time management and work in chapter 7.

8. *The Power of a Positive No: How to Say No and Still Get to Yes*, by W. Ury, 2007, New York: Bantam Books.

9. *The Hidden Injuries of Class*, by R. Sennett and J. Cobb, 1973, New York: Vintage.

10. *A Sense of Urgency*, by J. P. Kotter, 2008, Cambridge, MA: Harvard Business Press.

11. *It's Not the BIG That Eat the SMALL . . . It's the FAST That Eat the SLOW: How to Use Speed as a Competitive Tool in Business*, by J. Jennings and L. Haughton, 2002, New York: Harper Business.

12. *Flow: The Psychology of Optimal Experience*, by M. Csíkszentmihályi, 1990, New York: Harper and Row.

13. *Ask the Children: What America's Children Really Think about Working Parents*, by E. Galinsky, 1999, New York: William Morrow.

14. "Research on Household Labor: Modeling and Measuring the Social Embeddedness of Routine Family Work," by S. Coltrane, 2000, *Journal of Marriage and the Family*, 62, 1208–1233.

15. "Money, Housework, Sex, and Conflict: Same-Sex Couples in Civil Unions, Those Not in Civil Unions, and Heterosexual Married Siblings," by S. E. Solomon, E. D. Rothblum and K. F. Balsam, 2005, *Sex Roles*, 52, 561–575.

16. *For Better: The Science of a Good Marriage,* by T. Parker-Pope, 2010, New York: Dutton.
17. "The Division of Household Labor and Wives' Happiness—Ideology, Employment, and Perceptions of Support," by D. L. Piña and V. L. Bengston, 1993, *Journal of Marriage and the Family, 55,* 901–912.
18. *Present Moment, Wonderful Moment: Mindfulness Verses for Daily Living,* by T. Nhat Hanh, 1990, Berkeley, CA: Parallax Press.
19. *Wherever You Go There You Are: Mindfulness Meditation in Everyday Life,* by J. Kabat-Zinn, 2005 (10th anniversary ed.), New York: Hyperion.
20. *The Power of Now: A Guide to Spiritual Enlightenment,* by E. Tolle, 1999, Novato, CA: New World Library.
21. *Mindfulness and Psychotherapy,* ed. C. K. Germer, R. D. Siegel, and P. R. Fulton, 2005, New York: Guilford Press. See also *Dialectical Behavior Therapy Skills Workbook: Practical DBT Exercises for Learning Mindfulness, Interpersonal Effectiveness, Emotion Regulation, & Distress Tolerance,* ed. M. McKay, J. C. Wood, and J. Brantley, 2007, Oakland, CA: New Harbinger Publications.
22. *Peace Is Every Step: The Path of Mindfulness in Everyday Life,* by T. Nhat Hanh, 1991, New York: Bantam Books.
23. "Couples' Sharing Participation in Novel and Arousing Activities and Experienced Relationship Quality," by A. Aron, C. C. Norman, E. N. Aron, C. McKenna, and R. E. Heyman, 2000, *Journal of Personality and Social Psychology, 78,* 273–284.
24. *Kaironomia: On the Will-to-Invent,* by E. C. White, 1987, Ithaca, NY: Cornell University Press.
25. *Flow,* by Csíkszentmihályi, 1990.
26. *Why We Love: The Nature and Chemistry of Romantic Love,* by H. Fisher, 2004, New York: Henry Holt.
27. "Love at First Sight or Friends First?," by D. P. H. Barelds and P. Barelds-Dijkstra, 2007, *Journal of Social and Personal Relationships, 24,* 479–496.
28. *After the Ecstasy, the Laundry: How the Heart Grows Wise on the Spiritual Path,* by J. Kornfield, 2000, New York: Bantam Books.
29. "Love at First Sight or Friends First?," by Barelds and Barelds-Dijkstra, 2007.
30. *Getting to Yes: Negotiating Agreement without Giving In,* by R. Fisher, R. L. Ury, and B. Patton, 1991 (2nd ed.), New York: Penguin.

3   *The Tortoise and the Hare*

1. *Organizing from the Inside Out,* by J. Morgenstern, 2004 (2nd ed.), New York: Henry Holt.
2. *It's Not the BIG that Eat the SMALL . . . It's the FAST that Eat the SLOW: How to Use Speed as a Competitive Tool in Business,* by J. Jennings and L. Haughton, 2002, New York: Harper Business.
3. *A Sense of Urgency,* by J. P. Kotter, 2008, Boston: Harvard Business Press.
4. *Slow Is Beautiful: New Visions of Community, Leisure and Joie de Vivre,* by C. Andrews, 2006, Gabriola Island, B.C., Canada: New Society Publishers.
5. *In Praise of Slowness: How a Worldwide Movement Is Challenging the Cult of Speed,* by C. Honoré, 2004, New York: HarperCollins.
6. *Temporal Matters in Social Psychology: Examining the Role of Time in the Lives of Groups and Individuals,* by J. E. McGrath and F. Tschan, 2004, Washington, DC: American Psychological Association.
7. *Faster: The Acceleration of Just about Everything,* by J. Gleick, 1999, New York: Pantheon.
8. "Attention and the Evolution of Hollywood Film," by J. E. Cutting, J. E. DeLong, and C. E. Nothelfer, 2010, *Psychological Science, 21,* 432–439.

9. *American Mania: When More Is Not Enough,* by P. C. Whybrow, 2005, New York: W. W. Norton.

10. *The Long Shadow of Temperament,* by J. Kagan and N. Snidman, 2009, Cambridge, MA: Belknap Press of Harvard University Press.

11. "Temperament and Emotion," by J. E. Bates, J. A. Goodnight, and J. E. Fite, in *Handbook of Emotions* (3rd ed.) (pp. 485–496), ed. M. Lewis, J. M. Haviland-Jones, and L. Feldman Barrett, 2008, New York: Guilford Press.

12. "Emotion Regulation: Conceptual Foundations," by J. J. Gross and R. A. Thompson, in *Handbook of Emotion Regulation* (pp. 3–24), ed. J. J. Gross, 2007, New York: Guilford Press.

13. *Handbook of Attachment: Theory, Research, and Clinical Applications* (2nd ed.), ed. J. Cassidy and P. R. Shaver, 2008, New York: Guilford Press.

14. Other drummers say the same: See John Riley's *The Art of Bop Drumming,* 1994, Miami, FL: Manhattan Music Publications.

15. There are many wonderful, practical books by Thich Nhat Hanh. Excellent introductions to the practices of mindful breathing, walking, eating, and other daily practices are *Being Peace,* 1987/1996, Berkeley, CA: Parallax Press; and *Peace Is Every Step: The Path of Mindfulness in Everyday Life,* 1991, New York: Bantam Books.

16. *Wherever You Go There You Are,* by J. Kabat-Zinn, 2005 (10th anniversary ed.), New York: Hyperion; also by Kabat-Zinn, *Guided Mindfulness Meditation,* 2004, Lexington, MA: Stress Reduction CDs and Tapes.

17. One issue we'll discuss in chapter 8 is the negative effects of overwork on sexual arousal and intimacy. See also *Mating in Captivity: Reconciling the Erotic and the Domestic,* by E. Perel, 2006, New York: HarperCollins.

18. See chapter 7 in Carl Honoré's *In Praise of Slowness* for a humorous and informative inside view of Tantric sex courses.

4 *Syncing Your Relationship Rhythms*

1. Interview with Shelly Manne, *Downbeat Magazine,* 1964, quoted in *The Art of Bop Drumming* (p. 9), by J. Riley, 1994, Miami, FL: Manhattan Music Publications.

2. *Webster's New Collegiate Dictionary,* 1976, Springfield, MA: G. & C. Merriam.

3. "Comments on the Significance of Interaction Rhythms," by A. E. Sheflen, in *Interaction Rhythms: Periodicity in Communicative Behavior* (p. 14), ed. M. Davis, 1982, New York: Human Sciences Press.

4. "Rhythms of Dialogue in Infancy," by J. Jaffe, B. Beebe, S. Feldstein, C. L. Crown, and M. D. Jasnow, 2001, *Monographs of the Society for Research in Child Development, Series 264, vol. 66,* 1–132.

5. "The Cross-cultural Variation of Rhythmic Style," by A. Lomax, in *Interaction Rhythms* (pp. 149–174), ed. M. Davis, 1982. Also see *Cantometrics: An Approach to the Anthropology of Music,* by A. Lomax, 1976, Berkeley, CA: University of California Extension Media Center.

6. "Temporal Patterning in the Family," by R. E. Cromwell, B. P. Keeney, and B. N. Adams, 1976, *Family Process, 15,* 343–348.

7. I wrote what is widely considered the first comprehensive scientific article on couples and rhythm: "Time and Rhythm in Couples," by P. Fraenkel, 1994, *Family Process, 33,* 37–51. My other academic articles on the topic include: "The Rhythms of Couplehood: Using Time as a Resource for Change," by P. Fraenkel, 1996, *The Family Therapy Networker, 20,* 65–77. "Time and Couples, Part I: The Decompression Chamber," by P. Fraenkel, in *101 Interventions in Family Therapy, vol II* (pp. 140–144), ed. T. Nelson and T. Trepper, 1998, West Hazleton, PA: Haworth Press. "Time and Couples, Part II: The Sixty Second Pleasure Point," by P. Fraenkel, in *101 Interventions in Family Therapy, vol II* (p. 145–149), ed. T. Nelson and T. Trepper, 1998,

West Hazleton, PA: Haworth Press. "Getting a Kick out of You: The Jazz Taoist Key to Love," by P. Fraenkel, in *Why Do Fools Fall in Love* (pp. 61–66), ed. J. Levine and H. Markman, 2001, San Francisco: Jossey-Bass. "The Beeper in the Bedroom: Technology has become a Therapeutic Issue," by P. Fraenkel, 2001, *The Psychotherapy Networker*, 25, 22–29, 64–65. "The Place of Time in Couple and Family Therapy," by P. Fraenkel, in *Minding the Time in Family Experience: Emerging Perspectives and Issues* (pp. 283–310), ed. K. J. Daly, 2001, London: JAI. "Clocks, Calendars, and Couples: Time and the Rhythms of Relationships," by P. Fraenkel and S. Wilson, in *Couples on the Fault Line: New Directions for Therapists* (pp. 63–103), ed. P. Papp, 2000, New York: Guilford Press.

8. "Time and Rhythm in Couples," by Fraenkel, 1994.
9. "A Chronography of Conversation: In Defense of an Objective Approach," by S. Feldstein and J. Welkowitz, in *Nonverbal Behavior and Communication* (pp. 435–439), ed. A. W. Siegman and S. Feldstein, 1987 (2nd ed.), Hillsdale, NJ: Lawrence Erlbaum Associates.
10. There is a large literature on the relationship of chronobiology to physical and mental health. Some of the early classics: *Body Time: The Natural Rhythms of the Body*, by G. G. Luce, 1973, St. Albans, England: Paladin; *Body Clock: The Effects of Time on Human Health*, by M. Hughes, 1989, Abingdon Oxon, England: Andromeda Oxford; "Rhythms in Human Performance: 1-½ Hour Oscillations in Cognitive Style," by R. Klein and R. Armitage, 1979, *Science, 204,* 1326–1328; "Implications of the Rest-Activity Cycle: Implications for Organizing Activity," by N. Kleitman, in *Sleep and Dreaming* (pp. 46–73), ed. E. Hartmann, 1970, Boston: Little, Brown; *Biological Rhythms and Mental Disorders*, by D. Kupfer, T. Monk, and J. Barchas, 1988, New York: Guilford Press.
11. *The 20-Minute Break: Reduce Stress, Maximize Performance, and Improve Health and Emotional Well-being Using the New Science of Ultradian Rhythms* (p. 14), by E. Rossi, 1991, Los Angeles: Jeremy P. Tarcher.
12. These levels overlap with but are not identical to the micro, molar, and macro human interaction rhythms I describe later. For instance, within the broad chronobiological category of ultradian rhythms are those I'd categorize as micro, lasting milliseconds to seconds, as well as molar activities that last minutes to hours but are shorter than the circadian 24-hour cycle.
13. *The 20-Minute Break*, by Rossi, 1991.
14. *The Clocks That Time Us*, by M. C. Moore-Ede, F. M. Sulzman, and C. A. Fuller, 1982, Cambridge, MA: Harvard University Press.
15. "Nonstandard Work Schedules and Marital Instability," by H. B. Presser, 2000, *Journal of Marriage and Family, 62,* 93–110.
16. *The Sabbath: Its Meaning for Modern Man*, by A. Heschel, 1951, New York: Farrar, Straus and Giroux.
17. "A Review of 50 Years of Research on Naturally Occurring Family Routines and Rituals: Cause for Celebration?," by B. H. Fiese, T. J. Tomcho, M. Douglas, K. Josephs, S. Poltrock, and T. Baker, 2002, *Journal of Family Psychology, 16,* 381–390.
18. *Black Families in Therapy: Understanding the African American Experience*, by N. Boyd-Franklin, 2003 (2nd ed.), New York: Guilford Press.
19. "A Review of 50 Years of Research on Naturally Occurring Family Routines and Rituals," by Fiese et al., 2002. See also "Family Time and Routines Index (FTRI)," by H. I. McCubbin, M. A. McCubbin, and A. I. Thompson, 1996, in H. I. McCubbin, A. I. Thompson, and M. A. McCubbin, *Family Assessment: Resiliency, Coping and Adaptation—Inventories for Research and Practice* (pp. 325–340), Madison: University of Wisconsin System.
20. "Who Took My Hot Sauce? Regulating Emotion in the Context of Family Routines and Rituals," by B. Fiese, in *Emotion Regulation in Couples and Families: Pathways to Dysfunction and Health* (pp. 269–290), ed. D. K. Snyder, J. Simpson, and J. N. Hughes, 2006, Washington, DC: American Psychological Association.

21. "Organizing Principles of Interaction from Infant Research and the Lifespan Prediction of Attachment: Application to Adult Treatment," by B. Beebe and F. Lachmann, 2002, *JicaP, 2 (4)*, 61–89.
22. *The Evolution of Useful Things*, by H. Petroski, 1992, New York, Vintage Books; *Success through Failure: The Paradox of Design*, by H. Petroski, 2006, Princeton, NJ: Princeton University Press.
23. "The Contribution of Couple Leisure Involvement, Leisure Time, and Leisure Satisfaction to Marital Satisfaction," by H. A. Johnson, R. B. Zabriskie, and B. Hill, 2006, *Marriage and Family Review, 40*, 69–91.
24. "Parent and Child Perspectives of Family Leisure Involvement and Satisfaction with Family Life," by R. B. Zabriskie and B. P. McCormick, 2003, *Journal of Leisure Research, 35*, 163–189.
25. "An Investigation of Life Satisfaction Following a Vacation: A Domain-Specific Approach," by L. L. Hoopes and J. W. Lounsbury, 1989, *Journal of Community Psychology, 17*, 129–140; "Moderating Effects of Vacation on Reactions to Work and Domestic Stress," by G. Strauss-Blasche, C. Ekmekcioglu, and W. Marktl, 2002, *Leisure Sciences, 24*, 237–249.
26. "Molar" is a term commonly used in anthropology to describe midrange-length activities. In the current context, it has nothing to do with your teeth, or with its use in economics. Weird word, but that's science jargon for you!
27. These levels overlap with the three levels discussed earlier that have been identified by chronobiologists. However, the micro and molar rhythms would both be examples of what chronobiologists call ultradian, while macro rhythms include both circadian (daily) and infradian (weekly, monthly, and yearly) rhythms.

5   Time Perspective

1. "Putting Time in Perspective: A Valid, Reliable Individual-Differences Metric," by P. G. Zimbardo and J. N. Boyd, 1999, *Journal of Personality and Social Psychology, 77*, 1271–1288 (quotation is from p. 1271).
2. See Barbara Ehrenreich's book *Bright-Sided: How the Relentless Promotion of Positive Thinking Has Undermined America* (2009, New York: Metropolitan Books) for an excellent description and trenchant critique of the belief in the power of positive thinking to affect health, career, economic, and other concrete outcomes.
3. See the wonderfully poignant poem by Langston Hughes entitled "Montage of a Dream Deferred," in which he asks, "What happens to a dream deferred? Does it dry up like a raisin in the sun?," *Selected Poems of Langston Hughes* (p. 268), by L. Hughes, 1959, New York: Vintage Books.
4. *Mindfulness and Psychotherapy*, ed. C. K. Germer, R. D. Siegel, and P. R. Fulton, 2005, New York: Guilford Press.
5. "Relationships between Mindfulness Practice and Levels of Mindfulness, Medical and Psychological Symptoms and Well-Being in a Mindfulness-Based Stress Reduction Program," by J. Carmody and R. A. Baer, 2008, *Journal of Behavioral Medicine, 31*, 23–33.
6. "The Influence of a Sense of Time on Human Development," by L. L. Carstensen, 2006, *Science, 312*, 1913–1915.
7. "Sacrifice as a Predictor of Marital Outcomes," by S. M. Stanley, S. W. Whitton, S. L. Sadberry, M. L. Clements, and H. J. Markman, 2006, *Family Process, 45*, 289–303.
8. "If I Help My Partner, Will It Hurt Me? Perceptions of Sacrifice in Romantic Relationships," by S. W. Whitton, S. M. Stanley, and H. J. Markman, 2007, *Journal of Social and Clinical Psychology, 26*, 64–92.

6   *Resolving Struggles about Punctuality*

1. "Who Is Late and Who Is Early? Big Five Personality Factors and Punctuality in Attending Psychological Experiments," by M. D. Back, S. C. Schmukle, and B. Egloff, 2006, *Journal of Research in Personality, 40,* 841–848 (quote from p. 842).

2. I am using the terms Generally Punctual Partner (GPP) and Rarely Punctual Partner (RPP) because it's the rare person who is always or never punctual. Rather, the differences are a matter of degree and context: A person may be frequently late in social situations or, more specifically, when it comes to meeting up with his partner, but on time for work; the partner who is almost always punctual for meetings with her mate may not be as concerned with being punctual for large parties.

3. "Family-of-Origin Frames in Couples Therapy," by R. Gerson, S. Hoffman, M. Sauls, and D. Ulrici, 1993, *Journal of Marital and Family Therapy, 19,* 341–354.

4. "Determinants of Employee Punctuality," by M. Dishon-Berkovits and M. Koslowsky, 2002, *Journal of Social Psychology, 142,* 723–739.

5. "Who Is Late and Who Is Early?," Back et al., 2006.

6. "A Meta-analytically Derived Nomological Network of Procrastination," by W. Van Eerde, 2003, *Personality and Individual Differences, 35,* 1401–1418.

7. "Why Not Procrastinate? Development and Validation of a New Active Procrastination Scale," by J. N. Choi and S. V. Moran, 2009, *Journal of Social Psychology, 149,* 195–211.

8. "Who Is Late and Who Is Early?," Back et al., 2006.

9. A large body of research has demonstrated that negative attributions about one's partner's behavior are among the strongest predictors of relationship distress and dissolution. See, for instance, "Research on the Nature and Determinants of Marital Satisfaction: A Decade in Review," by T. N. Bradbury, F. D. Fincham, and S. R. H. Beach, 2000, *Journal of Marriage and the Family, 62,* 964–980; and a classic first review, "Attributions in Marriage: Review and Critique," by T. N. Bradbury and F. D. Fincham, 1990, *Journal of Personality and Social Psychology, 107,* 3–33.

10. "Love at First Sight or Friends First?," by D. P. H. Barelds and P. Barelds-Dijkstra, 2007, *Journal of Social and Personal Relationships, 24,* 479–496.

11. "Only the Congruent Survive: Personality Similarities in Couples," by B. Rammstedt and J. Schupp, 2008, *Personality and Individual Differences, 45,* 533–535.

12. *A Geography of Time,* by R. Levine, 1997, New York: Basic Books.

13. Levine assessed the average "pace of life" of large cities in 31 countries through three measures: (1) surreptitiously timing people's average speed of walking alone for 60 feet on a flat, unobstructed, uncrowded, and sufficiently broad sidewalk on a clear summer day; (2) timing the speed with which it took postal clerks to respond to a request for stamps; and (3) documenting the accuracy of 15 randomly selected bank clocks as compared to an accurate indicator of the time. From these combined assessments, the top-paced countries were Switzerland, Ireland, and Germany; slowest paced were Brazil, Indonesia, and Mexico. It's important to note that Levine uses the term "pace of life" more broadly than I do. He defines pace of life as ". . . the flow or movement of time that people experience" (p. 3). Tempo, or the actual speed with which activities are conducted, he considers one component of the overall pace of life, which also includes the sense of the flow of time, rhythms (for instance, the pattern of work time and nonwork time), sequences (the typical order of activities), and synchronies (the degree to which people and their activities are connected in time). I use the term "life pace" to denote speed or tempo of activities. As you've seen in previous chapters, I consider rhythms to be different from pace (since rhythms can be carried out at different paces or tempos) and sequences to be one component of rhythm. I consider "synchronies" as the issue of whether people are linked in their rhythms.

14. *The Maria Paradox,* by R. M. Gil and C. I. Vazquez, 2002, New York: Random House.

15. *Acceptance and Change in Couple Therapy: A Therapist's Guide to Transforming Relationships,* by A. Christensen and N. S. Jacobson, 1998, New York: W. W. Norton.

7 *The Great Juggling Act, Part I*

1. "Time Clocks: Work Hour Strategies," by P. Moen and S. Sweet, in *It's about Time: Couples and Careers,* ed. P. Moen, 2003, Ithaca, NY: Cornell University Press.

2. "Why Study Working Families?," by B. Schneider and L. J. Waite, in *Being Together, Working Apart: Dual Career Families and the Work-Life Balance* (pp. 3–17), ed. B. Schneider and L. J. Waite, 2005, Cambridge: Cambridge University Press. Schneider and Waite write in their introduction to their report on a national study of 500 families, "Nearly all mothers and fathers report conflicts between work and family, and when these conflicts occur, the family is more likely to suffer than work. For most working parents, trade-offs and compromises between family and work obligations appear to be unavoidable" (p. 7).

3. *The Three Faces of Work-Family Conflict: The Poor, the Professionals, and the Missing Middle,* by J. C. Williams and H. Boushey, 2010, Washington, DC: Center for American Progress; *Families That Work: Policies for Reconciling Parenthood and Employment,* by J. C. Gornick and M. K. Meyers, 2003, New York: Russell Sage Foundation.

4. *Work to Live,* by J. Robinson, 2003, New York: Penguin Putnam.

5. *The Power of Full Engagement: Managing Energy, Not Time, Is the Key to High Performance and Personal Renewal* (p. 5), by J. Loehr and T. Schwartz, 2003, New York: Free Press.

6. *Families That Work,* by Gornick and Meyers, 2003.

7. *Parental Leave Policies in 21 Countries: Assessing Generosity and Gender,* by R. Ray, J. C. Gornick, and J. Schmitt, 2008, revised June 2009, Washington, DC: Center for Economic and Policy Research, retrieved May 22, 2010, from http://www.lisproject.org/publications/parentwork/parent-leave-report.pdf; "Case for Paid Family Leave: Why the United States Should Follow Australia's Lead," by L. Daly, *Newsweek,* Aug. 3, 2009, retrieved June 6, 2010, from http://www.newsweek.com/id/210252.

8. "Family and Medical Leave: Evidence from the 2000 Surveys," by J. Waldfogel, 2001, *Monthly Labor Review, 19,* 19–20.

9. *A Detailed Look at Parental Leave Policies in 21 OECD Countries,* by R. Ray, Sept. 2008, Washington, DC: Center for Economic and Policy Research, retrieved May 22, 2010, from http://www.emplaw.co.uk/content/index?startpage=data/20033221.htm. In her recent book, leading work-family legal scholar Joan Williams argues trenchantly that the male-centered culture of work and the general culture of heterosexual maleness that keeps men from more fully acting on desires to fulfill more equitable roles must change if greater work-family balance is to be achieved for both men and women. *Reshaping the Work-Family Debate: Why Men and Class Matter,* by J. C. Williams, 2010, Cambridge, MA: Harvard University Press.

10. *The Three Faces of Work-Family Conflict,* by Williams and Boushey, 2010. See also *Families That Work,* by Gornick and Meyers, 2003.

11. *Working Fathers: New Strategies for Balancing Work and Family* (pp. 16–17), by J. A. Levine and T. L. Pittinsky, 1997, New York: Harcourt Brace.

12. "Time Strains and Psychological Well-Being: Do Dual-Earner Mothers and Fathers Differ?," by K. M. Nomaguchi, M. A. Milkie, and S. M. Bianchi, 2005, *Journal of Family Issues, 26,* 756–792.

13. *Handbook of Attachment: Theory, Research, and Clinical Applications,* ed. J. Cassidy and P. R. Shaver, 2008 (2nd ed.), New York: Guilford Press.

14. *In Praise of Idleness,* by B. Russell, 2001, London: Routledge.

15. See http://www.timeday.org/right2vacation/care.asp.

16. *Overwork in America: When the Way We Work Becomes Too Much* (p. 7), by E. Galinsky, J. T. Bond, S. S. Kim, L. Backon, E. Brownfield, and K. Sakai, 2005, New York: Families and Work Institute.

17. Ibid., p. 7.

18. Ibid., p. 7.

19. Ibid., p. 8. A survey by Andersen Consulting found 63 percent of vacationing workers had contact with their main office through cell phones, pagers, voicemail, and laptops. "On the Next Vacation, Don't Forget the Laptop," by K. O'Brien, *New York Times,* Sept. 20, 2000, p. G1.
20. *Overwork in America* (pp. 8–9), by Galinsky et al., 2005.
21. The Families and Work Survey (*Overwork in America,* p. 9, by Galinsky et al., 2005) found that the 20 percent of employees who frequently work during nonwork hours are most likely to work on vacations.
22. *Overwork in America* (p. 8), by Galinsky et al., 2005; "When Work Interferes with Life: The Social Distribution of Work-Nonwork Interference and the Influence of Work-Related Demands and Resources," by S. Schieman, M. A. Milkie, and P. Glavin, 2009, *American Sociological Review, 74,* 966–988.
23. An enormous literature documents what sociologists and psychologists refer to as work-family conflict and work-life spillover. In addition to the other references for this chapter, a few prominent research articles specifically on couples are "The Contagion of Stress across Multiple Roles," by N. Bolger, A. DeLongis, R. C. Kessler, and E. Wethington, 1989, *Journal of Marriage and the Family, 51,* 175–183; "Effects of Daily Workload on Subsequent Behavior During Marital Interaction: The Roles of Social Withdrawal and Spouse Support," by R. L. Repetti, 1989, *Journal of Personality and Social Psychology, 57,* 651–659; and "Stress Crossover in Newlywed Marriage: A Longitudinal and Dyadic Perspective," by L. A. Neff and B. R. Karney, 2007, *Journal of Marriage and Family, 69,* 594–607. See also my recent chapter on work-family balance: "Contemporary Two-Parent Families: Navigating Work and Family Challenges," by P. Fraenkel and C. Capstick, in *Normal Family Processes* (4th ed.), ed. F. Walsh, 2011, New York: Guilford Press.
24. "Work-Family Conflict and Marital Quality: Mediating Processes," by L. S. Matthews, R. D. Conger, and K. A. S. Wickrama, 1996, *Social Psychology Quarterly, 59,* 62–79.
25. "Association Between Everyday Stress, Critical Life Events, and Sexual Problems," by G. Bodenmann, T. Ledermann, D. Blattner, and C. Galluzo, 2006, *The Journal of Nervous and Mental Disease, 194,* 494–501. See also "Sexual Compatibility and the Sexual Desire-motivation Relation in Females with Hypoactive Sexual Desire Disorder," by D. F. Hurlbert, C. Apt, M. K. Hurlbert, and A. P. Pierce, 2000, *Behavior Modification, 24,* 325–347.
26. "Stress, Communication, and Marital Quality in Couples," by T. Ledermann, G. Bodenmann, M. Rudaz, and T. N. Bradbury, 2010, *Family Relations, 59,* 195–206. See also "Economic Stressors," by T. M. Probst, in *Handbook of Work Stress* (pp. 267–297), ed. J. Barling, E. K. Kelloway, and M. R. Frone, 2005, Thousand Oaks, CA: Sage.
27. "Stress and Coping among Stable-Satisfied, Stable-Distressed and Separated/Divorced Swiss Couples: A 5-Year Prospective Longitudinal Study," by G. Bodenmann and A. Cina, 2006, *Journal of Divorce and Remarriage, 44,* 71–89. See also "Associations of Stressful Life Events and Marital Quality," by L. M. Williams, 1995, *Psychological Reports, 76,* 1115–1122. And for a comprehensive review of research, see "Understanding Marriage and Stress: Essential Questions and Challenges," by L. B. Story and T. N. Bradbury, 2004, *Clinical Psychology Review, 23,* 1139–1162.
28. "Linking Economic Hardship to Marital Quality and Instability," by R. D. Conger, G. H. Elder, Jr., F. O. Lorenz, K. J. Conger, R. L. Simons, L. B. Whitbeck, S. Huck, and J. N. Melby, 1990, *Journal of Marriage and the Family, 52,* 643–656.
29. "Stress, Sex, and Satisfaction in Marriage," by G. Bodenmann, T. Ledermann, and T. N. Bradbury, 2007, *Personal Relationships, 14,* 551–569.
30. See Organization for Economic Co-operation and Development (OECD), "OECD Stat Extracts, Average Annual Hours Actually Worked per Worker," retrieved May 12, 2010, from http://stats.oecd.org/Index.aspx?DatasetCode=ANHRS (sortable data showing U.S. among top 11 countries with longest work hours and longer work hours than Japan, each year from 2000 to 2008). "Death by Overwork in Japan, Jobs for Life," *The Economist,* Dec. 19, 2007, retrieved June 10, 2010, from http://www.economist.com/world/asia/displaystory.cfm?STORY_ID=10329261.

31. "Are Americans Really Abject Workaholics?," by R. Arora, Oct. 5, 2004, Gallup Poll Tuesday Briefing, 1–4.

32. Recent statistics from the ILO suggest that Great Britain may have usurped the U.S. as the Western world's leader in overwork. "Britons Top Poll for Longest Working Hours in Developed World," June 7, 2007, *Mail Online,* retrieved May 16, 2010, from http://www.dailymail.co.uk/news/article-460600/Britons-poll-working-hours-developed-world.html.

33. "Average Annual Hours Actually Worked per Worker," OECD Stat Extracts, retrieved Oct. 11, 2010 from http://stats.oecd.org/Index.aspx?DataSetCode=ANHRS.

34. "So Much Work, So Little Time," by S. Greenhouse, *New York Times,* Sept. 5, 1999, p. 1. See also *The Overworked American,* by J. B. Schor, 1991, New York: Basic Books.

35. "Work and Family in the 1990s," by M. Perry-Jenkins, R. L. Repetti, and A. C. Crouter, 2000, *Journal of Marriage and the Family, 62,* 981–998; "Work and Family Research in the First Decade of the 21st Century," by S. M. Bianchi and M. A. Milkie, 2010, *Journal of Marriage and Family, 72,* 705–725.

36. "Job Loss and Depressive Symptoms in Couples: Common Stressors, Stress Transmission, or Relationship Disruption?," by G. Howe, M. Levy, and R. Caplan, 2004, *Journal of Family Psychology, 18,* 639–650.

37. Jerry Jacobs and Kathleen Gerson offer statistics indicating little change in the length of the work week from 1960 until 2000. They argue that the increase in overall work hours for families is due to increased annual work hours for women (more weeks a year, rather than more hours per week). See *The Time Divide: Work, Family, and Gender Inequality,* by J. A. Jacobs and K. Gerson, 2004, Cambridge, MA: Harvard University Press.

38. *Highlights of the 2002 National Study of the Changing Workforce,* by J. T. Bond, C. Thompson, E. Galinsky, and D. Prottas, 2003 (No. 3), New York: Families and Work Institute.

39. "Overworked Individuals or Overworked Families? Explaining Trends in Work, Leisure, and Family Time," by J. A. Jacobs and K. Gerson, 2001, *Work and Occupations, 28,* 40–63 (quote from p. 46).

40. For excellent books on research about the factors that best predict happiness, see *The Happiness Hypothesis: Finding Modern Truth in Ancient Wisdom,* by J. Haidt, 2006, New York: Basic Books; *Stumbling on Happiness,* by D. Gilbert, 2007, New York: Vintage Books; *Psychology and Consumer Culture: The Struggle for a Good Life in a Materialistic World,* ed. T. Kasser and A. D. Kanner, 2004, Washington, DC: American Psychological Association.

41. *Overwork in America,* by Galinsky et al., 2005.

42. *Being Together, Working Apart* (p. 7), ed. Schneider and Waite, 2005.

43. *Highlights of the 2002 National Study of the Changing Workforce,* by Bond et al., 2003.

44. *Overwork in America* (p. 4), by Galinsky et al., 2005.

45. No, that's not a typo—sometimes it's just impossible to "grin" and bear it, and instead we have to harness our toughness, our true grit, to get through quite difficult periods at work. It's a jungle out there!

46. Books that provide step-by-step guides to negotiating for changes in work schedules, maternity or paternity leave, flextime, vacation, and other aspects of work time are *Ask For It: How Women Can Use the Power of Negotiation to Get What They Really Want,* by L. Babcock and S. Laschever, 2008, New York: Bantam Books; *Working Fathers,* by Levine and Pittinsky, 1997: *Work to Live,* by Robinson, 2003.

47. *Being Together, Working Apart* (p. 8), ed. Schneider and Waite, 2005.

48. "Individual Differences in Utilizing Control to Cope with Job Demands: Effects on Susceptibility to Infectious Disease," by J. Schaubroeck, J. R. Jones, and J. L. Xie, 2001, *Journal of Applied Psychology, 86,* 265–278. See also "When Work Interferes with Life," by Schieman et al., 2009.

49. *Temporal Matters in Social Psychology: Examining the Role of Time in the Lives of Groups and Individuals* (p. 69), by J. E. McGrath and F. Tschan, 2004, Washington, DC: American Psychological Association.

50. *Overwork in America* (p. 4), by Galinsky et al., 2005.

51. "Executive Control of Cognitive Processes in Task Switching," by J. S. Rubinstein, D. E. Meyer, and J. E. Evans, 2001, *Journal of Experimental Psychology: Human Perception and Performance, 27,* 763–797.

52. *Peace Is Every Step: The Path of Mindfulness in Everyday Life,* by T. Nhat Hanh, 1991, New York: Bantam Books.

53. "The Beeper in the Bedroom: Technology Has Become a Therapeutic Issue," by P. Fraenkel, 2001, *The Psychotherapy Networker, 25,* 22–65.

54. "Home Is Where the Office Is," by N. A. Ruhling, *American Demographics,* June 2000, 54–60. Ruhling estimates that in 2000, 21 million people worked at home and that by 2020, at least 40 percent of the American workforce will be telecommuters or home-office workers.

55. "A Wild Ride on the Swivel Chair," by L. Belkin, *New York Times,* Sept. 29, 1999, p. G1. Although advertisements for items related to home offices always depict smiling parents working away with their kids happily looking on (or working at an adjoining desk on their own computer), many home-office parents describe even more intense problems balancing their work and family time than when they worked in out-of-home offices. The physical boundary and commute between the workplace and home previously allowed a greater degree of regulation of the work-family boundary. When the office moves to the home, the temporal boundary becomes increasingly central, but it can be extremely challenging to maintain this boundary when pressure mounts to complete projects or to make "just a few" more phone calls.

56. "Foreign Affairs; Cyber-Serfdom," by T. L. Friedman, *New York Times,* Jan. 30, 2001, p. A23.

57. *Overwork in America* (p. 5), by Galinsky et al., 2005.

58. *Faster: The Acceleration of Just about Everything,* by J. Gleick, 1999, New York: Pantheon Books.

59. *The Time Divide,* by Jacobs and Gerson, 2004.

60. "Recovery, Well-Being, and Performance-Related Outcomes: The Role of Workload and Vacation Experiences," by C. Fritz and S. Sonnetag, 2006, *Journal of Applied Psychology, 91,* 936–945.

61. *The Clocks That Time Us,* by M. C. Moore-Ede, F. M. Sulzman, and C. A. Fuller, 1982, Cambridge, MA: Harvard University Press.

62. "The Job Demands-Resources Model of Burnout," by E. Demerouti, A. B. Bakker, F. Nachreiner, and W. B. Schaufeli, 2001, *Journal of Applied Psychology, 86,* 499–512; "Understanding Burnout: Work and Family Issues," by C. Maslach, in *From Work-Family Balance to Work-Family Interaction: Changing the Metaphor* (pp. 99–114), ed. D. F. Halpern and S. E. Murphy, 2005, Mahwah, NJ: Laurence Erlbaum Associates.

63. Few ideas are truly, completely new. Certainly not one that makes as much practical sense as using one's commuting to wind down. I want to acknowledge that among their many other great suggestions for achieving work-life balance, Jim Levine and Todd Pittinsky mentioned this one in their book *Working Fathers.* I know I won't get sued by these authors for plagiarizing their material—first, because I am citing it and including it in my list of sources; second, I must admit that I only recently read their book, published in 1997, and I have been writing about my ideas for work-life balance independently for many years. But third, and best of all for me, Jim is my literary agent!

64. See *Peace Is Every Step,* by Nhat Hanh, 1991.

8 *The Great Juggling Act, Part II*

1. *Work to Live,* by J. Robinson, 2003, New York: Penguin Putnam.

2. "Dual-Centric: A New Concept of Work Life," by E. Galinsky, executive summary of *Leaders in a Global Economy,* by E. Galinsky et al., 2008, New York: Families and Work

Institute, retrieved May 22, 2010, from http://familiesandwork.org/site/research/reports/dual-centric.pdf.

3. A doctoral student of mine, Mark Horney, took a first step in this research direction with his 2006 dissertation, "Organization Men: A Qualitative Study of Personal and Professional Issues among Male MBA Students," *Dissertation Abstracts International*, 67, no. 01B (2006): p. 546.

4. *Why We Love: The Nature and Chemistry of Romantic Love*, by H. Fisher, 2004, New York: Henry Holt.

5. "Nowhere, U.S.A.," by R. Rayner, *New York Times Magazine*, March 8, 1998, p. 27; *The Power of Commitment*, by S. Stanley, 2005, San Francisco: Jossey-Bass; *Mating in Captivity: Unlocking Erotic Intelligence*, by E. Perel, 2006, New York: HarperCollins.

6. "Do You Go to Work Sick?," by K. Lorenz, Sept. 2007, retrieved May 9, 2010, from http://www.careerbuilder.com/Article/CB-755-The-Workplace-Do-You-Go-to-Work-Sick. See also Society for Human Resource Management, SHRM® Special Expertise Panels 2005 Trends Report, retrieved May 9, 2010, from http://shrm.org/Research/FutureWorkplaceTrends/Documents/05FullPanelTrendsReport.pdf.

7. "Reconsidering Work Time: A Multivariate Longitudinal Within-Couple Analysis," by R. C. Barnett, K. C. Gareis, and R. T. Brennan, 2009, *Community, Work & Family*, 12, 105–133. Most studies find greater negative spillover from work to family than from family to work. "Spillover," by P. V. Roehling, P. Moen, and R. Batt, in *It's about Time: Couples and Careers* (pp. 101–121), ed. P. Moen, 2003, Ithaca, NY: Cornell University Press.

8. "Associations between Marital Distress and Work Loss in a National Sample," by M. S. Forthofer, H. J. Markman, M. Cox, S. Stanley, and R. C. Kessler, 1996, *Journal of Marriage and the Family*, 58, 597–605. As reported by J. C. Williams and H. Boushey: "Extensive research documents that the mismatch between work and life today leads to very high and very expensive levels of absenteeism and attrition as well as to decreases in productivity. Indeed, the 'business case for workplace flexibility' is extensively documented at the microeconomic level . . . Replacing these workers is extremely costly, given that replacing workers earning less than $75,000 costs 22 percent of their annual salary. Research suggests that the turnover rate for employees who lack the flexibility they need is twice that of those who have it" (p. 5). *The Three Faces of Work-Family Conflict: The Poor, the Professionals, and the Missing Middle*, 2010, Washington, DC: Center for American Progress. See also "One Sick Child Away from Being Fired: When 'Opting-Out' is Not an Option," by J. C. Williams, 2006, Center for Work-Life Law, University of California, Hastings College of the Law, pp. 25–30, retrieved May 20, 2010, from http://www.worklifelaw.org/pubs/OneSickChild.pdf.

9. "Women, Men, Work, and Family," by R. C. Barnett and J. S. Hyde, 2001, *American Psychologist*, 56, 781–796. See also *She Works/He Works: How Two-Income Families Are Happy, Healthy, and Thriving*, by R. C. Barnett and C. Rivers, 1996, Cambridge, MA: Harvard University Press; *Times Are Changing: Gender and Generation at Work and at Home: The 2008 National Study of the Changing Workforce*, by E. Galinsky, K. Aumann, and J. T. Bond, 2009, New York: Families & Work Institute; *The Unfinished Revolution: How a New Generation Is Reshaping Family, Work, and Gender in America*, by K. Gerson, 2010, New York: Oxford University Press.

10. *Ask the Children: What America's Children Really Think about Working Parents*, by E. Galinsky, 1999, New York: William Morrow.

11. "Work Demands of Dual-Earner Couples: Implications for Parents' Knowledge about Children's Daily Lives in Middle Childhood," by M. F. Bumpus, A. C. Crouter, and S. M. McHale, 1999, *Journal of Marriage and the Family*, 61, 465–475.

12. Jane C. Gornick and Marcia K. Meyers have proposed reforming work-family policies so that we can attain what they call a "dual-earner-dual-career society," in which men and women couples are able to participate in both roles: See especially pp. 84–111 in *Families that Work: Policies for Reconciling Parenthood and Employment*, 2003, New York: Russell Sage Foundation.

13. "The Effects of Infant Child Care on Infant-Mother Attachment Security: Results of the NICHD Study of Early Child Care," by NICHD Early Child Care Research Network, 1997a, *Child Development*, 68, 860–879; "Maternal Employment and Child Cognitive Outcomes in the First Three Years of Life: The NICHD Study of Early Child Care," by J. Brooks-Gunn, H. Wen-Jui, and J. Waldfogel, 2002, *Child Development*, 73, 1052–1072; *The High Cost of Child Care Puts Quality Care out of Reach for Many Families*, by K. Schulman, 2000, Washington, DC: Children's Defense Fund.

14. "American Child Care Today," by S. Scarr, 1998, *American Psychologist*, 53, 95–108.

15. *Ask the Children*, by Galinsky, 1999. In contrast, successful coping by dual-career couples is enhanced when men and women hold gender-equitable attitudes about work and family life—demonstrated by supporting and valuing one another's work, as well as by sharing child care, housework, and emotional care-taking of one another, children, and extended family members. See *The Unfinished Revolution* by Gerson, 2010. Also see "Intimate Partnership: Foundation to the Successful Balance of Family and Work," by T. S. Zimmerman, S. A. Haddock, L. R. Current, and S. Ziemba, 2003, *The American Journal of Family Therapy*, 31, 107–124.

16. My esteemed colleague Bill Doherty has been a leading passionate advocate for the need to preserve time for the marriage and to protect that time from intrusion of work, children, extended family, and friends. See *Take Back Your Marriage*, by W. J. Doherty, 2001, New York: Guilford Press.

17. "Time and Couples, Part II: The Sixty Second Pleasure Point," by P. Fraenkel, in *101 Interventions in Family Therapy*, vol. II (pp. 145–149), ed. T. Nelson and T. Trepper, 1998, West Hazleton, PA: Haworth Press.

18. "Emotional Transmission in the Daily Lives of Families: A New Paradigm for Studying Family Process," by R. W. Larson and D. M. Almeida, 1999, *Journal of Marriage and the Family*, 61, 5–20.

19. "Time and Couples, Part I: The Decompression Chamber," by P. Fraenkel, in *101 Interventions in Family Therapy*, vol. II (pp. 140–144), ed. T. Nelson and T. Trepper, 1998, West Hazleton, PA: Haworth Press.

20. "The Family Work Day," by S. L. Nock and P. W. Kingston, 1984, *Journal of Marriage and the Family*, 46, 333–343; "Individual and Crossover Effects of Work Schedule Fit: A Within-Couples Analysis," by K. C. Gareis, R. C. Barnett, and R. T. Brennan, 2003, *Journal of Marriage and Family*, 65, 1041–1054; "Work Time, Work Interference with Family, and Psychological Distress," V. S. Major, K. J. Klein, and M. G. Ehrhart, 2002, *Journal of Applied Psychology*, 87, 427–436.

21. *Lights Out: Sleep, Sugar, and Survival*, by T. S. Wiley and B. Formby, 2000, New York: Pocket Books.

22. *The Twenty-Four Hour Society*, by M. Moore-Ede, 1993, Reading, PA: Addison-Wesley.

23. *The Time Divide: Work, Family, and Gender Inequality*, by J. A. Jacobs and K. Gerson, 2004, Cambridge, MA: Harvard University Press.

24. *Working Fathers: New Strategies for Balancing Work and Family*, by J. A. Levine and T. L. Pittinsky, 1997, New York: Harcourt Brace. See the more recent reports on men's increased participation in child care and housework in *Times Are Changing*, by Galinsky et al., 2009; *The Unfinished Revolution*, by Gerson, 2010; and "Gender, Time, and Inequality: Trends in Women's and Men's Paid Work, Unpaid Work, and Free Time," by L. C. Sayer, 2005, *Social Forces*, 84, 285–303.

25. "Measuring the Division of Household Labor: Gender Segregation of Housework among American Couples," by S. L. Blair and D. T. Lichter, 1991, *Journal of Family Issues*, 12, 91–113. See also *Time for Life: The Surprising Ways Americans Use Their Time*, by J. Robinson and G. Godbey, 1997, University Park: Pennsylvania State University Press; "Work and Family Research in the First Decade of the 21st Century," by S. M. Bianchi and M. A. Milkie, 2010, *Journal of Marriage and Family*, 72, 705–725.

26. *Transit Markets of the Future: The Challenge of Change, Report 28*, by S. Rosenbloom, 1998, Washington, DC: National Academy Press.

27. "Research on Household Labor: Modeling and Measuring the Social Embeddedness of Routine Family Work," by S. Coltrane, 2000, *Journal of Marriage and the Family, 62,* 1208–1233; *The Unfinished Revolution: How a New Generation is Reshaping Family, Work, and Gender in America,* by K. Gerson, 2010, New York: Oxford University Press.

28. "Research on Household Labor," by Coltrane, 2000.

29. "When Does Gender Trump Money? Bargaining and Time in Household Work," by M. Bittman, P. England, L. Sayer, N. Folbre, and G. Matheson, 2003, *American Journal of Sociology, 109,* 186–214.

30. "Maternal Gatekeeping: Antecedents and Consequences," by R. Gaunt, 2008, *Journal of Family Issues, 29,* 373–395.

31. So-called "maternal gatekeeping" is often a response to men overriding or ignoring the home and child care systems women work hard to create and sustain. "All about Fathers," by P. Fraenkel, *NYU Child Study Center Newsletter,* Nov./Dec. 1999, 4, 1–4.

32. "The Opt-Out Revolution," by L. Belkin, *New York Times,* Oct. 26, 2003, retrieved June 7, 2010, from http://www.nytimes.com/2003/10/26/magazine/26WOMEN .html?pagewanted=all.

33. *The Unfinished Revolution,* by Gerson, 2010; *Highlights of the 2002 National Study of the Changing Workforce,* by J. T. Bond, C. Thompson, E. Galinsky, and D. Prottas, 2003, New York: Families and Work Institute.

34. *The Time Bind: When Work Becomes Home and Home Becomes Work,* by A. R. Hochschild, 1997, New York: Henry Holt; "Women, Men, Work, and Family," by Barnett and Hyde, 2001.

35. "The Division of Household Labor and Wives' Happiness—Ideology, Employment, and Perceptions of Support," by D. L. Piña and V. L. Bengston, 1993, *Journal of Marriage and the Family, 55,* 901–912. See other studies in "Research on Household Labor," by Coltrane, 2000.

36. "Whistle while You Work? The Effect of Household Task Performance on Women's and Men's Well-Being," by J. Robinson and G. Spitze, 1992, *Social Science Quarterly, 73,* 844–861.

37. "The Ethic of Care: Leisure Possibilities and Constraints for Women," by K. A. Henderson and K. R. Allen, 1991, *Society & Leisure, 14,* 97–113; *Balancing Work and Caregiving for Children, Adults, and Elders,* by M. B. Neal, N. J. Chapman, B. Ingersoll-Dayton, and A. C. Emlen, 1993, Newbury Park, CA: Sage; "Care-Giving and Employment: Competing or Complementary Roles?," by A. E. Scharlach, 1994, *The Gerontologist, 34,* 378–385.

38. *The Unfinished Revolution,* by Gerson, 2010; *Times Are Changing,* by E. Galinsky et al., 2009.

39. *Peer Marriage: How Love between Equals Really Works,* by P. Schwartz, 1994, New York: Free Press.

40. Having a child under the age of 6 in the home reduces women's labor participation. The Bureau of Labor Statistics found only 64.2 percent of mothers with children under 6 years old worked, whereas 77.3 percent of mothers with children ages 6 to 17 worked. Mothers with infants are even less likely to work (56.6 percent). Another way to view the statistics is that in 36.6 percent of two-parent heterosexual families with children less than 6 years old, fathers worked but mothers didn't, whereas only 23 percent of families with children between 6 and 17 years of age had this arrangement. *Employment Characteristics of Families in 2009,* U.S. Bureau of Labor Statistics, 2010, retrieved Nov. 6, 2010, from http://www.bls.gov/news.release/famee.nr0.htm. A study by the Institute for Women's Policy Research (cited by Galinsky and colleagues) showed women's markedly lower salaries over a period of 15 years were due mostly to women reducing work hours or leaving jobs temporarily to take care of children. *Times Are Changing,* by E. Galinsky et al., 2009. Thus, one major strategy dual-earner couples use to handle child care needs is women temporarily cutting back or leaving work. "Scaling Back: Dual-Earner Couples' Work-Family Strategies," by P. E. Becker and P. Moen, 1999, *Journal of Marriage and the Family, 61,* 995–1007.

41. "Effective Work/Life Strategies: Working Couples, Work Conditions, Gender, and Life Quality," by P. Moen and Y. Yu, 2000, *Social Problems, 47,* 291–326.

42. "Research on Household Labor" (p. 1225), by Coltrane, 2000.
43. *What Predicts Divorce: The Relationship between Marital Processes and Marital Outcomes*, by J. M. Gottman, 1994, Hillsdale, NJ: Lawrence Erlbaum.
44. "Money, Housework, Sex, and Conflict: Same-Sex Couples and Heterosexual Married Siblings," by S. E. Solomon, E. D. Rothblum, and K. F. Balsam, 2005, *Sex Roles, 52,* 561–575.

9 Syncing and Flowing as a Couple

1. "Teaching Family Therapy-Centered Integration: Assimilation and Beyond," by P. Fraenkel and W. M. Pinsof, 2001, *Journal of Psychotherapy Integration, 11,* 59–85.
2. *Playing and Reality* (p. 54), by D. W. Winnicott, 1971, London: Routledge. See also *Attachment, Play and Authenticity: A Winnicott Primer,* by S. Tuber, 2008, New York: Jason Aronson.
3. "Getting a Kick out of You: The Jazz Taoist Key to Love," by P. Fraenkel, in *Why Do Fools Fall in Love* (pp. 61–66), ed. J. Levine and H. J. Markman, 2001, San Fransisco: Jossey-Bass.
4. *Funk, Blues, & Straight-Ahead Jazz Instructional DVD for Drums,* by M. Clark, 2007, Milwaukee, WI: Hal Leonard.
5. *Fighting for Your Marriage,* by H. J. Markman, S. M. Stanley, and S. L. Blumberg, 2010 (3rd ed.), San Francisco: Jossey-Bass. PREP® was created and has been research-tested for over 30 years by my colleagues Howard Markman and Scott Stanley, their colleagues at the University of Denver's Center for Marital Studies, and others around the world. For 12 years, I directed and researched PREP® at the New York University Medical School and Child Study Center.
6. These terms come from earlier versions of the PREP® program and do not appear in the most recent edition of the classic book *Fighting for Your Marriage.* I continue to use these terms because they make a lot of sense to couples and help them identify the particular "flavors" of escalation, and that aids the partners to more quickly stop escalating.
7. Available along with other materials for couples at www.prepinc.com.
8. One of the reasons couples sometimes are reluctant to use the Speaker-Listener Technique is that it does feel artificial. With practice, it becomes more natural. One of the things I tell my hip, artsy New York City couples who are reluctant to try the technique, is that this technique is quite similar to a piece by a famous video artist, Bruce Naumann, called "World Peace (projected)." When I saw it in SoHo in New York, it involved a room filled with large video monitors. Each showed a man or woman of a different race, ethnicity, and age, all slowly saying, "I'll talk, and you'll listen. You'll talk, and I'll listen. We'll talk, and they'll listen. They'll talk, and we'll listen," and on and on. Each person starts the sequence at a different time, so it has the effect of what is called a "round" in classical music. Very cool. Just like the Speaker-Listener Technique, it's all about talking and listening, and taking turns. Most hip and artsy couples are willing to do the Speaker-Listener after I make this connection.
9. *Fighting for Your Marriage,* by Markman et al., 2010.
10. In the current version of PREP®, the third step of problem solving is listed as Agreement and Compromise. I find it useful to remind couples that their first step should be to "harness their differences" and look for how they may each bring a useful perspective that can be combined. I also still include the term "contracting," which appeared in an earlier version of PREP®, because I find that without getting concrete about who will carry out which part of the plan and by when, these plans often go by the wayside.
11. "Sacrifice as a Predictor of Marital Outcomes," by S. M. Stanley, S. W. Whitton, M. L. Clements, and H. J. Markman, 2006, *Family Process, 45,* 289–303.

12. *Influence: The Psychology of Persuasion,* by R. B. Cialdini, 2007 (rev. ed.), New York: HarperCollins.

13. *Acceptance and Change in Couple Therapy: A Therapist's Guide to Transforming Relationships,* by N. S. Jacobson and A. Christensen, 1996, New York: W. W. Norton.

14. *The Developing Mind: How Relationships and the Brain Interact to Shape Who We Are,* by D. Siegel, 1999, New York: Guilford Press; *Handbook of Attachment: Theory, Research, and Clinical Applications,* by J. Cassidy and P. R. Shaver, 2008 (2nd ed.), New York: Guilford Press.

15. *After the Honeymoon: How Conflict Can Improve Your Relationship,* by D. B. Wile, 2008, Oakland, CA: Collaborative Couple Therapy Books.

16. *Seven Principles for Making Marriage Work,* by J. Gottman, 1999, New York: Three Rivers Press.

17. "What Shamu Taught Me About a Happy Marriage," by A. Sutherland, *New York Times,* "Fashion and Style" section, Oct. 25, 2006, Retrieved July 24, 2010, from http://www.nytimes.com/2006/06/25/fashion/25love.html?_r=1&pagewanted=all.

18. *Flow: The Psychology of Optimal Experience,* by M. Csíkszentmihályi, 1990, New York: Harper & Row.

19. *Finding Flow: The Psychology of Engagement with Everyday Life,* by M. Csíkszentmihályi, 1997, New York: Basic Books.

20. *Flow,* by Csíkszentmihályi, 1990.

21. *Mating in Captivity: Reconciling the Erotic and the Domestic,* by E. Perel, 2006, New York: HarperCollins.

22. "A Systems View of Family Interaction and Psychopathology," by P. Steinglass, in *Family Interaction and Psychopathology: Theories, Methods and Findings* (pp. 25–65), ed. T. Jacob, 1987, New York: Plenum Press.

23. *Flow,* by Csíkszentmihályi, 1990.

24. *Finding Flow,* by Csíkszentmihályi, 1997.

25. *Fighting for Your Marriage,* by Markman et al., 2010; *Seven Principles for Making Marriage Work,* by Gottman, 1999.

26. *Influence,* by Cialdini, 2007.

27. "The Death of 'Till Death Us Do Part': The Transformation of Pair-Bonding in the 20th Century," by W. M. Pinsof, 2002, *Family Process, 41,* 135–157.

28. *Shattered Assumptions: Towards a New Psychology of Trauma,* by R. Janoff-Bulman, 2002, New York: Free Press.

29. *The Relational Trauma of Incest: A Family-Based Approach to Treatment,* by M. Sheinberg and P. Fraenkel, 2001, New York: Guilford Press.

30. Ibid.

31. For two excellent guides to addressing the impact of an affair, see *After the Affair: Healing the Pain and Rebuilding Trust When a Partner Has Been Unfaithful,* by J. Abrahms Spring with M. Spring, 1996, New York: HarperCollins; *Infidelity: A Survival Guide,* by D. Lusterman, 1998, Oakland, CA: New Harbinger Press.

32. *Seven Principles for Making Marriage Work,* by Gottman, 1999.

33. "Marital Stability and Spouses' Shared Time," by M. S. Hill, 1988, *Journal of Family Issues, 9,* 427–451.

34. *Predicting Success or Failure in Marriage,* by E. Burgess and L. Cottrell, 1939, New York: Prentice Hall; *Husbands and Wives: The Dynamics of Married Life,* by R. Blood and D. Wolfe, 1960, New York: Free Press; "Age at Marriage and Marital Satisfaction: A Multivariate Analysis with Implications for Marital Stability," by G. Lee, 1977, *Journal of Marriage and the Family, 39,* 439–504.

35. "Compatibility and the Development of Premarital Relationships," by R. M. Houts, E. Robins, and T. L. Huston, 1996, *Journal of Marriage and the Family, 58,* 7–20; "Joint and Separated Lifestyles in Couple Relationships," by M. Kalmijn and W. Bernasco, 2001, *Journal of Marriage and Family, 63,* 639–654; "Marital Stability and Spouses' Shared Time," by Hill, 1988; *Personal Relationships: Their Structures and Processes,* by H. Kelley, 1979, Hillsdale, NJ: Lawrence Erlbaum; "The Reciprocal Relationship

Between Marital Interaction and Marital Happiness: A Three-Wave Study," by J. Zuo, 1992, *Journal of Marriage and the Family*, 54, 870–878; "Dyadic Exploration of the Relationship of Leisure Satisfaction, Leisure Time, and Gender to Relationship Satisfaction," by E. C. Berg, M. Trost, I. E. Schneider, and M. T. Allison, 2001, *Leisure Studies*, 23, 35–46; "Family and Leisure: A Review of the Literature with Research Recommendations," by T. B. Holman and A. Epperson, 1984, *Journal of Leisure Research*, 16, 277–294; "Compatibility, Leisure, and Satisfaction in Marital Relationships," by D. W. Crawford, R. M. Houts, T. L. Huston, and L. J. George, 2002, *Journal of Marriage and Family*, 64, 433–449.

36. "Discriminating Interaction Behaviors in Happy and Unhappy Marriages," by G. R. Birchler and L. J. Webb, 1977, *Journal of Consulting and Clinical Psychology*, 45, 494–495; "Multimethod Analysis of Social Reinforcement Exchange between Maritally Distressed and Nondistressed Spouse and Stranger Dyads," by G. R. Birchler, R. L. Weiss, and J. P. Vincent, 1975, *Journal of Personality and Social Psychology*, 31, 349–360. "Self-Expansion and Flow in Couples' Momentary Experiences: An Experience Sampling Study," by J. M. Graham, 2008, *Journal of Personality and Social Psychology*, 95, 679-694.

37. "The Reciprocal Relationship Between Marital Interaction and Marital Happiness," by Zuo, 1992.

38. "Role Balance among White Married Couples," by S. R. Marks, T. L. Huston, E. M. Johnson, and S. M. MacDermid, 2001, *Journal of Marriage and Family*, 63, 1083–1098.

39. "Working Status and Leisure: An Analysis of the Trade-off between Solitary and Social Time," by G. Kraaykamp, W. van Gils, and T. van der Lippe, 2009, *Time & Society*, 18, 264–283.

40. "Timestyles: Role Factor Influences on the Convergence and Divergence of Couples' Complementary and Substitute Activity Patterns," by T. A. Anderson, L. L. Golden, U. N. Umesh, and W. A. Weeks, 1992, *Psychology & Marketing*, 9, 101–122.

41. "An Exploration of Women's Leisure within Heterosexual Romantic Relationships," by K. L. Herridge, S. M. Shaw, and R. C. Mannell, 2003, *Journal of Leisure Research*, 35, 274–291.

42. "Compatibility, Leisure, and Satisfaction in Marital Relationships," by Crawford et al., 2002.

43. "An Exploration of Women's Leisure within Heterosexual Romantic Relationships," by Herridge et al., 2003.

44. "Compatibility, Leisure, and Satisfaction in Marital Relationships," by Crawford et al., 2002.

45. "Rising to the Challenge: Fathers' Role in the Negotiation of Couple Time," by V. Dyck and K. Daly, 2006, *Leisure Studies*, 25, 201–217; "Role Balance among White Married Couples," by Marks et al., 2001; "Predicting Relationship Satisfaction from Couples' Use of Leisure Time," by G. T. Smith, D. K. Snyder, T. J. Trull, and B. R. Monsma, 1988, *American Journal of Family Therapy*, 16, 3–13.

46. "Role Balance among White Married Couples," by Marks et al., 2001.

47. "Compatibility, Leisure, and Satisfaction in Marital Relationships," by Crawford et al., 2002.

48. "Marital Satisfaction: An Examination of Its Relationship to Spouse Support and Congruence of Commitment among Runners," by J. H. Baldwin, G. D. Ellis, and B. Baldwin, 1999, *Leisure Sciences*, 21, 117–131.

49. "Compatibility, Leisure, and Satisfaction in Marital Relationships," by Crawford et al., 2002.

50. "Joint and Separated Lifestyles in Couple Relationships," by M. Kalmijn and W. Bernasco, 2001, *Journal of Marriage and Family*, 63, 639–654; "The Reciprocal Relationship Between Marital Interaction and Marital Happiness," by Zuo, 1992.

51. "No Fun Anymore: Leisure and Marital Quality across the Transition to Parenthood," by A. Claxton and M. Perry-Jenkins, 2008, *Journal of Marriage and Family*, 70, 28–43; "Leisure and Fatherhood in Dual-Earner Families," by E. Such, 2006, *Leisure Studies*, 25, 185–199.

52. "Leisure and Fatherhood in Dual-Earner Families," by Such, 2006.
53. Ibid.
54. "Rising to the Challenge," by Dyck and Daly, 2006.
55. "No Fun Anymore," by Claxton and Perry-Jenkins, 2008.
56. "The Influences of Family Leisure Patterns on Perceptions of Family Functioning," by R. B. Zabriskie and B. P. McCormick, 2001, *Family Relations: Interdisciplinary Journal of Applied Family Studies, 50,* 281–289.
57. "Everyday Interaction in Marital Relationships: Variations in Relative Importance and Event Duration," by M. Dainton, 1998, *Communication Reports, 11,* 101–109.
58. "The Contribution of Couple Leisure Involvement, Leisure Time, and Leisure Satisfaction to Marital Satisfaction," by H. A. Johnson, R. B. Zabriskie, and B. Hill, 2006, *Marriage & Family Review, 40,* 69–91.
59. "Compatibility and the Development of Premarital Relationships," by Houts et al., 1996.
60. "No Fun Anymore," by Claxton and Perry-Jenkins, 2008; "Self-Expansion and Flow in Couples' Momentary Experiences" by Graham, 2008; "Joint and Separated Lifestyles in Couple Relationships," by Kalmijn and Bernasco, 2001; "Leisure and Fatherhood in Dual-Earner Families," by Such, 2006.
61. "Self-Expansion and Flow in Couples' Momentary Experiences," by Graham, 2008.
62. "Couples' Shared Participation in Novel and Arousing Activities and Experienced Relationship Quality," by A. Aron, C. Norman, E. Aron, C. McKenna, and R. Heyman, 2000, *Journal of Personality and Social Psychology, 78,* 273–284.
63. *Love and the Expansion of Self: Understanding Attraction and Satisfaction,* by A. Aron and E. N. Aron, 1986, New York: Hemisphere.
64. "Self-Expansion and Flow in Couples' Momentary Experiences," by Graham, 2008.

Index

housework, 12, 22, 37, 66, 77, 90, 96, 103–4, 107, 161, 179, 193–204, 207, 234, 236
Housework-Fun Incompatibility, Myth of, 37, 39–41, 193, 204
Hughes, Langston, 248n.3
humors, four, 68–9

In Praise of Slowness (Honoré), 55, 246n.18
Internet, 61, 152, 170, 189
intimacy, sexual and emotional, 1, 6–7, 12–4, 22–6, 34–40, 57, 87, 92, 131, 160, 183, 189–91, 205–6, 217, 220, 223–6, 232–3, 238
invalidation, 14–7, 207–9, 230
It's Not the BIG that Eat the SMALL... (Jennings and Haughton), 55

Jackson, Janet, 206
Jacobs, Jerry, 161, 252n.37
jazz, 1, 19, 30, 87, 91, 174–5, 196, 206, 221, 223, 226, 239–40, 242, 244n.3–4
Judiasm, 81, 116, 121

Kabat-Zinn, Jon, 80
kairos, 32, 46–54, 223
Kanner, A. D., 252n.40
Kasser, T., 252n.40
Kierkegaard, Søren, 47
Kornfield, Jack, 47

Laschever, S., 252n.46
Lee, Ang, 46
leisure, 4, 23, 34, 61, 65, 92–3, 97–8, 123, 130, 156, 185, 222, 225, 227, 233–8
Levine, James, 155–6, 186, 253n.63
Levine, Robert, 138–9, 249n.13
Life Pace Questionnaire, 57–9, 67, 75
Loehr, Jim, 154, 174
Lomax, Alan, 88
Luce, Gay Gaer, 91

mal-intent, theories of, 14, 17. *See also* negative interpretations
Manne, Shelly, 87
Markman, Howard, 10, 257n.5

maternity/paternity leave, 153–5, 252n.46
Matrix, The (film), 46, 133
meditation, 27–8, 43–4, 78–9, 82, 115, 190. *See also* Buddhism; mindfulness
Meyers, Marcia K., 254n.12
mindfulness, 41–4, 47, 78–82, 84–5, 115, 168–9, 175, 246n.15
Modern Times (film), 33
money, 23, 28, 36, 60, 63, 65, 109–10, 124, 130, 133, 161, 195–6, 200, 208–9, 212–5, 222, 238
morning routines, 89, 101
multitasking, 36, 67, 167–8
Murray, Bill, 44
mutual awareness, 13–8

negative interpretations, 14, 17–8, 158, 207–8, 232
neuroticism, 57, 133–4, 136, 140, 243n.10
New York University Medical School, 1, 257n.5
Nhat Hanh, Thich, 43, 80–1, 246n.15
no pressure zones, 74
no-tech zones, 171–2

pace:
    activities to expand range of, 76–86
    assessing, 57–61
    differences in, 2–3, 9–12, 18–21, 26, 55–7, 66–86
    emotional temperament and, 68–75
    Four R's and, 75–9
    life, 2–3
    society and, 61–6
peer marriage, 11, 200
Perfection, Myth of, 35–7, 183–4, 188, 190, 204
Pittinsky, Todd, 155–6, 186
polarizing patterns, 6–13, 18, 23, 49, 213, 231
    blamer-placater, 132–3, 136
    overfunctioning/underfunctioning, 8–11, 23, 215, 231–2
    pursuer/distancer, 6–11
pop psychology, 217
post-traumatic stress disorder (PTSD), 111
Power of Full Engagement, The (Loehr and Schwartz), 154